Serving a City

The Story of Cork's English Market

Manifestly, one does not treat a meat market in quite the same fashion as a thoroughfare where statesmen trod and orated, or places which saw military history in the making. The Market, however, has seen history of a different type ...

'Grand Parade and Princes Street Markets',
Cork Evening Echo,
2 April 1958

Serving a City

The Story of Cork's English Market

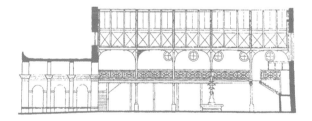

Diarmuid Ó Drisceoil & Donal Ó Drisceoil

The Collins Press

First published in 2005 by
The Collins Press,
West Link Park,
Doughcloyne,
Wilton,
Cork

British Library Cataloguing in Publication Data

O Drisceoil, Diarmuid
    Serving a city : the story of Cork's English market
    1. Food industry and trade – Ireland – Cork 2. Markets – Ireland – Cork
    I. Title II. O Drisceoil, Donal
    381.4156413100941956

ISBN : 19093464722

Design and typesetting: Stuart Coughlan @ edit+
Cover design: Stuart Coughlan @ edit+
Font: Sabon, 12 point

Printed in Ireland by ColourBooks Ltd

Contents

Preface

Cork's English Market has been operating on the same site since 1788, the year the 'first fleet' reached Australia and established a settlement there. The world was on the cusp of the transformation heralded by the French Revolution and Britain's industrial revolution; the Act of Union that created the modern United Kingdom was a dozen years into the future and the newly-created United States of America had not yet elected its first president, George Washington, when stalls first opened for trade in the original Grand Parade meat market. Over the following year fish, fowl, fruit and vegetable stalls were added, and the Market that we still know today was born. As the modern world emerged around it, more immediately the modern city of Cork was also coming into being. The familiar streetscape of today was being created, and the new flagship municipal market was located at the heart of the new commercial city centre. It was the creation of the Protestant or 'English' corporation that controlled the city until the fourth decade of the nineteenth century; when local government was reformed in 1840 and the representatives of the city's Catholic, 'Irish' majority took over, they established another covered food market, St Peter's, which was sometimes known as the 'Irish Market' to distinguish it from its older counterpart, which remained associated with its English creators. The name 'English Market' dates from this era of transition.

The Market has entered its fourth century in relatively healthy shape, having stubbornly survived revolution and war, fire and famine, depression and boom, changing tastes and intensifying competition, and a rapidly changing socio-economic, food and retail environment. It has undergone numerous changes in its external and internal appearance, its management and customer base, and in the nature and range of its fare, but it remains essentially what it always was: a food market serving the people of Cork. In that role it has acted both as a bastion of tradition, a showcase and a vehicle of change – a haven for offal and olives, a shopping space for native Corkonians of all ages and classes and, increasingly, for the city's burgeoning immigrant population. But while it is and always has been primarily a food market, the Market was and is much more. It is a place of commerce, but also a civic space, owned by the corporation on behalf of the citizens of Cork. It is a meeting place, a thoroughfare, a venue and gallery, a bustling social hub of the city. Cork playwright Johnny Hanrahan, whose play *Crystal* was performed in the theatrically atmospheric night-time Market in 2004, explained why he chose this space for his drama of the Cork everyday:

In its layout, in the kinds of encounters you have with stallholders surrounded by religious icons, dead birds, cheeses you could build houses with, with your brother, the man from the tax office, your old teacher, fourteen screaming teenagers and a bemused foreign journalist, camera crew lost forever in the sea of Corkonians, all talking at the top of their voices, the market is where it's at.[1]

It is an historical place that refuses to stagnate and a cultural space that mocks pretension, a jewel of shabby charm and a bulwark against the vulgar tide of homogenising commercialisation. The diversity and variety of its products, the primacy of small traders, the personalised service, the growing emphasis on organic products and reliance on small-scale producers, its mix of traditional Cork fare and exciting new foods from afar, and longstanding family-run stalls with newcomers from outside, all contribute to its unique appeal, which is celebrated widely, especially by visitors to the city. Municipal authorities in Ireland and Britain are seeking to revitalise and recreate similar markets that have been abandoned or put to other uses and look to Cork's English Market as a model. Historical Cork has bequeathed the city a unique legacy which it is now coming to appreciate, and which must be protected, resourced and encouraged as part of ongoing efforts at urban renewal and regeneration.

This book, which is part of the growing appreciation of the Market's importance, was commissioned by The Collins Press on the initiative of a number of Market traders, especially Kay Harte and Mary Rose. We would like to thank them for placing their trust in us. Kay and Mary have been a constant source of support and help in our research, and we are grateful for their efforts. Thanks also to all the other Market stallholders, traders, workers and customers, past and present, who have spoken to us and shared memories, insights, photographs and other material, especially: Ken Barrett, Driss Belmajoub, Michael Bresnan, Jack and Marian Burke, Seán Calder Potts, Jenny Rose Clarke, Eileen Crowley, Josephine Kennedy, Glenys Landon, Pauline Noonan, George Martin, William Martin, Helen McDonnell, Jack and Mary Mulcahy, Michael Murphy, Paul Murphy, Donal O'Callaghan, Pat and Paul O'Connell, Katherine O'Mahony, Ashley O'Neill, Tim O'Sullivan, Eddie Sheehan, Isabelle Sheridan, Toby Simmonds. Simon and Patrick O'Flynn were most generous with their time in arranging meetings and interviews, and in discussing our work as it progressed.

We are grateful to the staff at the Valuation Office, Dublin; the National Library of Ireland; the National Archives of Ireland; the Cork Public Museum, and Examiner Publications, especially Des O'Driscoll. Special thanks to those in Special Collections, Boole Library, UCC; Local Studies, Cork City Library; and the Cork Archives Institute. Thanks to Peter Foynes, Larry Geary and Marita Foster for access to unpublished papers; Nell McCafferty for permission to publish her article, 'The Vegetable Seller'; Maurice

Hurley, Cork City Archaeologist, for advice and suggestions; Gina Johnson for her invaluable aid with maps; Noel Murphy for his time and insights, access to his unpublished accounts of trade disputes, and to the minute books of the Cork Operative Butchers' Society (COBS); Jim Cosgrave, former Market worker and past president of COBS, for sharing his memories and knowledge. The following kindly supplied photographs, and though space restrictions meant that only a selection could be used, we are very grateful to them all: Tony O'Connell, Daphne Pochin-Mould, Dori O'Connell, Claire Keogh, Janice O'Connell, Tanya Bauman, Peter Barry, Tony Barry, Johnny Hanrahan, Mick Hanningan, Derek Foott, Chris Ramsden, Gloria Monteleone and Joe Creedon. Wendie Young spent many days in the Market on her photographic assignment and the images she produced for this book are graphic testament to her talent.

Thanks to Stuart Coughlan, the book's designer, whose skill and professionalism made working with him a pleasure, and all at The Collins Press. We are especially indebted to Colman O'Mahony, without whose unrivalled knowledge of Cork's newspapers and unfailing generosity in sharing it this book would be much the poorer. Finally, we are, as always, grateful to and appreciative of our respective families – Miriam, Méabh and Aonghus, and Orla, Kim and Fionn – who put up with our obsessions.

Publisher's Note

The publishers wish to acknowledge the contribution of all who supported the publication of this book, both sponsors and willing helpers. In particular we thank the following:

Janssen Pharmaceutical
Bank of Ireland
Henry Ford and Son, Limited
Barry's Tea
Cork City Council

Bresnan Butchers
Bubble Brothers
James Clancy
Coffee Central
Farmgate
Moynihans Poultry
Paul and Alan Murphy, Butchers
O'Mahony Family Butcher
The Chicken Inn
The Real Olive Company
West Cork Smoke-House

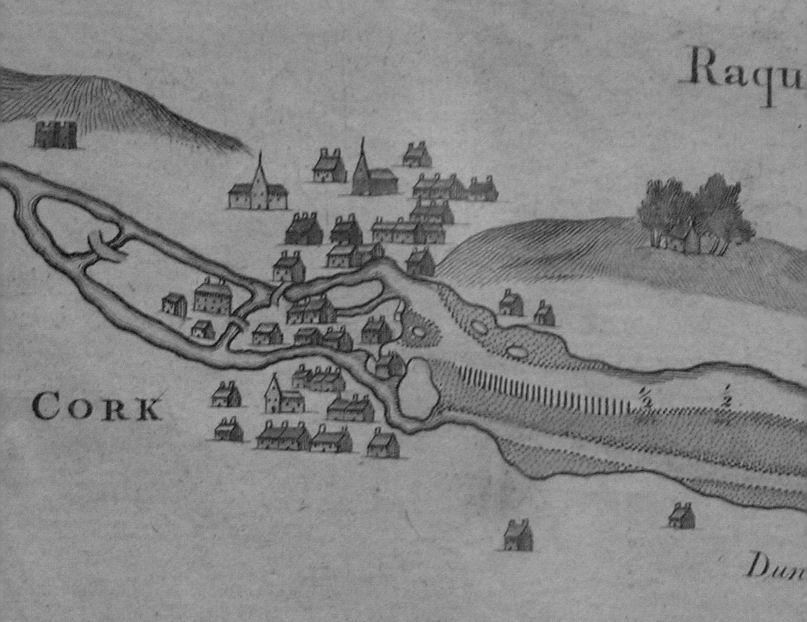

Raqu

CORK

St. Phinbarry Parifh

Douglafs

Marrowborough

1 Cork: The Making of a City

Markets are an intrinsic part of the history of Cork city, from its earliest emergence as a settlement. A centre of population, whether town, monastery or military encampment, attracts trade: people must eat and if sufficient food cannot be produced or carried, it has to be acquired. A conquering or occupying army takes by force, but a settled population, wishing to prosper in comfort and peace, must trade. The trading of goods in a set place, governed by accepted rules and behaviour, constitutes a market. When people first gathered to settle and live in what became the city of Cork, a market or markets evolved. The relationship between town and market is interdependent, and as this town grew into a city, so its markets grew, multiplied and became more specialised, contributing to and reflecting its evolving physical, social, economic and political landscape.[1]

Origins

In the present state of knowledge it is not possible to say precisely when the town of Cork first became established. A monastery existed from at least the seventh century, probably on the higher ground to the south of the river in the region of the present St Finbarr's cathedral. This monastery was sufficiently developed and wealthy to attract the attentions of Viking raiders during the ninth century. Archaeological excavation has shown that a town was growing on a marshy island in the area of the present South Main Street by the eleventh century. Viking settlers were the probable driving force in this development and Cork became part of the wider network of trading posts and towns set up by them in many parts of Europe. The nearby monastery, the town's location at an important crossing point on the River Lee, and the fact that the river was not

Opposite page: Detail from a marine chart, 'The South Coast of Ireland, from Cable Island to Galley Head, surveyed and navigated (1775)', by Murdoch Mackenzie Snr. (Port of Cork)

11

navigable for larger boats above this point were also factors in the location and growth of the town. By the twelfth century the population of Cork was a mixture of Irish and Hiberno-Norse or settled Vikings. Norman occupation and expansion began in Ireland around 1170 and two Anglo-Norman lords besieged Cork in 1177. This indicates that it was by then a defended, walled town. King Henry II of England granted the town to these two lords, Miles de Cogan and Robert FitzStephen, and Cork became a royal city. The Normans brought financial organisation, discipline and a political administration to Cork and instigated a period of expansion.

Bridges were built between the two main islands of the city and also at the northern and southern entrances. Today's North and South Gate Bridges mark those entrances. The principal street of the city ran for over 600 metres between these two bridges. Houses of wattle construction fronted the street with long narrow plots running east and west and these houses were gradually replaced with fully framed timber houses, many of more than one storey. Numerous narrow laneways ran east and west from the principal street and evolved into mini-streets with residential and commercial buildings. Cork's defensive wall had been extended in the thirteenth century to also enclose the north island, centred around what is now North Main Street. Earthen banks and timber and wattle walls were replaced over time by a much more substantial stone wall with towers and gates, including a watergate where present-day Castle Street joins Daunt's Square. The form of the medieval city was now established and it retained this until the end of the seventeenth century. Even at the earliest stages of its development Cork had suburbs on the higher ground to the north and south of the city proper.

Norman conquest and occupation brought improvements in agriculture and increased commercialisation during the thirteenth century. Cork's economic development was dependant on its trade in agricultural produce and even at this early stage in its history the city was exporting oats, wheat, beef, pork, fish, malt, wool and hides. Imports included wine, cloth and manufactured utensils. Cork's trade with England and France is reflected in the large quantities of pottery from these countries recovered from excavations in the city. Political instability, a decline in trade and the Black Death brought about a downturn in the fortunes of the city during the fourteenth century and it was not until the middle of the following century that any recovery occured.

During the medieval period, and indeed up to the eighteenth century, the wealthy merchants and the poor of the city lived side by side, all confined to the streets and laneways held within the city walls. However, wealthy families were able to build substantial stone houses and some, such as the Skiddys and Roches, erected tower houses or small castles within the medieval city. Churches were also built in the city and a number of friaries and churches were established outside the walls. Analysis of the skeletal remains of those buried during the medieval period at the Dominican friary of St Mary's of the Isle, immediately to the west of the walled city, has given us a flavour of what life was like for the people of Cork at that time. It is probable that only half of the children born survived to adulthood. It was rare for adults to live beyond 50 years of age. Most people had severe dental problems and many suffered degenerative joint disease. Poor nutrition and heavy physical labour took a toll on both men and women. Many skeletons showed signs of trauma, injuries more usually associated with violence than accident.

Up to the seventeenth century Cork's external trade was modest and the port was less significant than Youghal, Waterford and Wexford, the other principal ports on Ireland's southern coast. Skins, hides, woollen mantles, fish and wood are the exports most mentioned in the records. During the sixteenth century Cork was essentially loyal to the English Crown and the city's political and economic life was controlled and dominated by an elite that was English in its identity. Cork's hinterland was frequently torn by strife, famine, plague, drought and other misfortunes. The upheavals of the Reformation affected Cork, especially after 1530 and the Augustinian, Dominican and Franciscan friaries, which lay outside the city walls, were dissolved and their properties were acquired by city merchants. With the accession of Elizabeth I to the throne in 1558 England's policies of conquest and colonisation intensified. There was an increase in the English Protestant presence in Cork and in the south of Ireland generally, as a result of the Munster Plantation and the English military and civil establishment in the region also grew. In the latter part of the century war had a severe impact. During the Desmond rebellion of 1579 to 1583, for example, trade and commerce all but collapsed and famine was common both in the country and within the walls of the city.

A map of Cork, in reality a pictorial representation, dating to *c.*1587 gives a good impression of the general layout of the city at the time. This map comes from the book *Pacata Hibernia*, first published in 1633. The city is viewed from the east. The bridges and gates at the southern and northern entrances are shown to the left and right respectively. A watergate with portcullis in the middle of the eastern city wall protects an inner dock, present-day Castle Street. The main street of the city runs between the entrance gates and crosses the waterway that divided the two islands by way of a bridge. To the right, or north, of this bridge the base of a cross is shown (see page 15 and detail page 29). This marked Cork's market place. An earlier, simpler map of 1545 also shows the position of the cross and the surrounding open space is called Cross Green. It was here that traders and merchants gathered to do business and where the inhabitants could buy food. While most of the city's requirements were brought in from the surrounding countryside, some animals were reared within the walls and there was a successful fishery on the river and its channels. In the bottom left-hand corner of the map fishermen are shown at work. There were large open spaces within the walls also, especially in the northeastern quadrant, and gardens are shown here. Presumably vegetables, fruit and herbs were grown here and elsewhere in the city. A map dating to 1602 depicts Cork, viewed from the west, and shows an extensive range of gardens in the southeastern quadrant of the city. Other maps from the early seventeenth century show that the northeastern marsh, the area bounded today by Paul Street, Emmet Place, Lavitt's Quay and Cornmarket Street, was being reclaimed. It is not possible to accurately measure the population of the city when these maps were drawn, but a figure of between 2,000 and 2,500 seems likely for the years around 1600.

Seventeenth-century Cork

During the seventeenth century Cork became a major Atlantic seaport and established an export trade in provisions that laid the foundation of the great expansion and improvements in the city in the subsequent century. There was now extensive English settlement in Munster; old towns and villages were improved and developed, and new ones established. These provided markets for agricultural and other produce. There was an increase in agricultural production and exports of woollen goods, hides, tallow and wood grew ten-fold in the decades up to 1641. Exports of provisions, mostly to England initially, began to grow also. Beef, pork and fish were processed in the city. In 1614 the corporation of Cork banned the operation of slaughterhouses in the city, such was the volume of meat being processed, and that work was relocated to the suburbs, mainly those to the north.

By 1641 Cork's population had grown to 8,200. Although there were many 'new' English settlers in the city and surrounding areas, the 'old' English elite retained control of the corporation and thereby protected their wealth and influence. The 1640s saw great upheaval and Cork suffered some dramatic changes. Following the rebellion of 1641-2 and an unsuccessful siege of the city in 1642, Lord Inchiquin, the commander of the Crown forces in Munster, ordered the expulsion of all Catholics from Cork and the forfeiture of their property in 1644. Some of the old elite managed to stay and retain their property for a time, but by the early 1650s most of the city's real estate and resources were in Protestant hands. In 1656 the corporation of Cork was restored by Oliver Cromwell, it having lapsed following the expulsion of the Catholic population in 1644. From then until the 1840s, except for 1687-90, the corporation of the city was the preserve of a Protestant elite, which owned most of the property of the city and suburbs, monopolised trade and controlled commercial life. Catholic involvement in trade, commerce and political life was severely restricted.

The disruption caused by war, famine and disease during the 1640s and 1650s devastated trade. Following the restoration of the British monarchy in 1660, relative stability facilitated a new growth in the economy and Cork's exports of provisions to England began to grow again. This success was undermined following the protectionist

Opposite page: A pictorial representation of Cork, c.1587, from *Pacata Hibernia* (1633).

CORKE

S.Peters

Skyddes Castell

Christ Churche

S.Queen Castell

S watergate

A marshe.

A marshe,

Galwaies Castell

Platte of Kerey whytte

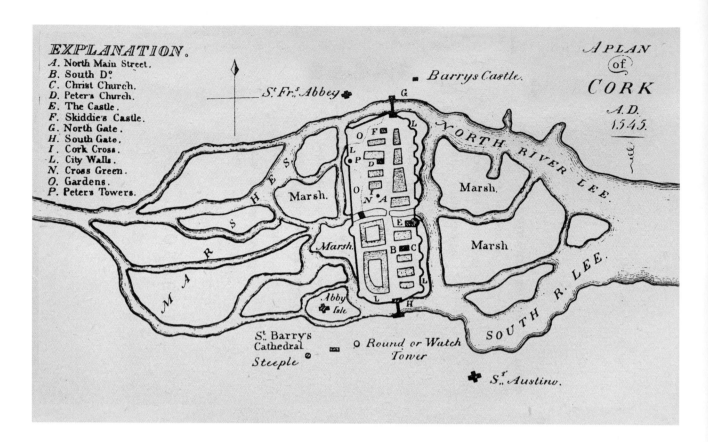

EXPLANATION.
A. North Main Street.
B. South D.°
C. Christ Church.
D. Peter's Church.
E. The Castle.
F. Skiddie's Castle.
G. North Gate.
H. South Gate.
I. Cork Cross.
L. City Walls.
N. Cross Green.
O. Gardens.
P. Peter's Towers.

A PLAN of CORK A.D. 1545.

Above:
'A Plan of Cork A.D. 1545'
reproduced in F.H. Tuckey,
*The City and County of
Cork Remembrancer*
(Cork, 1837).

Cattle Acts of 1665 and 1667, which banned the import of Irish provisions into England. Merchants were forced to look elsewhere for markets and trade with France and with the English colonies in the Caribbean and North America grew rapidly. In the later seventeenth century Cork became the principal Irish port for the importation of tobacco and sugar from the Americas. Customs returns more than doubled between 1664 and 1683 and the city's quays were extended. GA Story's map of 1690 shows quays running along the south side of the north channel of the Lee from present-day Emmet Place westwards to Kyrl's Quay. These quays replaced the protected dock that lay within the city walls at present-day Castle Street, this waterway having been at least partially infilled by the end of the seventeenth century.

Economic progress also resulted in other building in Cork. Meat markets, a fish market and a corn market were established. A meat shambles, or market, was built on the south side of Castle Street. This is shown on city maps from 1690. A bridge was built in 1699 from Tuckey's Lane eastwards across the channel of the river that ran where Grand Parade is today. This bridge gave access to Dunscombe's Marsh. This large marsh lay to the east of the walled city and was so called as it had been leased by Alderman Noblett Dunscombe in 1686. Reclamation work was even then in progress on the marsh as Story's map of 1690 shows a large bowling green, which appears to occupy at least part of the space now covered by the English Market.

Cork's fortunes suffered a setback in 1690 when the city sided with the Catholic Jacobites and was besieged by an army led by John Churchill, Duke of Marlborough. In 1687 Cork's corporation had been dissolved and reconstituted with a Catholic majority. This was a result of the accession of the Catholic King James II to the throne of England. James landed in Kinsale in 1689 and was given a great welcome in Cork. Churchill's force was loyal to the Protestant King William and in September of the following year bombarded and burned the northern and southern suburbs of Cork. The southeastern section of the city walls was destroyed and the city surrendered. The Protestant corporation was restored and for the following 150 years Catholics were excluded and could not become freemen.

By 1700 the city was beginning to outgrow its walls. For centuries suburbs had been growing on the higher ground to the north and south of the walled city, but now marshes were being reclaimed to the west and more especially to the east. It was on this new ground that the merchants, businessmen and wealthy professionals of the eighteenth century city lived and pursued their commercial and professional activities.

Eighteenth-century Cork: growth and development

At the beginning of the eighteenth century Cork was essentially a small walled city of medieval appearance with one principal street and a virtual web of laneways. Extensive marshes, largely unreclaimed, lay to the east and west and two bridges connected the city and its suburbs to the north and south. By the century's end the city had grown to become Ireland's most significant Atlantic port and had spread far beyond its original limits. The old walls had disappeared and new ground for development was created on the reclaimed marshes. A new commercial centre developed to the east. Wide streets replaced the river channels and waterways, which were filled in or arched over and new quays, bridges, churches, commercial and public buildings were built. Fortunes were made in trade and large houses appeared on the city's outskirts. The city took on a form it still retains.

In 1706 Cork's population is estimated to have been about 17,600. By 1725 it had doubled, and reached almost 60,000 by 1800. This growth was made possible by the almost uninterrupted economic prosperity the city enjoyed in the period. Cork was favoured with a number of significant advantages. The city had a productive agricultural hinterland and a good natural harbour. It was the last port of significance between Britain and the Americas. Cork's corporation was controlled by merchants, and their priorities became the city's priorities. Costs were low relative to competitor countries and an entrepreneurial spirit drove many to take the risks necessary for success. Salted beef, butter and pork, processed and barrelled in the city, became the principal exports.

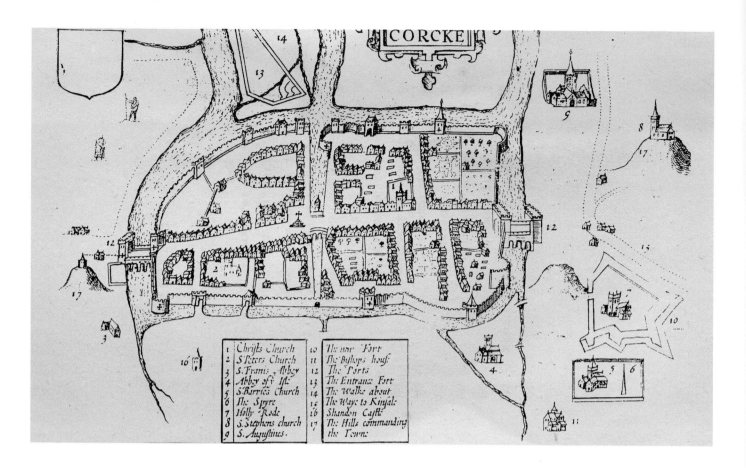

Key to map:
1 Chryfts Church
2 S.Peters Church
3 S.Francis Abbey
4 Abbey of y Ifl:
5 S.Barries Church
6 The Spyre
7 Holly Rode
8 S.Stephens church
9 S.Auguftines
10 The new Fort
11 The Bifhops houf
12 The Ports
13 The Entrance Fort
14 The Walke about
15 The Way to Kinfale
16 Shandon Caftl
17 The Hills commanding the Towne

Above:
Map of Cork 1602. (Cork City Library)

These went to Britain and Europe but increasing quantities were also exported to the growing British colonies in America and the Caribbean. During the first half of the century the volume of beef exported through Cork exceeded the combined total for all other Irish ports. The Irish trade in pork to continental Europe was controlled entirely by Cork merchants. Up to 1782 Cork was the sole centre for provisioning British army and navy supply ships and even after that date continued to be a main supplier. The Revolutionary wars in America and the later Napoleonic wars in Europe in the late eighteenth and early nineteenth centuries kept this demand high. While the processing of these provisions employed many directly, by-products such as hides, tallow, candles and soap also contributed to the city's economy.

The city's role as a meat provisioning centre earned it titles such as 'the Slaughterhouse of Ireland' and 'the shambles of the kingdom'.[2] The predominance of victualling led to an increase in meat consumption locally – good cuts for the wealthy, cheap offal for the poor. Many of the traditional foods associated with Cork, and today increasingly available only in the English Market, have their origins in this history of provisioning: corned and spiced beef, buttered eggs and salted ling reflect preservation techniques from this era, while offal and blood products such as tripe and drisheen, skirts and kidneys, bodice, and so on were by-products of the city's massive meat export industry. Most

18

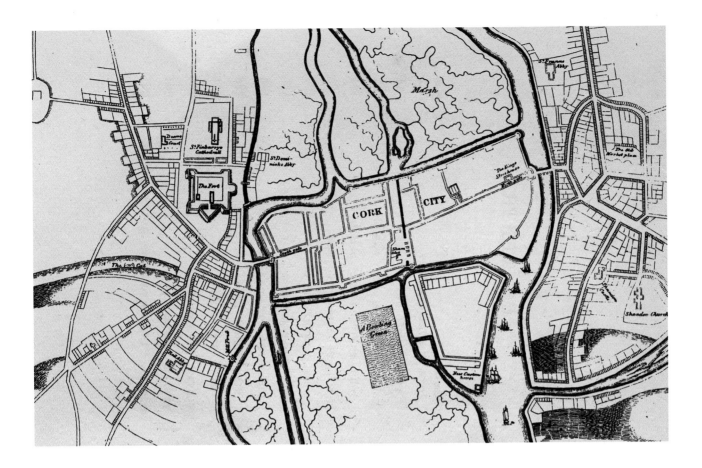

Above:
Map of Cork 1690, from G.A. Story, *An Impartial History of the War In Ireland with a Continuation thereof* (1693).

of the slaughterhouses, packing yards and related activities were located near Blarney Lane in the northern suburb. The processing and export of butter became very well managed, and the city's butter merchants organised their rural suppliers, guaranteed a constant supply, standardised prices and made the quality of their product a priority. They set up the Cork Butter Market in 1769 and it quickly became the largest such market in the world. For the following century Cork butter enjoyed a worldwide reputation while enriching its exporters. Hundreds of coopers were employed in the making and repair of barrels, the basic packaging for provisions, beer and whiskey. The quantity of shipping using the port led to the establishment of shipbuilding and repair yards. A sailcloth industry was established in the village of Douglas, to the southeast of the city, which employed 750 by the 1750s. Textile manufacture became a significant employer also. In the later eighteenth century thousands were employed in the manufacture of woollen, cotton and linen goods. The growth of arable farming, especially to the east of the city, facilitated the supply of barley, and brewing and distilling grew in importance. Large-scale concerns were set up in the city and supplied the local and export markets.

While the export boom in provisions fuelled growth in Cork and its surroundings, the growing population led to local demand for agricultural produce, manufactured goods as well as commercial and professional services. The city was an important market for flour, beer, spirits, leather, textiles, meat, fish and vegetables. Imports of tobacco, tea, wine, brandy, sugar, spices and other luxuries satisfied the exotic demands of the wealthy. These imports led to a four-fold increase in customs receipts for the port of Cork between 1750 and 1800. The travel writer Richard Twiss commented in 1775 that:

> the *forte* of the citizens does not lie in the sciences of painting, sculpture, architecture, music or such trifles, but in the more essential arts relative to eating and drinking; such as the slaughter of hogs, oxen and sheep, in order to exchange the superfluous pork, beef, and mutton, for wine, &c.[3]

The eighteenth century saw a great physical transformation of the city. The cost of the upkeep of the walls of medieval Cork had always been a burden on the city's citizens. The damage done to those walls during the siege of 1690 coupled with the changes

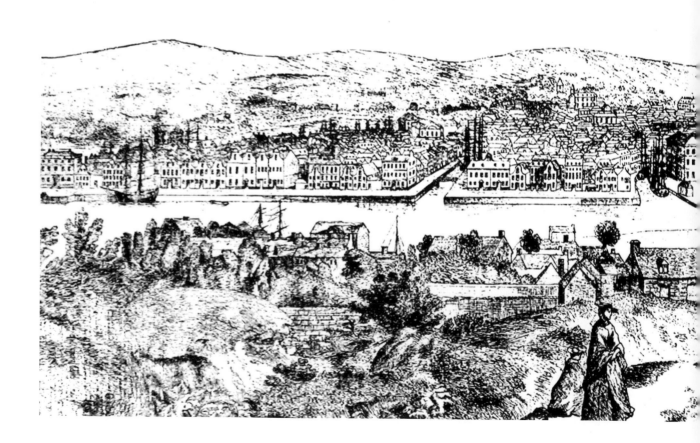

in warfare and how towns were defended made them superfluous. John Carty's map of Cork (1726) shows small lengths of wall surviving in the northeast, northwest and southwest, but by then a substantial amount of building had taken place outside the walls. The North Gate Bridge was replaced in 1712 with a stone bridge of five arches. The following year the bridge at the South Gate was also replaced. Bridges were built to give access to the reclaimed marshes. Tuckey's or Dunscombe's Bridge, leading eastwards from Tuckey's Lane across the waterway that later became the Grand Parade, had been built in or about 1699. This bridge led from the old city to the newly developing streets on Dunscombe's Marsh. The Berwick Fountain on Grand Parade marks the site of that bridge. This marsh was reclaimed and George's Street (now Oliver Plunkett Street) was built as far as Cold Harbour (Parnell Place), and a number of other streets were also built running north and south from it.

Until the eighteenth century a waterway ran along the eastern walls of the city, connecting the principal south and north channels of the River Lee. The course of this waterway is today marked by Grand Parade, Daunt's Square and Cornmarket Street.

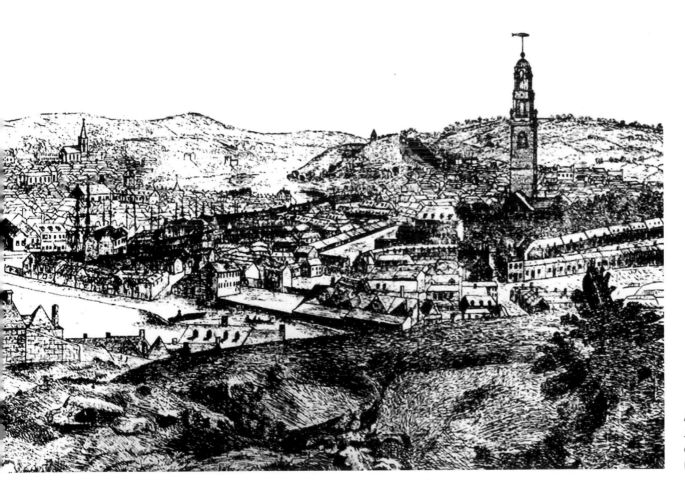

A view of Cork by John Butts from the late eighteenth century. (Cork City Library)

By 1726 the area where Castle Street, Cornmarket Street and the Grand Parade meet had been arched over. A bridge, known as Daunt's Bridge, had previously crossed the waterway at this point. Between 1759 and 1771 the waterway from this point south as far as Tuckey's Bridge was culverted and the eastern side of this new street was known as The Mall (not to be confused with the later South Mall). It was planted with trees and was a favoured promenade for the genteel residents of the newly developing area. By 1789 the remainder of the waterway south to the south channel of the Lee was covered and the Grand Parade, as the new street came to be known, was complete.

The channel that ran from the northern end of Grand Parade eastwards and then curved northwards to the north channel of the Lee was arched over by the end of the 1780s also and St Patrick's Street was created. The first St Patrick's Bridge was built between 1788 and 1791 and became only the second bridge of significance, apart from that at the North Gate, to cross from the flat of the city to the north side of the river.

This new access facilitated traffic to and from the new commercial centre of the city.

The South Mall today runs eastwards from the southern end of Grand Parade. This was a waterway until the early nineteenth century. With the development of Dunscombe's Marsh during the previous century a quay had been built along the south side of the marsh and warehouses and offices, with residential accommodation overhead, were built along it. This corresponds to the north side of today's South Mall. In the years after 1761 a bridge was built between this quay and the island to the south, known as Lavitt's Island, later Morrison's Island, from where Princes Street met the South Mall. Another bridge was built from the south side of this island to Red Abbey Marsh. This latter bridge was the forerunner of today's Parliament Bridge. A bridge also spanned the waterway that was to become the South Mall further east at Cook Street and later at Pembroke Street. The South Mall waterway was infilled in 1801-2.

During the 1700s Cornmarket Street was created through the culverting of the waterway that ran northwards from Daunt's Square. While it was still open the east side was known as Newenham's Quay and the Potato Quay lay opposite. Another dock off the north channel of the Lee was King's Dock. A Custom House was built here in 1724 and today it constitutes the older section of the Crawford Art Gallery. The dock was filled in later in the century to create the area now called Emmet Place, and a new Custom House was built further east on Lapp's Island between 1816 and 1818. The eighteenth century also saw the reclamation of Pike's and Hammond's Marshes to the west of the old city and the arching over and infilling of former waterways to create new streets. The Mansion House (now the Mercy Hospital), the official residence of the Mayor, was built here in 1767. Clarke's Bridge was built in 1776 and connected Wandesford Quay and Clarke's Marsh to the city.

An enlightened approach to the problems of planning in the rapidly expanding city is seen in the establishment of the Wide Street Commissioners in 1765 to instigate and oversee projects to improve and widen existing streets and to draw up plans for new thoroughfares. They were responsible for the layout of South Terrace, Dunbar Street, and the widening of

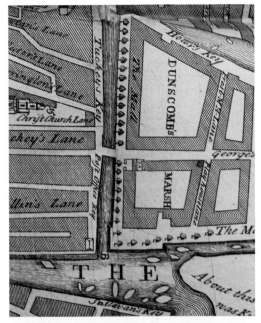

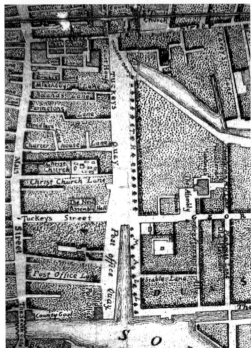

Opposite page:
North Gate Bridge in the late eighteenth century. Etching by Nathaniel Grogan (the elder). (Crawford Municipal Art Gallery)

Above:
Details from the maps of Charles Smith (1750) and John Rocque (1773), showing the development of the Grand Parade.

Top: Detail from John Rocque's map (1773), showing the dock that later became Cornmarket Street.

Bottom: General street scene in Cork, *Illustrated London News*, 3 March 1888.

Castle, Tuckey and Shandon Streets. Their greatest achievement is considered to be the construction of Great George's Street (now Washington Street) in the 1820s. The quays along the main channels of the river were gradually improving as the reclamation of marshes, the infilling and culverting of water channels and the construction of new streets proceeded. However, it was not until the Harbour Commissioners were set up in 1813 that a co-ordinated approach to the problems of navigation on the river and the proper construction and maintenance of quays was properly addressed.

Eighteenth-century Cork society

Great prosperity made some wealthy, but the vast majority of people led miserable lives in the crowded tenements and narrow lanes of the city. Access to a clean water supply was difficult. The majority of the city's population got their water directly from the river and its associated channels, and these same channels were used as dumps and also drained the city's sewage. The waste from the numerous slaughterhouses, tanneries and other industrial concerns also ended up in those waters. In 1734 Dr Joseph Rogers attributed the epidemics that ravaged the city in the eighteenth century partly to:

> The great number of slaughterhouses both in the North and South suburbs, especially on the North Ridge of Hills, where are vast Pits for containing the putrifying Blood and Ordure, which discharge by the Declivities of those

Hills, upon the great Rains, their fetid contents into the River: The Streams and Vapours of the said Pits, even corrupting the most wholesome Northern Blasts, when they are pour'd down on the City ... The unwholesome, foul, [...] corrupted Waters, that great Numbers of the Inhabitants, are necessitated to use during the dry Months of the Summer ... [and] the vast Quantitites of Animal Offals used by the meaner sort during the slaughtering Seasons.[4]

Piped water was first supplied in the 1770s but its cost put it beyond the means of all but the wealthy. The first public fountain to supply water to the poor free of charge was not erected until 1815. The streets and lanes were also filthy; ash and 'night filth' was thrown from windows and doorways, and dung was a constant problem owing to the volume of horse traffic as well as cattle and other animals being driven through the streets. Pigs roamed freely and were regarded by many as doing a public service in that they ate much of the night filth and other waste thrown onto the streets. The corporation attempted to deal with the problem by appointing scavengers, sweepers and barrow-men to keep the streets clean, but their efforts were only occasionally successful. A visitor in the 1770s had been forewarned that Cork was 'the magazine of nastiness', and as late as 1825 it was reported that 'the city and its suburbs from end to end, exhibit a scene of unexampled filth and feculence and mire and dirt, through which the passenger can scarcely wade', with 'sickness and contagion engendered by the accumulated heaps of all kinds of foetid and noxious matter, which are to be found in every part of the city'.[5] It is not surprising that outbreaks of typhus, smallpox, tuberculosis, rabies and other unnamed 'fevers' were common.

Bad weather and consequent crop failure led to frequent food shortages in the 1790s. Disturbance and riot usually resulted as the poor protested and attempted to raid food warehouses. Charitable initiatives such as the setting up of soup kitchens and public ovens gave a little relief to some in times of need. More permanent efforts were made with the opening of the Foundling Hospital in 1747 and the House of Industry in 1777. A dispensary for the poor was set up in 1787 and the Benevolent Society for the Relief of Sick Poor began work in the 1790s. Petty crime was very common in eighteenth-century Cork and punishment was severe. Imprisonment was the fate of some but public whipping, transportation or hanging awaited others. Prostitution was a cause of frequent comment in the newspapers of the time as raids on brothels and 'bawdy-houses' often led to violence and uproar. As well as suffering degradation and brutality many women and girls fell victim to sexually transmitted diseases and the birth of unwanted children multiplied the misery that was life for many.

Up to the later eighteenth century the wealthy minority of the city's inhabitants, largely merchants, shared the narrow and crowded streets with their poorer neighbours. The expansion of the city beyond its medieval confines and on to the reclaimed marshes to the east and west gave these wealthy people the opportunity to live in larger, more elegant houses on new and wide streets. Many had business offices, stores or shops on their ground floors and residential accommodation overhead. A number of the merchant elite moved further from the city centre and built substantial houses in Blackrock and Douglas to the southeast and in Sunday's Well, Montenotte and Tivoli to the north of the River Lee. These houses had stabling for horses, and better roads and bridges made commuting to the city by carriage more feasible. The Protestant minority, together with a small number of Quakers, dominated the trade and commerce of Cork, owned most industrial concerns and made up the majority of the professional classes. Until the middle of the nineteenth century Catholics, who made up over 80 per cent of the population, were successfully excluded from positions of power. Catholics did not have a vote and could not become members of the city's corporation or of parliament. They were also officially excluded from trade and craft guilds. The Friendly Club, a clique of Protestant families founded in the 1760s, maintained a monopoly of municipal power. It controlled the election of Mayor, senior Sheriff and members of the city's grand jury. The club indirectly controlled the distribution of the more important municipal posts such as Town Clerk, Chamberlain and Superintendent of Toll-collectors. The first half of the nineteenth century saw a Catholic ascendancy in commerce and industry, but political power remained the monopoly of this small clique. It was this 'English' corporation which took the decision in the 1780s to construct the flagship markets in the new commercial city centre that survive today as the English Market, a name that refers back to this period before the Catholic merchant and middle class finally achieved political power in the city.

2 A City of Markets

Archaeological and historical evidence reveals Cork's past as a city of markets. Besides the occasional street market on Cornmarket Street, the English Market alone survives into the twenty-first century as a living testimony to this aspect of Cork's rich history and heritage, including its distinctive food traditions.

The emergence and development of markets in Cork city

Medieval town dwellers enclosed their settlements with defensive walls and protected themselves, their rights and privileges from the real and imagined dangers that lay outside. But they also depended on this outside world, near and remote, for their supply of food and other necessities. While a limited amount of animal husbandry and fruit and vegetable growing was carried on within the walls of medieval Cork, it was the rural hinterland that supplied most of its basic needs. There were many informal and casual arrangements for the supply and sale of such goods, but a centrally located market, held regularly, best suited the needs of townspeople. Such a market could more easily be protected and used as a source of revenue for the body that controlled it.

The development of markets, market towns and associated commercial activity began in the Cork region with the spread and consolidation of Anglo-Norman power in the thirteenth century. Markets undoubtedly existed before then. Cork had a large and powerful monastery located on the high ground immediately to the southwest of the central islands of the city. While this monastery, and others like it, were not towns proper, they were centres of population and power prior to the foundation of Ireland's first towns by the Vikings. Basic economic activities, such as the trading and bartering of goods and labour, took place at such locations. This type of economic exchange, carried on at a time before the introduction of money, constituted a market at its most basic level. Viking trading posts, later to become towns, began to be established at significant Irish port sites, including Cork, during the ninth and tenth centuries. The embryonic town of Cork became permanent and as its population grew, so too did trade with the hinterland. Producers were attracted to the town for trade and it may be assumed that a market place came to be defined within the enclosed settlement. The Vikings were the first to use money in Ireland and this made exchange and trade more sophisticated.

The Anglo-Normans who arrived in Ireland in the late twelfth century quickly established control over much of the east and south of the country. The Hiberno-Norse town of Cork was taken in 1177 and during the following century the influx of people into the region, coupled with agricultural innovation and the production of surpluses, led to a growth in internal and external trade. Anglo-Norman lords who established boroughs on their newly acquired lands sought royal licence to establish weekly markets or yearly fairs to promote the economic fortunes of their boroughs and to generate revenue for themselves. Such markets were held in definite locations at specific times and needed protection and regular supervision if they were to attract trade and render tax to a lord. Markets were essential to the existence of boroughs and urban areas. A succession of royal charters, from that of Henry III in 1242 onwards, conferred on the successive corporations of Cork the exclusive right to hold markets within the city. In 1299 the Sheriff of Cork listed 36 markets and market towns that by then formed a network of commercial activity, especially in the north and east of what is now County Cork.[1] In addition to Cork, Shandon, barely a few hundred metres to the north of the medieval city, and del Fayth, a similar distance to the south, are also listed as having their own markets. The use of money expanded in the thirteenth century; in rural areas it began to replace rents in kind and labour and in a variety of other transactions also, but was still more widely used in an urban context, especially in markets. Payments, taxes and tolls could now be rendered in coin, a portable and convenient method of measuring and moving wealth.

The location of medieval Cork's market place is indicated on a map of 1545.[2] An open space is shown within the city walls just north of the junction of the two central islands of the city. This corresponds approximately to the area to the north of today's Liberty Street. It is called Cross Green on the map and the market cross, called the Cork Cross, is marked in the centre of this area. No buildings are indicated, which suggests that it was an open market place. The plan of Cork in *Pacata Hibernia* dates to about 1590 and seems to show the base of the market cross just north of the central crossing between North and South Main Streets. The open market space shown for 1545 no longer exists. However, this is a stylised representation and there may still have been sufficient room for a market place in the area. A map of Cork from 1602 shows the cross in position and a relatively large open space to the east of it, which may have been a market place. Cork had then, or shortly thereafter, a market house. In 1620 the corporation of the city mortgaged it and much else at a time of great financial difficulty. An entry in the *Council Book* for 6 December 1630 states that Alderman Dominick Roche was to build 'a good and convenient Market house in the New Street and nowhere else'.

By the late seventeenth century Cork was enjoying a boom. The city and its suburbs had a population approaching 20,000 and the trading of foodstuffs, wares and services was becoming more sophisticated and specialised. The city had many shops and outlets dealing in a more defined range of goods as retailing developed. But markets remained important and were a significant source of revenue for the corporation, which built, maintained and regulated them. They also became more specialised and wholesale and retail markets for the sale of meat, fish, corn and other produce were either built, developed or improved at this time. This era of specialisation was reflected in the trades, which were becoming more defined. Guilds were increasingly organised for carpenters, bakers, tanners, skinners, goldsmiths and for many more of the trades then prospering in Cork. The butchers of the city had their own guild and the charter and bye-laws of the Society of Butchers in Cork was discussed by the city's corporation in January 1695.[3] Following the fall of the city to Williamite forces in 1690, all Catholic freemen were disenfranchised, which meant they were excluded from the guilds, could not become apprentices and were restricted in retailing:[4] thus, the Society of Butchers would have been restricted to Protestant or English butchers.

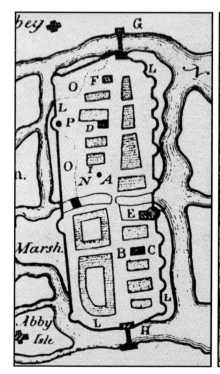

From left to right:
Details from 'A Plan of Cork AD 1545', the *Pacata Hibernia* map of c.1587, and the 1602 map of Cork. (Cork City Library)

The building and maintenance of markets by the municipal authorities was motivated not only by the desire to regulate trade and secure revenue, but also by issues of public health. Cork's economic success was based principally on the provisioning trade and the slaughtering of cattle had grown to such an extent that the corporation prohibited the operation of slaughterhouses inside the city walls in 1614. When the butchers of Youghal were regulated in 1623, they had to pay towards the cleaning of streets and water channels near their stands. The 'English butchers' of Kinsale were incorporated in 1657 and were forbidden to slaughter animals within the town walls, except for their own use, as a measure to ensure streets and watercourses were kept free of blood, bones and offal. In 1670 butchers in Waterford were ordered not to slaughter animals in the streets as 'excrements' and 'filthy and infectious matter' was draining into watercourses.[5] It had been common practice to slaughter and butcher animals in the street or open market place and to offer the meat for sale at standings there. Meat markets were built in an effort to separate the slaughtering and retail aspects of the trade. Purpose-built meat markets became common in the seventeenth and eighteenth centuries and were generally known as 'shambles' or 'flesh shambles'. The word 'shamble' or 'shambles' originally meant a bench and came to be specifically associated with butchers' blocks, benches or stalls. Cork had two such shambles by 1680 when Sir Richard Cox noted that 'The both shambles cost £465, *anno* 1680' in his description of the 'most memorable things' in the city.[6]

The Castle Street Shambles

At least one of the shambles mentioned by Cox was located on the south side of present-day Castle Street. It was an important public amenity and is one of the few features noted by Thomas Phillips on his map of 'Corke Citty' in 1685. This street had been created when the dock that lay within the city walls had been arched over. Story's map of 1690 again shows the Shambles as a significant feature. It is not possible to identify the location of the second shambles mentioned by Cox, but it was probably located in the

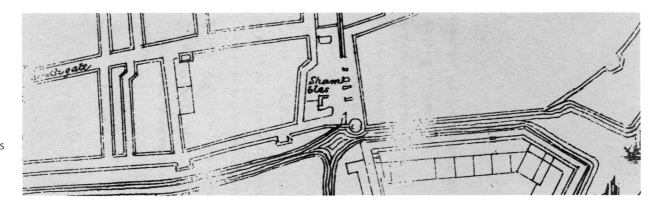

Right:
Detail from G.A. Story's map of Cork in 1690, showing the Castle Street Shambles.

suburb immediately north of the old city. This was where many of the slaughterhouses that fed the growing provisions trade were located and there was an important market place there, noted as 'The Old Market Place' on Story's map.

A description of a shambles in the *Historical Memoirs of the City of Armagh* by James Stuart, published in 1819, explains the typical layout:

> ... ranges of slated shades, so disposed as to ensure an area which is paved and kept perfectly clean in every season of the year. The shades are subdivided into various stalls, which are allocated to different butchers, whose names are inscribed in front, so that the stand of every individual is generally known. No cattle are ever killed here; and the place is free from everything offensive to the sight or smell ... The crane master and clerk of the market are always in attendance, to adjust the weights ... [7]

By 1693 the city-centre shambles on Castle Street was 'daily falling to decay' and the corporation ordered that 'the remaining part of the Shambles be pulled down, and the timber and other materials safely kept, which will go a great way in the new building of same'.[8] It was estimated that the new building would cost £200. Work did not start for another two years, when a *Council Book* entry for 9 April 1695 notes that Alderman Rogers was then building the shambles. By 25 June of that year £260 had been spent on the work and in August the butchers of the city were to choose their stalls in the new building.[9] However, some butchers were reluctant to give up their street standings and on 16 November 1699 the *Council Book* records 'that Mr. Mayor suffer no Butchers to stand in the street for whom he can provide stalls in the Shambles'.

As well as keeping butchers from trading in the street the corporation was also anxious that the Shambles be well run and kept clean. The *Council Book* for 12 June 1701 records that:

> Forasmuch as the Flesh Shambles of this city are kept so nasty, chiefly occasioned by keeping of live sheep therein by night, and partly by killing sheep and calves therein, that there is danger of infection, for preventing whereof, and that the Shambles may be kept clean and sweet, it is ordered, as a standing bye-law, that after 14 June, inst., no sheep or other beasts be kept alive by night nor slaughtered or dressed day or night within said Shambles, except lambs, upon pain of six pence for each sheep or other beast so kept or slaughtered, ... that said Shambles be well cleaned, swept, and the dirt carried away at least twice every week ... by the respective tenants.

Despite being provided with a purpose-built market, some butchers were still reluctant to use the facilities. In 1710 it was ordered that the stalls 'against the walls of the Exchange, and all those against the walls of the Flesh Shambles, be pulled down ... ' and in April 1712 action was again taken against butchers who had deserted the Shambles in favour of stalls in the street outside.[10]

The problem of falling revenue from the Shambles led the corporation to form a committee of investigation in January 1711, and in 1713 it was decided to initiate improvements. The Shambles was an open market area with stalls ranged along walls beneath lean-to roofs. Such 'penthouses', as the *Council Book* terms them, were in a state of disrepair and 'the Butchers and those that come to market are much incommoded'. It was decided to raise a roof over the whole market area so that 'the whole will be dry and clean, and all encouraged to keep their stalls therein'. The principal butchers were prepared to pay an increased rent for these improvements, and when the works were completed in late 1715, rents were raised by 2d per week.[11] This shambles, occasionally called the English Shambles, was the principal city-centre retail market for meat until the opening of the Grand Parade Market in 1788. In 1750 Charles Smith described the Shambles as 'an excellent flesh-market of all kinds of Butcher's meat, which is generally very reasonable and cheap in this city'.[12] The *Council Book* for 22 February 1738 records an effort by the corporation to prevent butchers from holding more than one stall each in the Shambles and also shows how Protestant control of municipal government extended to restrictions on the religious beliefs of its chosen butchers:

> It appears to this board that several of the Butchers are now in possession of two stalls in the English Shambles, which is found very inconvenient; ordered, that when the leases of the present stalls shall expire, leases shall be drawn with such restrictions as shall prevent any Butcher from holding two stalls, and that no stall shall be let to a papist, nor under 18 pence per week.

Such religious discrimination is evidenced again nearly 40 years later in 1772, when the corporation insisted that the stalls in a fowl market that was being converted to use as a meat market '... be set to Protestant Butchers for one year'.[13] The Shambles on Castle Street continued in use until the opening of the Grand Parade Market in 1788. A *Council Book* entry for 7 July 1789 refers to it as 'the late market', suggesting that all business had ceased there.

While the Castle Street Shambles was the principal meat market in the city centre, there were two other significant meat markets on the immediate outskirts. One was located to the north, at the junction of Shandon Street and what is now called Blarney Street, and is generally referred to as the North Shambles. The other, usually called the

South Shambles in the records, was located on the eastern side of Barrack Street, to the south of the old walled city, opposite the junction with Fort Street.

The South Shambles

The South Shambles was the older of the two. The *Council Book* for 27 June 1733 records that 'Mr. Thomas Daunt's proposal for the building of the Meat and Milk Market on the ground near the Barracks be agreed to. He shall be paid, according to his proposals, the sum of £140'. The stalls in this new market were let five months later at 7d per week. This is less than half of what was charged at the Castle Street Shambles, where stalls were let at 18d per week in 1738, indicating the relative status of the two markets. The corporation again insisted that no butcher keep standings in the street. The market was also used for the sale of milk, and like the butchers, sellers of milk were forbidden from 'keeping churns in the street without the South Gate'. In May 1737 an order was agreed for the building of a dedicated milk market adjacent to this meat market.[14] The opening of the Grand Parade Market in 1788 and the later growth of butchers' shops in the city took from the trade in meat in this and other markets. By the second half of the nineteenth century the Ordnance Survey maps are naming the former Barrack Street Shambles 'Potato Market'.

This part of Barrack Street was also the location of an open general market. This market occupied the space outside the eastern wall of Elizabeth Fort fronting the street.

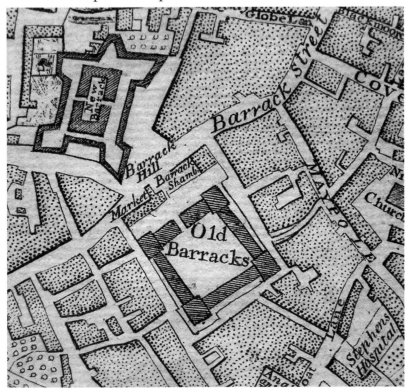

John Rocque's map of 1773 shows a market area and indicates the meat and milk markets as 'Barrack Shambles'. This open market space was walled in 1843 and named St Finnbarr's Market. The site today is occupied by a coal yard. This general area had long been associated with market activity. As noted above, a market, known as del Fayth, was functioning in this area as early as the thirteenth century. Markets continued to operate on Barrack Street well into the

Left:
Detail from John Rocque's map (1773), showing the location of the Barrack Street markets.

twentieth century, but the records of income of the various corporation markets show that their contribution was not significant, often as little as one-thirtieth of the income derived from the English Market.

The North Shambles

The building of the North Shambles was first proposed in 1735. On 4 March of that year the *Council Book* records that Alderman Austin produced plans for a market in the Shandon area. His plans were mentioned again on 19 February 1736 and on 2 December it was decided that 'Mr. Mayor, both Sheriffs, Ald. Knapp, and Austin do measure the waste ground opposite Shandon Church and report if it be a fit place to build a meat market'. The market was built soon afterwards and on 22 February 1738 it is recorded that 'Jo. Huleat shall provide three beams, scales and weights sufficient that one of them shall be fixed in the new Shambles out of the North Gate ... '. A stone from the North Shambles, now in Cork Public Museum, is inscribed:

This Shambles was erected at the expense of Corporation Corke Anno D N I 1737 Thomas Farren Esq. Mayr. and Dan Crone Esq. and Richd. Bradshaw Esq. Sheriffs

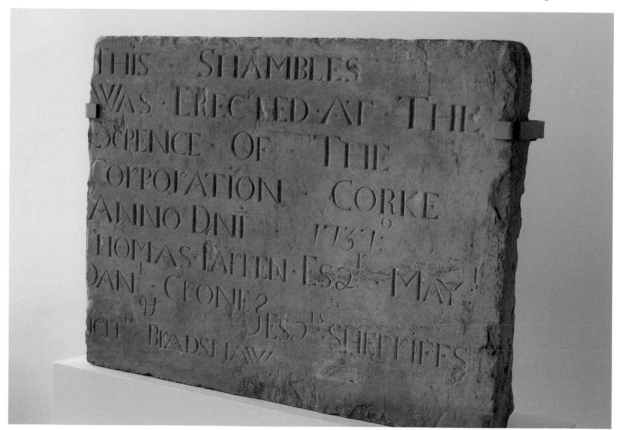

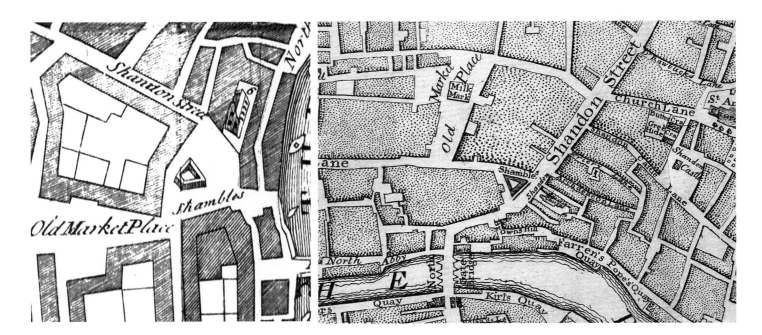

Above:
Detail from the maps of Charles Smith (1750) (left) and John Rocque (1773), showing the North Shambles and Old Market Place.

This shambles is shown on Charles Smith's map of 1750 as an open space with a four-sided building at its centre. John Rocque's maps from later in that century, and all subsequent maps, show the space as having a triangular arrangement of buildings within it. It continued to be used well into the nineteenth century and is named 'Shambles' on the large-scale Ordnance Survey map of the city of 1872.

Fish Markets

A narrow street or lane running west from North Main Street, which corresponds to present-day Liberty Street, is named on maps from 1750 as Fishamble Lane. This indicates the presence of a fish shambles or market in the vicinity and probably predates the fish market that formed part of the Castle Street Shambles, built in the early 1690s. A description of Cork from 1748 notes that the Fish Market lay near the Exchange, or Tholsel, and that 'this situation is very convenient, a double-cut stream running on each side, which is a means of rendering it sweet and clean'. This visitor also wrote of the range of fish available: 'Crayfish I have seen, of thirty ounces, bought for threepence, salmon at a penny a pound, turbot under threepence, and all other fish in proportion ... What rich town in Europe can produce the same?'[15] Charles Smith in 1750 described the fish shambles as 'very convenient, being erected on a branch of the river which runs thro' arches under the middle of the town, by which means they are kept clean, cool and sweet. This market is well supplied with fish, chiefly from Kingsale.'[16] Both these accounts indicate that the water channel arched over to create Castle Street was partly open, or at least accessible, to those using the Fish Market.

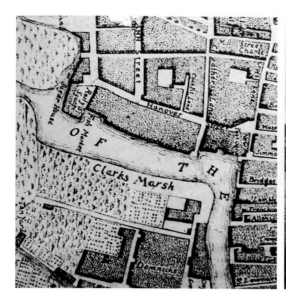 

Above:
Location of Cork's
eighteenth-century
Fish Market as shown
on John Rocque's map
(1759), and a view of
the site today from
Wandesford Quay.

In March 1735 the corporation approved the preparation of a plan for a new 'Fishambles'.[17] However, the proposed development does not seem to have gone ahead as the possibility of building a 'Fish Market' was mentioned again on 3 December 1736. The *Council Book* records no further activity in relation to this matter until twenty years later when, on 2 September 1756, a group of corporation members was asked to look about the city and report 'where they can find a proper place to erect a new Fish Market, the present one being small'. A location was found and on 30 October it was recorded that a plot of ground running southwards from the western end of Hanover Street to the South Channel of the river would be acquired for the purpose. An entry for 13 December 1758 shows that the new market was ready to be occupied and it was ordered 'that the fish be immediately removed to the present Fish Market'. The vacated premises on Castle Street were to be used for the sale of fowl and eggs. Rocque's map of 1759 and Connor's of 1774 both show the new 'Fish Market' at the location indicated in the *Council Book*.

This market was still functioning in 1789, a year after the opening of the Grand Parade Market, as indicated in a *Council Book* entry for 6 February of that year, when one Robert Travers was appointed 'to sweep Gratton Street and all the streets to the west of it, together with Anne Street, and from thence to the Fish market'. Soon afterwards plans were made to move the fish market to a new site, adjacent to the Grand Parade Market, and the new Fish Market was built in 1789. A number of entries in the *Council Book* suggest that this market lay to the north of the Grand Parade Market, between Mutton Lane and Meat Market Lane and was accessed initially from St Patrick's Street and later from the Princes Street Market also. It corresponds to what later became known as the Little or Back Market. In 1792 it was decided that the ground on which the old Fish Market stood, off Hanover Street, was to be 'set by public auction for 500 years'.[18]

Milk Markets

Milk, a very perishable commodity, was sold daily door-to-door, at standings in the street and in the various markets where the corporation set aside specific space for its sale. During the eighteenth century there were at least four milk markets operating in the city. The earliest reference to a dedicated milk market is to a 'Milk Market in the North Suburbs' on 25 April 1732. In 1733 the corporation agreed to the building of a meat and milk market on Barrack Street and it was decided that vendors would be charged a half-penny 'for every pair of churns that come into the New Milk Market'. Four years later it was decided to separate the sale of meat and milk at Barrack Street and a specific milk market was established.[19] A *Council Book* entry for 6 May 1737 refers to yet another milk market at an unspecified location, and the description suggests an arrangement similar to that used at a meat shambles:

> That the piece of vacant ground lately in the possession of Abraham Morris, *dec.*, be immediately inclosed with a wall built of stone, lime and sand, the ground to be ten feet in the clear; the front to be converted into a Milk Market for the profit of this Corporation, to be roofed linney-wise, supported by stone pillars, and a door to be fixed in the centre of the east wall.

In 1747 another milk market was built at Old Market Place, off Blarney Lane in the northern suburb. The plan was by Alderman Croker and a mason, Thomas Clemmens, was employed to do the building.[20] This milk market is shown in the centre of Old Market Place on Rocque's map of 1759 and on subsequent editions also. Daniel Murphy's map of 1789 also shows it in this position, however the Ordnance Survey map of 1872 shows 'Milk Market' as a different building to the southeast of the main market place. In 1887 the corporation built Ryan's Buildings on the site of Old Market Place, a housing development for labourers and their families. In 1754 the Brocklesby family granted a walled plot of over one acre in extent in Blackpool to the corporation for use as a market place.[21] A milk market was established here and functioned for over 100 years while the site was also used as a cattle market. In the 1860s part of the market area was used by the corporation as a storage area for dung cleared from the streets of the city, something that local residents understandably resented.[22] In 1886 the corporation built 76 labourers' dwellings (Madden's Buildings on Watercourse Road) on this site. The *Council Book* for 24 September 1790 indicates that a milk market had operated in the vicinity of the Bridewell on Potato Quay, which was located on the western side of present-day Cornmarket Street. By the date of the entry the market had ceased operations.

Other Markets

Many other lesser markets are mentioned in the *Council Book* for the years 1690 to 1800. An herb market is mentioned in 1706 and in 1718 a new herb market was ordered to be built 'at the end of the New Corn Market'. In 1758 a new market was built near the City Court House, then located to the south of Castle Street, east of the Shambles, and 'several standings of Frize and other woollens, of bandle cloath, and other linens, of gartering and other small wares' were ordered to be removed from the 'Public Street' into the market. This market is later referred to as the Frize Market and in 1760 it became a fowl market, while the existing fowl market became a market for butter and eggs.[27] A Bandle Cloth market is again mentioned on 7 November 1788 and on 18 March 1791 it was suggested that the new Grand Parade and Princes Street markets would 'be made more complete by bringing the Butter and other Markets, such as the Frize and Bandle Cloth Markets and Worstead Market to adjoin' them. A fruit market and an apple market are also mentioned in the records, but no locations are given for them.[28]

Revenues and regulation

Expenditure on the building and improvement of markets by the corporation was regarded primarily as an investment, though the provision of a service to its citizens was also a consideration. The income generated for the corporation by rents paid for stalls or standings in the markets and by tolls collected on goods sold there was the return. Tolls, called gateage, were also collected on goods brought into the city for sale and toll collection stations were set up on all principal entry points to the city. The tolls paid on cattle made up the major part of these. The significance of this income can be seen from figures noted by Charles Smith in 1750. He estimated the revenues collected by the corporation at between £1,200 and £1,300 per year, of which gateage tolls, rents of stalls in markets and the tolls paid by street sellers amounted to £790. In the 1780s the gateage tolls yielded an average of between £1,800 and £2,000 per year. Fifty years later the relative importance of tolls and market-generated income in the corporation's revenues was similarly significant. Averaged over five years to 1833, total annual revenue was £6,237, £4,976 of which came from tolls and market rents.[29] It was clearly in the corporation's interest to maintain well-regulated markets. The corporation forced butchers to trade in the official markets rather than at standings in the street, and the *Council Book* records a number of decisions in this regard.[30] Hawkers, pedlars and other casual street sellers were a constant presence on the streets of Cork and were an important element in the distribution and sale of food and other commodities, especially to the less well off. Though they too had to pay tolls for the right to sell in the street,

Above:
'The Irish resisting the toll at Roche's Castle, Cork' by John Fitzgerald, showing the dock, now occupied by Castle Street, viewed from the west.
(Port of Cork)

they were frequently seen as an obstruction to the free passage of people and, literally, more trouble than they were worth. Occasional efforts were made to move them to the markets. On 13 December 1758 the corporation noted:

> Whereas the petty dues received by the Corporation for pitching or standing in the street hath been a pretence for crowding the street with standings, to the great inconvenience of the public passage; and whereas Markets have been erected by the Corporation for articles formerly sold in the street; ordered, that no standings be suffered in the Public Street, or on the Bridges, and that the Pitching pence for standings in the street shall not from henceforth be collected until further order to the contrary.

The *Cork Hibernian Chronicle* of 7 October 1773 reports another attempt by the corporation to protect its citizens from the nuisance of street sellers and the added danger of reckless drivers:

M&E. SHEEHAN

Grand Parade, Fish Market
Cork.

M. & E. Sheehan – Eddie Sheehan

Eddie Sheehan was born in 1933 and started work in the market in 1951 at the age of eighteen, having completed his Leaving Certificate. Prior to that he had worked part-time at his father's stall as a schoolboy for 5s per week but Eddie's mother did not want him working there: 'Keep out of that bloody place!', she said. Eddie did not heed her advice and worked in the Market until 2000, when he retired and the business of M. & E. Sheehan ceased trading. The business was founded by Eddie's grand-uncle and grandfather, Edward and Michael Sheehan, and the minutes of the Tolls and Markets Committee of the Corporation first mention this partnership in 1906, although Michael Sheehan was trading in his own name in the market from 1887. M. & E. Sheehan also traded in St Finnbarr's Market on Barrack Street and had a fish smokehouse there. Michael Sheehan died in 1919 and Edward continued the business, to be succeeded in time by his son Jack, Eddie's father. In his 50 years in the Market, Eddie worked with his father Jack, his mother Cissy, Paddy Hickey, Davey Hurley, his grand-aunt Annie, his wife Sheila and son Michael. The Market was an integral part of all their lives.

The busiest trading day for the fish stalls was Friday. 'You almost couldn't cope', Eddie remembers. 99 per cent of the customers were women and the principal varieties bought were whiting, plaice, cod, white sole, mackerel and herring. The more expensive varieties such as smoked salmon, brill, turbot and black sole were more frequently bought by restaurants and hotels. Customers did not want to buy pre-prepared fish. The fish had to be cleaned and filleted at the counter while the customer watched. Buying pre-prepared fish could mean you were buying another's leavings. At the busiest times, for example after morning mass in nearby St Augustine's church, the crush at the counter brought cries of 'I was here first!' or 'I was before her!' and there was little evidence of restraint or courtesy as customers elbowed their way to the counter. Like a barman in a busy pub, the staff learned to keep their eyes downcast while filling an order, as to make eye contact with a customer would necessitate acknowledgement and immediate attention. Lent was a very busy time. The overwhelming majority of customers were Catholic and strictly observed the rules of abstinence for Lent, not eating meat on Wednesdays or Fridays and eating fish as an alternative. Most fish was sold fresh, but there was a market for smoked haddock or cod, commonly called yellow fish, and kippers, which are smoked herrings. These were generally supplied from Scotland by the firm of Allen & Day. The Sheehans smoked salmon to satisfy the limited demand for it at the time. Another popular cured fish was salted and dried ling, commonly known as battleboard. This was popular during Lent and was traditionally eaten also in the days before Christmas. The Sheehans also had a significant business supplying hotels, restaurants and a number of hospitals in Cork and Tralee.

Fresh fish was sourced from a number of different suppliers. Eddie Sheehan recalls the depots of Bord Iascaigh Mhara and that of Clayton Love in the city. Fish was also supplied by the Dingle Fishermen's Co-operative and by the Coastal Fish Company at the Dublin Fish Market. In the years before Sheehans had their own van, two carriers, George Hallissey and Leslie Cuttris, who had horses and drays, transported the fish from the depots or from the railway station to the Market. Fish ordered from the Dublin market at 7 am arrived in Cork by 3 pm. Fresh fish also came from abroad, from Russell & Hancock in Milford Haven in Wales and plaice from Holland. The Sheehans had a refrigerated store in Market Avenue, formerly Pump Lane, adjacent to the Market. Many

Above: Edward and Michael Sheehan.

stallholders did not have any refrigeration and sometimes used the Sheehans' facility. Eddie remembers a florist, Betty Fell, storing roses there. Ice was bought from O'Sullivan's Cold Storage.

Messenger boys were an essential feature of the fish trade. M. & E. Sheehan had two messenger boys and on Fridays employed an extra one. A plate, fixed below the crossbar of the messenger's bicycle carried the name of the stall or shop. Eddie recalls an incident when a Garda (policeman) came to the Market and reported to Jack, Eddie's father, that he had seen an M. & E. Sheehan bicycle speeding down Shandon Street with four people 'on board' – one driving, another behind on the saddle, a third sitting on the handlebars and a fourth in the basket in front. Jack was asked to deal with the matter. His solution was to paint over the nameplate so that the bicycle would not be easily identified in any future incidents!

Those manning the stall of M. & E. Sheehan wore white coats, wellington boots and yellow oilskin aprons. Each worker had two knives, a larger heavy knife for chopping and a smaller sharper filleting knife. These knives were the essential tools of the trade and were closely guarded. Borrowing another's knife was frowned upon. These knives were generally supplied by the firm of Broderick of Sir John Rogerson's Quay in Dublin. Mr Kelly was the representative of the firm who visited the Market regularly.

In reflecting on his 50 years in the Market, Eddie notes some significant changes from when he first started work. The requirement to abstain from meat on Wednesdays and Fridays during the 40 days

of Lent lapsed, as did the Friday abstinence during the rest of the year. This impacted on trade and fish became a food of choice rather than a compulsory one. Poverty became less obvious also. In the 1950s and 1960s many people struggled to provide for their families and lived very much on a day-to-day basis. In more recent years it became rare to see hungry and malnourished people. Eddie recalls regular visits from nuns of charitable orders visiting the Market with buckets to collect fish, meat and vegetables.

Eddie says: 'You had to be born into the market to work there.' He was, and worked there for 50 years until the stall of M. & E. Sheehan closed in 2000.

Opposite page, bottom: Jack Sheehan. *Above:* The former stall of M. & E. Sheehan, as it now looks.

3 The English Market 1788-1899

Why 'English'?

The appellation 'English Market' for the new city-centre covered markets, established in the late 1780s and early 1790s by Cork Corporation, appears to have been retrospectively applied, certainly in the official sense. In contrast to the occasional usage of 'English Shambles' for its Castle Street predecessor as the main municipal market, none of the surviving municipal records or contemporary accounts from its early decades uses the term. It was not an official title, but a popular name, which may have been in general usage from the outset, if and when, as is likely, the religious restrictions on traders was applied as in the English Shambles and the clientele was predominantly from the relatively large Protestant population of the city centre. It is also possible that the name gained currency following the reform of the corporation under the 1840 Municipal Reform Act, after which the previously all-Protestant/unionist/conservative/Ascendancy (or 'English') body had a Catholic/liberal/nationalist (or 'Irish') majority and identity. This hibernicised, reformed corporation oversaw the building and official opening in 1843 of a new municipal covered food market, St Peter's, which fronted onto North Main Street and backed onto Cornmarket Street. This apparently became known as the 'Irish Market', presumably to distinguish it from the 'English Market', and visa-versa. It is unlikely that the distinction is linguistically based. While Cork city had a relatively significant Irish-speaking population, which increased with immigration from the countryside in the mid-nineteenth century, the census returns for the second half of the century show that the number of Irish-only speakers in the city declined from a minuscule 126 in 1851 to 96 in 1871; those who spoke both languages declined from 10,258 in

1851 to 5,294 in 1871, in an average population of around 80,000.[1] The vast majority of Irish speakers were poor and Catholic, so would have been more likely to shop and trade in St Peter's, but not in sufficient numbers to offer a solely linguistic explanation for the terms 'Irish' and 'English'. The earliest reference to 'the English Market' that we have encountered is in a newspaper report of 1855.[2] The reformed corporation's own Tolls and Markets Committee minutes first feature the term in 1887 in a reference to 'the butchers of the Back English Market'; there are only two subsequent usages – one in 1894 and another in 1895.[3] The markets were denoted, initially, as the New Market or Markets, the Corporation Market, and subsequently as the Grand Parade Market and later the Grand Parade, Back or Little, and Princes Street Markets.

The location of the new market was significant and symbolic. It was situated at the heart of the newly developed commercial centre of the expanding city. This was where the bulk of Cork's affluent merchant and professional elite lived, worked and shopped, and the shops and services in the streets around the Market reflected this. Variety, specialisation and luxury distinguished the area's retail profile from the basic, general and low-grade concerns in the old medieval city area, where the majority of the poor lived and shopped (and later its Shandon Street and Barrack Street extensions, where the migrant poor congregated). This pattern intensified through the first half of the nineteenth century. A trade directory of 1787 lists the wine merchants, cigar divans, jewellers and goldsmiths, upmarket outfitters and toy shops in St Patrick's Street, Princes Street, the Grand Parade and George's Street. All but one of Cork's eleven perfumers were located in this area; most of the pawn shops were in the old city, on and about North and South

Above:
Woodford Bourne & Co. on the corner of St Patrick's Street, Stratten & Stratten's *Dublin, Cork, and South of Ireland.* (London, 1892)

51

Main Streets.[4] A century later, a visitor described the area as 'filled with well-stocked shops, handsome buildings and well-dressed people intent on business'.[5] Along with the significant expense of purchasing the required property and land, and constructing the new market, the choice of location indicates the intention of the corporation that it cater for the better off. This was to be an upmarket market. Was it also to be an exclusively Protestant market? No surviving records suggest this. The new city centre did have a disproportionately high Protestant population, but wealth rather than religion was the key determinant of social and economic (though still not political) acceptability and respectability. The Catholic upper and middle classes were increasing in numbers and wealth from the late eighteenth century and it is likely that they patronised the new markets from the outset. What gave the Market its Protestant or English identity was its administration: the Market managers and operatives were appointees of the Protestant corporation, beneficiaries of the discriminatory and exclusionary patronage system that characterised municipal administration. As an extension of this, it is likely that Protestant traders were given priority in the allocation of stalls. There was probably a strong protectionist impulse at work here. Cork's victuallers or butchers, the core Market traders, were overwhelmingly Catholic, and while these 'papists' may not have been completely excluded as they were in the late English Shambles, they were likely to have been in a minority in the infant English Market.

The plans take shape

In January 1785 the corporation ordered the taking of four buildings fronting the Grand Parade, together with their 'back concerns' and 'all the large tract of ground backwards of said houses' for a term of 999 years at a yearly rent of £196 18s 6d. These were 'the house now inhabited by Mrs Kennedy, the house and concerns occupied by Mr Marrett, now in the possession of Mr Burnett, the dwelling-house in the tenancy of Mrs Jappie, and the dwelling house in the possession of the Miss Johnsons'.[6] The process of creating the new markets had begun. On 30 June the following year, it was recorded that

> Whereas this board [the Corporation] is of opinion that for effectually completing the markets intended to be built, some of the adjacent grounds and houses may be necessary to be added to that already taken, ordered, that the Mayor, &c., be at liberty to purchase the interests of any person or persons in any way interested in such adjacent grounds and houses be thought necessary to be added, or take the same on lease or leases ...

In August 1786 it was agreed to pay Thomas Bewley £190 for his interest in the premises held by him from Robert Dennis in St Patrick's Street, 'extending backwards to the ground whereon the New Markets are intended to be built'. A sum of £60 was ordered to be paid to Bewley for his interest in the adjoining house on St Patrick's Street and £40 to Edward Hart Hope for his part of the same premises. A further £150 was paid to Rev John Pick for his dwelling house and surrounding ground in Princes Street.[7] Samuel Andrews was commissioned to draw a map of the grounds in this area between Grand Parade, St Patrick's Street, Princes Street and George's Street where the markets were to be built. Clearance of the grounds began and the materials from the area were sold by public auction.[8] On 29 September 1786, 'The mayor, the late mayor, the sheriffs, the late sheriffs, the aldermen and burgesses, with the city regalia, went in procession to lay the new foundation of the new meat market'.[9]

The preparation for this major work of municipal construction proceeded in 1787. In March the corporation decided that the markets would be flagged instead of paved, and an advertisement was placed in the Dublin, Cork and Waterford newspapers seeking a proposal from stonecutters and building providers for the supply of '1,000 square yards of stone, which must be of a gritty quality, from 3 to 4 inches thick, that will not wear smooth; the persons proposing must undertake to have them completely squared and laid by the first day of January next'. The acquisition of necessary buildings on the site continued with the purchase, for £60, of Joseph Morgan's interest in the dwelling house on Grand Parade taken by him from Mr Jappie.[10] In September the proposal of Samuel Hobbs and William Flaherty for the supply of flagstones was accepted; they were paid 7s 6d per square yard 'for so many square yards of flagging as the markets be found to contain when finished'. Hobbs and Flaherty furnished the corporation with estimates for the construction of:

> one division, one counter, and three racks, to go against two sides, and one stall intended for the New Meat Market, the division to be 8 feet in depth, and ten feet high each in the clear, as also providing and fixing tables to each stall, the whole expense of finishing one stall agreeable to such estimate, amounting to £5 7s 6d, to which they agree.[11]

The Market is born

Several stalls according to this design were set up in July 1788 and offered for rent, paid weekly, for one year. (In September 1789 it was decided to lease the stalls for seven years, at a weekly rent of 5s) It was specified that they were for the sale of meat only. On 1 August 1788 the city fathers gathered for the grand opening of the new market, which was still a work-in-progress. After the ceremonies, they retired to Blackrock Castle for

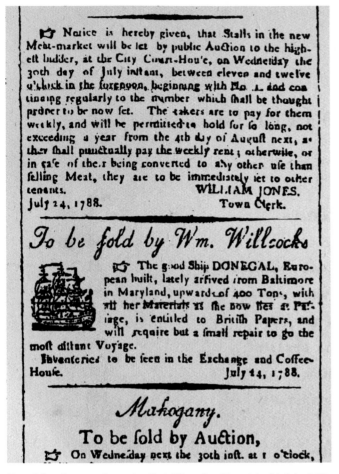

Top: Advertisement from the *Cork Hibernian Chronicle*, 24 July 1788, announcing a public auction of market stalls.

Bottom: Detail from a map of Cork by Dan Murphy (1789). The Grand Parade Market was in place at this time, but the first Princes Street Market had not yet been built. The building shown on Princes Street is the Presbyterian Church.

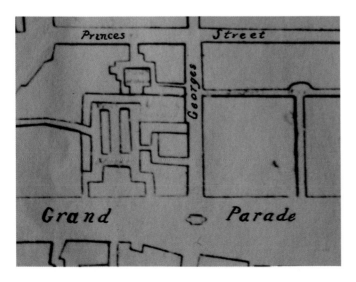

a celebration hosted by the mayor, Richard Purcell, having set aside the substantial sum 30 guineas to fund the occasion.[12] On its first Christmas, the mayor visited it and the other city markets to collect for the poor,

> and the butchers, bakers, root-sellers, &c., most cheerfully contributed in aid of so laudable a request. A quantity of the provision was in consequence sent to the City gaol, the House of Industry, and to many very wretched room keepers, which his Worship sought out with great attention, and happily relieved their distress.[13]

The original Market gradually took shape over the following years, under the supervision of a special corporation committee under former mayor, Sir John Franklin, who was paid 100 guineas per year for his 'very great trouble'. It was decided to create fish, fowl and vegetable markets as appendages to the core meat market. A proposal that 'the whole may be made more complete by bringing the Butter and other Markets, such as the Frize [sic] and Bandle Cloth Markets and the Worsted Market to adjoin the other Markets' was not proceeded with.[14] In 1789 the city's central fish market was relocated to a new site adjoining the Grand Parade meat market. The 'New Fish Market', which was fitted out with specially constructed stone tables, was located to the north of the Grand Parade Market, between Mutton Lane and Meat Market Lane, and was accessed initially from St Patrick's Street and soon after from the new, adjoining Root Market, off Princes Street. It had space for over twenty stalls and later became known variously as the Back Market, Little Market and Little English Market. During the early nineteenth century the Back Market became an extension of the main meat market.

A 'Fowl Market', for the sale of poultry, and 'Green' or 'Root Market' for vegetables, were developed and extended in appended areas towards Princes Street.

A narrow passage from Princes Street into these markets was created in the early 1790s.[15] The vegetable and fowl market that this passage accessed was not roofed over, though peripheral shelter was provided by linney-type roofing around the edges of the market space. Here women sold vegetables and poultry from a chaos of standings, sittings and stalls, for which they paid much lower rent than the victuallers and mongers in the more formalised stalls of the adjoining covered meat and fish markets. It continued in this form until 1862 when the new, covered Princes Street Market was opened.

The new markets, along with all the others in the city, were overseen by a Market Jury, which in 1791 was empowered by the Mayor (Henry Puxley) to visit the markets, as well as storehouses, shops, cellars and anywhere else where 'Provisions and Victuals are sold, or made up' and to seize any that were 'unwholesome', 'bad', or 'illegally made up'.[16] The habit of butchers 'of selling Meat blown, varnished, and particularly the kidneys of Veal, turned and stuffed' was the subject of a clampdown by the Mayor and Market Jurors in 1797.[17] Besides fraud, which the latter practices were deemed to be, the Market faced a variety of difficulties, natural and political, in its first decade. On Saturday, 17 January 1789 it had to be shut down as Cork was hit by serious flooding, a recurrent danger in the marsh-based city. The entire flat of the city was reportedly under water, which was at least five feet high in most places. The markets, which normally

closed on Sundays, were ordered by the mayor to be opened following the receding of the flood waters, 'as the inhabitants would have been otherwise much distressed for provisioning.'[18] A decade later, in the aftermath of the 1798 rebellion, the high level of

Left:
Flood in Cork, January 1789, from Archibald G. Stack *The South of Ireland in 1850.* (Dublin, 1850)

military deployment led to another form of distress, as soldiers of the Cork garrison engaged in the harassment and robbery of country people bringing potatoes and other supplies into the city for sale. The head of the garrison, Major General Myers, was forced to station a guard of a trustworthy sergeant and twelve soldiers at each of the city's markets to maintain order. It was not until May 1800 that the mayor felt able to announce the success of the measures: 'The Mayor of Cork has the pleasure to inform all those who are in the habits of supplying the Markets of this City with Provisions, that the measures hitherto taken by him ... have at length proved effectual, and that no soldier or other person presumes now to seize Cars bringing Provisions hither.'[19]

Market fare

While the city markets were supplied from the agricultural hinterland, the extensive market gardens on the city's outskirts, such as those in Blackrock and the Friar's Walk area, were also major suppliers of vegetables and some fruit. Lewis' *Topographical Dictionary* of 1837 recorded that Blackrock 'supplies the Cork market with a large proportion of its vegetables'. Horatio Townsend's survey of 1810 notes that:

> In the neighbourhood of the town some of the land is laid out for kitchen garden and brings a very good profit; but less fruit is raised than might be expected in such a place, though there are numberless excellent situations for producing it: common vegetables are in consequence abundant and reasonable, the more valuable kinds of fruit very dear.[20]

While the potato was the staple food of the poor, it was also popular among the better off who shopped in the Market, though only as one part of a varied diet which included meat and breads, dairy produce, fish, fruit and other vegetables. The diet of the poor was far less varied. In the early 1830s an unemployed cooper and his family, for example, lived on a daily diet of potatoes and milk, with the occasional addition of herrings. Meat was sometimes eaten, but only on Sundays.[21] The main vegetables in the Market were cabbages and onions, though carrots, turnips, parsnips, celery and 'greens' were also sold. The apple was the commonest fruit, though pears, plums and strawberries made occasional, seasonal appearances. Imported oranges, lemons and bananas came later.

Townsend in 1810 mentions that in the Market, 'the price of butcher's meat has of late years risen considerably, and the prime kinds vary less in their prices throughout the year than formerly. From seven pence to eight pence per pound for beef and mutton may be reckoned the general rate of selling'. Beef and mutton were the most popular meats, followed by veal, lamb, poultry, pork and bacon, and offal, in that order. Chickens

predominated in the fowl trade, though ducks, turkeys and geese also featured, the latter two especially at Christmas. Eggs and fresh butter were also sold, usually from the same stalls, and the Cork favourite, buttered eggs. Buttering freshly laid eggs was a traditional preservation technique, but the rich flavour produced made them desirable in their own right. Today, the Market is the main outlet for this traditional Cork food. Although offal meats were increasingly associated with poverty, some remained in demand with the middle and upper classes; tongues were a particular favourite, preserved with salt or spices. Spiced tongue is still sold in the English Market. The sale of offal in the Market partially reflected the minority taste for offal among the better off.

The rich also purchased offal for their domestic staff and servants, and also their animals. For many of these domestic employees, shopping in the Market was part of their job. Almost half the approximately 40 per cent of the female population of the city in gainful employment across the nineteenth century were employed as domestics. A further fifteen per cent was engaged in 'dealing', which included the running of market stalls.[22] Women dominated the outdoor 'dealing' trade: 417 of the 494 'huxters

K. O'Connell Ltd. – Pat and Paul O'Connell

K. O'Connell Ltd is the largest of the three fresh fish stalls left in the Market and has built a reputation and recognition for itself and for the Market throughout Ireland and abroad. Kathleen, or Kay, O'Connell started the business in 1962 when she rented her first stall. Kay grew up on Mary Street in the Laurel Bar, which was owned by her mother. The family had another business on nearby George's Quay where fish, fruit and vegetables were sold and Kay worked there from an early age before taking a job at McCarthy's fish stall in the Market. Her determination to be independent and her shrewd eye for a business opportunity led Kay to take her first stall in 1962 and her husband John fitted it out, putting rainwater gutters around the table-top to take the water run-off, sheeting the front of the table and wallpapering the back wall of the stall. Kay bought her table, its marble top and weighing scales from Russell's provisions shop on Princes Street, which had ceased trading and her first purchase of stock at the Cornmarket Street fish auction cost £3 6s 0d.

In her first years in the Market Kay relied on the fish auctions in the city for her supplies but having acquired a car and trailer she travelled to the fishing ports of Union Hall and Castletownbere to buy her fish directly. Kay's son Paul remembers being collected early from school to accompany his mother on her trips to Castletownbere, 75 miles away, often leaving the city at 1pm for the Friday 7pm auction. Buying at the port gave a wider choice and more control over quality and price. Paul joined his mother in the Market when he was sixteen and Pat followed in 1978. Business grew and adjoining stalls were acquired as they fell vacant. The difficult economic conditions of the later 1970s and 1980s and the fall in the consumption of fish following the relaxation of the strict rules on abstinence from meat on Fridays led to the closure of many Market fish stalls. Kay O'Connell and her sons, and the fish traders that survived, adapted to the changing conditions. The growth of foreign travel, increasing affluence and more adventurous eating led to a renewed interest in fish. Television cookery programmes and the endorsement of the Market by celebrity chefs like Keith Floyd and Rick Stein also contributed to this change. Pat and Paul O'Connell remember the interest of customers and media when shark, swordfish and tuna were first offered for sale. Now the O'Connells deal in about 60 different varieties of fish and on an average day up to 40 varieties are on offer at the stall.

Pat and Paul O'Connell usually work sixteen hours, six days a week to maintain their successful business. As well as serving their customers in the Market they often drive to the distant ports of Castletownbere, Clogher Head or Killybegs for supplies. Fish is more readily available today in contrast to earlier decades and better transport enables the importation of exotic species. Boats are bigger now and better equipped and weather does not impact on supply as much as it did in the past. Pat and Paul see a change in the range of customers they serve as Cork's growing immigrant population has brought Asians, Africans and Eastern Europeans to the stall to join their loyal Cork clientele. Another change they remark on is that some of the newer customers would like to haggle when they buy and find it strange that the price given is the price to be paid.

When Kay O'Connell died in 1998 responsibility for the business fell to her sons Pat and Paul and they are proud to carry on the tradition of hard work and enterprise begun by their mother. The success of their Market stalls has played a significant part in the elevation of fish from a virtual penitential food to a dish of first choice for lovers of good and wholesome food.

and provision dealers' in Cork in 1841 were women, as were 453 out of 578 'dealers'.[23] Within the Market, women monopolised vegetable selling, predominated in the fowl, butter and egg sectors, and had a small minority presence among the butchers and fishmongers.

Pig meat increased in popularity in the late nineteenth century, a by-product of the growth of the bacon curing industry in the Cork region. This was also reflected in the increasing supply of and demand for pig offals – crubeens or pigs' feet, skirts and kidneys, bodice, pig's heads, and so on – which were supplied to the markets by the principal bacon curing factories of Ludhams, Dennys and Murphy's Evergreen.[24] Fish was far less popular than meats, and the fish market was much less significant than the dominant meat section. Fish was a minority taste in urban areas, and was often consumed by the better off as a supplement to meats at large meals. The growing Catholicisation of Irish society in the nineteenth century was a boon to the fishmongers, who benefitted from the abstinenence restrictions on Fridays, Wednesdays and holy days, and most significantly, those of the 40 days of Lent. The downside of this was the negative popular association of fish with abstinence and penitence. Nevertheless, a wide variety of fish was always available in the Market, sourced from the fish wholesalers at daily auctions held in the city. These supplies increased significantly from the mid-nineteenth century due to the development of the railway network. Such centralisation made economic sense, as individual fishmongers would not have been in a position to access the coasts (or rivers) on a regular basis. It was not until the 1960s that Market fishmongers began to source their fish directly, a situation made possible by transport improvements, later supplemented by refrigeration. Cod, ling, hake, whiting, turbot, herrings, mackerel, trout and salmon were staples. Windele, writing in the 1840s, described salmon as:

> always abundant in the [Grand Parade] fish-market, and [it] also forms an important article of exportation. It is obtained not only from the three principal rivers of the county, but also from those of Kerry, as well as the Shannon, etc. The Lee salmon especially is much prized for its delicacy and superior flavour and ... is said to be always in season.[25]

In 1867 fish merchant Daniel Cleary of Cornmarket Street, among those who supplied the Market, advertised his range as including: 'Prime Newfoundland cod fish, Irish and Shetland ling, summer hake, Scotch, Norway and Newfoundland herrings, etc.'[26]

Below:
Advertisement from *Guy's Directory* for 1893.

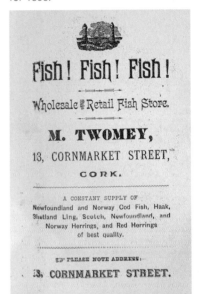

Above: Princes Street Market by Sóirle MacCana, used as a cover illustration for the *Holly Bough* of 1960.

Early nineteenth-century commentators praised the Market's abundance and lay-out. In 1810 Townsend wrote: 'The principal market place, nearly in the centre of town, is large, convenient, and well planned. It is extremely well supplied with meat, fish, poultry, and vegetables.' Pigot's directory of 1824 comments that it is 'judiciously arranged' and 'most plentifully supplied', while Lewis, in his *Topographical Dictionary* of 1837, noted its convenient location and the 'spacious entrances from Patrick-street, Princes-street, and the Grand Parade ... [it] comprises several detached buildings suitably arranged; it is divided into separate departments and is abundantly supplied daily with every kind of provisions'.[27] The latter describes the Market following its renovation and internal expansion at the close of the 1820s. The significant sum of £2000 was made available by the corporation, which advertised in December 1827 for 'Plans and Estimates for improving the Markets and ornamenting the front of the Parade'. These improvements resulted in a 'great increase in accommodation' by 1830.[28] There are no available records detailing the number of stalls before and immediately after the renovation. The first comprehensive listing is for 1855, when 72 stalls are listed for the main market, twenty in the Back Market, and an unspecified number of vegetable and fish stalls and open standings in the Root Market, Back Market and peripheries.[29]

Successive mayors, though some were far more diligent than others, took a direct interest in maintaining the Market and clamping down on fraudulent practices. In October 1814, for example, John George Newson, following numerous complaints, issued a notice warning that if

... any Meat, Poultry, Fish, or other articles of Provisions exposed for Sale in any of the markets of this City, shall be in any manner fraudulently or improperly dressed and prepared for Sale, the same shall be seized and forfeitted, and the penalty prescribed by Law for such offence, strictly enforced.

I also require and direct, that every person having a Stall in the MEAT, FISH, or FOWL MARKETS, shall keep the same in the cleanest order, and not suffer any Offal, Dirt, or other Filth to remain therein; and I further give Notice, that all FISH brought into Town for Sale, shall be immediately taken to the Market and not stored; and if any person shall offend in this particular, he or she shall be indicted or prosecuted as the Law directs.[30]

Below:
Advertisement from the *Cork Mercantile Chronicle*, 7 October 1814.

NOTICE.

WHEREAS, it has been represented to me, that various Frauds are practiced in the MARKETS in this City, in preparing and dressing MEAT and POULTRY for Sale, and in other instances which it is necessary to prevent a continuance of.

Now, I do hereby give Notice, that if after this Day, any Meat, Poultry, Fish, or other articles of Provisions exposed to Sale in any of the Markets of this City, shall be in any manner fraudulently or improperly dressed and prepared for Sale, the same shall be seized and forfeited, and the penalty prescribed by Law for such offence, strictly enforced.

I also require and direct, that every person having a Stall in the MEAT, FISH, or FOWL MARKETS, shall keep the same in the cleanest order, and not suffer any Offal, Dirt, or other Filth to remain therein; and I further give Notice, that all FISH brought into Town for Sale, shall be immediately taken to the Market and not stored; and if any person shall offend in this particular, he or she shall be indicted and prosecuted as the Law directs.

Dated at the Mansion-House, Cork, this 5th Day of October, 1814.
JOHN GEORGE NEWSOM
Mayor.

The *Cork Constitution* reported that under the mayoralty of Richard Parker in 1826-7, '[t]he Markets of the city may now bear a comparison with the United Kingdom for cleanliness, good order and regularity in every particular!'. Apparently, he was to be found 'as soon as day light appears in the morning, inspecting the different Markets throughout the city, and seeing that they are kept in proper order, and that no frauds are practiced'.[31]

Management, administration and revenue

The city's Superintendent of Markets was based in a purpose-built office, replete with desk and fireplace, in the Grand Parade Market. His duty was to 'collect the stallage rents in all city markets' and also, from 1829, the market tolls in the English Market. The latter had previously been leased out. In late 1830, the corporation appointed a superintendent, or inspector, specifically for the English Market. Under him were two beadles, or constables, who policed the Market, two collectors and three weighmasters, later re-titled scalesmen. There was also a general weighmaster for the city. The collectors and beadles were paid 8s per week; the three Market weighmasters were paid no salary, but supplied with beams, scales and weights by the corporation and then 'paid for their trouble by agreement with the butchers who employ them'. The scales were located at central points in the meat market. The Superintendent was paid a guinea a week. He also held many other prestigious positions, which paid handsomely. He was the Assay Master, or inspector of weights and measures, in the markets and the city generally (and had a nice sideline authorising weights for private citizens), as well as being one of the city's High Constables and a 'serjeant at mace', or mace bearer. The patronage system meant that the lesser Market positions were also allocated to Protestants, though in these cases, those of lower social status. Similar positions such as water bailiffs and turnkeys at the city gaol were likewise allocated.[32] This situation epitomised the corruption that characterised the corporation in its years under the control of the Friendly Club.

Combined rental income from the corporation's six other markets was an average of £1300 per annum in the years 1827-33, while the English Market alone yielded £968. Tolls on produce entering the Market in 1831 yielded £1354. City-wide markets and tolls revenue combined represented over 80 per cent of the corporation's annual income of £6237; the English Market alone represented over one-third, which explains why the corporation felt compelled to massively extend its debt in order to extend and refurbish in the late 1820s. Following the improvement work in 1830, toll collection was taken over directly by the corporation, which obviously felt that Caesar had not been rendered all that was due to him by the toll lessees. The highest sum produced from tolls in the years 1827-30 was £833 5s 2d; in the next two years, when the tolls were collected by the Superintendent for the corporation, they yielded an average of £1334, a 62 per cent increase that could not be accounted for solely by 'the great increase in accommodation in the market'. A parliamentary commission appointed to investigate municipal corporations in Ireland in 1833 was scathing in its report, published in 1835, on Cork Corporation and its sectarian system of patronage and the linked practices of profiteering and overcharging. Special mention was made of the Grand Parade Market, where nothing coming in was exempt from toll and 'several articles pay both toll and stallage'. The overall implication of the report was that suppliers, traders and ultimately customers were being exploited by unscrupulous officials and their cronies for private profit and gain.[33]

A new era: the Reformed Corporation

The old corporation, characterised, in the words of the historian of Cork Protestant society and politics, by 'inefficiency, corruption and family jobbery',[34] was doomed following the publication of the parliamentary commission report. The 1840 Reform Act altered and extended the franchise (though it was still limited to substantial property-holding males), and the elections of October 1841 saw the return of a Catholic majority and the creation of the Reformed Corporation. This heralded a new era in the political history of Cork, and also in the history of its markets. A Market Committee (later 'Markets and Tolls' and then 'Tolls and Markets') was established to oversee administration. In 1842 almost £5000 was earmarked for the building of new markets and renovation of

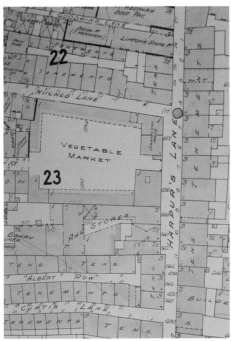

Left:
Harpur's Lane Market, as shown on the Goad Insurance map of 1897 (Cork City Library), and the houses that now occupy the site, off St Paul's Avenue.

many of the existing ones, most of which, with the exception of the English Market, had been neglected by the previous corporation. By late 1843 the committee reported to the corporation on the completion of its major projects:

> The St Finn Barr's or Barrack street market and the St. John's [Douglas Street] market are now in satisfactory condition. The people have commodious and well-sheltered Potato Markets, as well as convenient Fish, Milk, Flesh and, Vegetable Markets, with Offices and other improvements which they could hardly have anticipated ... St. Peter's Market, between the North Main and Market streets, is now nearly completed ... the Committee directed several alterations and repairs for the improvement of the Grand Parade Market, which will not interfere with a more extensive improvement in that market at a future time.'[35]

Improvements were also made to the North Cattle Market and an additional cattle market was established on Barrack Street. Another new market, St John's, was created off Douglas Street 'for the accommodation of the people of that improving neighbourhood'. The Harpur's Lane market was converted into a potato market, and the ground on the north side of the St Peter's, in the area of today's Kyle Street, was 'fitted up as a

Below:
The former Bazaar Market, Cornmarket Street.

Below right:
Street traders outside St Peter's Market.

Milk Market'. Plans were also made for a 'Bazaar, for the sale of ware, iron work and clothes'.[36] The Bazaar Market, located in the buildings occupied today by the Coal Quay Bar and The Loft furniture warehouse, was completed in 1851 or 1852.

The building of St Peter's as Cork's second central indoor food market, at a cost of approximately £3000, was the major act of the new corporation. With the main entrance on North Main Street and the rear entrance on Cornmarket Street, this huge building, covering half an acre and which today houses the Bodega bar complex and Maher's sports shop, was designed by Alexander Deane and modelled on St John's Market in Liverpool. Its hundreds of stalls sold meat, fish and vegetables to the Cork working class. It was described at the time of its opening as 'a sort of covered street'. St Peter's and the Bazaar provided 'accommodation for the numerous dealers who occupy the centre of [Corn]Market-street'.[37] The creation of these new markets was part of ongoing measures by the authorities to regulate dealing and minimise street selling. It was also an attempt by the new corporation to distinguish itself from its predecessors by providing facilities for the majority working class population, who had been ill served in the past. At the laying of the foundation stone for the new St Mary's potato market on Harpur's Lane, the mayor told the crowd that 'the Market Committee was anxious to do what they could to cheapen provisions for the people and had given directions that no person

Left:
The former St Peter's Market, Cornmarket Street.

67

purchasing a bag of potatoes in the market should be allowed to retail them at a higher price to the poor'.[38] The initiative for building the potato market came from councillors in 1842 who condemned the practice of buying potatoes from boats on the quays as 'both a dangerous and fraudulent one, and also a source of riot'.[39] The price of potatoes in the city had doubled in that year due to scarcity; apparently, farmers were afraid to bring them into the city. In June of that year there was a food riot on North Main Street, when over 1,000 hungry people attempted to storm a potato store.[40]

Rents, prices and food quality in St Peter's were lower than in the English Market. This was the 'poor man's market' and was referred to as the 'Irish Market', as mentioned earlier, probably to distinguish it from its grander Grand Parade counterpart, the 'English Market'. Special shield-shaped plaques were attached to the new markets, most of which were named after saints (St Peter's, St Finnbarr's, St John's, St Mary's), branding them as the creation of 'the Reformed Municipal Corporation of Cork'. The promised 'extensive' improvements to the Grand Parade Market were put on the long finger, as the new city fathers concentrated on their own creations.

Cork's butchers

Above:
Attack on a Potato
Store, from the
*Illustrated London
News,* 1847.

Not suprisingly, the new regime was not universally popular. In May 1846 the following advertisement, in the form of an open letter, appeared in the *Cork Constitution*, signed by the Grand Parade Market victuallers:

Sir, Presuming on your sense of justice, and confident that you are ready to defend the weak against the strong, we take the liberty of laying a grievance before you and the public which we feel we unjustly labour under. We, the VICTUALLERS of the Grand Parade Market, have been carrying on trade there from our infancies – we have in many instances been obliged to bring up our sons to the trade, and we expected that, having done so, the Corporation would have aided our efforts, and when a Stall became vacant, would have given our sons the preference, instead of a person who never served an apprenticeship to the business, or knew anything of the trade. About a week since, a Stall in the market became vacant – it was to be let. Several victuallers applied for it – one in particular, a respectable man of fifty years standing under the Corporation, sought it for one of his sons. Another person, by trade a *Wool-comber* [a craftsman who prepared wool for spinning], also looked for it. We are under the impression that the latter would have no claim against the Victualler above referred to, but, fearing that any undue influence should be at work to obtain the Stall from him, FIFTY-ONE Victuallers respectfully memorialled the Market Committee, that in disposing of the Stall a preference at least be given a Victualler. Judge of our surprise, Mr. Editor: our memorial was unheeded – the Stall was given away, not to a Victualler, but to a WOOL-COMBER.

Having put these facts before you, we leave it to your good sense and that of the public, to say whether this is the treatment we should have received?

In an editorial comment, the Protestant *Constitution* suggested that

If a landed proprietor, especially did he chance to be a Protestant, happened to act thus by the son of a respectable tenant, there would be no end to the uproar in the Papal Press, and doubtless the gentlemen of the Committee would be ready to join in denouncing him. But "circumstances alter cases".[41]

The paper is clearly intimating a sectarian dimension to the decision. The controversy also suggests that Protestant butchers remained a significant presence in the Market, though trade protection was obviously a major consideration among the protesting butchers, a majority of whom were Catholic. Up to 60 angry butchers disrupted a Town Council meeting on 6 June protesting against the decision; they threatened to unseat councillors, particularly the three they had helped to elect, pointing out that they could muster up to 100 votes and would use their power. [42]

Cork's victuallers had a long, tangled history of organisation, which awaits its historian. The importance of butchering meant that they probably formed one of the early guilds that were established under the royal charters for Anglo-Norman towns like Cork from the late twelfth century. The early guilds included both masters and journeymen, who

Left:
This photograph from the Day Collection shows Cornmarket Street in the late 1890s.

came together to regulate their common trade and protect their common interests. Control of the guilds reflected the shifts in religious/political power in the city, and Catholics did have brief periods of ascendancy through the seventeenth century. After 1690, however, when Cork was secured by the Williamite forces and became a 'Protestant city', the Society of Butchers was limited to Protestant or 'English' butchers, as Catholics were prevented from becoming freemen and, therefore, members of guilds. As well as discrimination against Catholics, there was increasing discrimination against journeymen, and many came together in 'combinations' to defend their interests in the early eighteenth century. A series of acts from 1729 criminalised these combinations, and severe penalties were meted out to workers who attempted to organise, including imprisonment and public whipping. An extortionist taxation system called 'quarterage' had led to the decline in most of the city's guilds by the 1760s, but there was revival in 1787 when a number of them re-emerged, including the Company of Butchers. Sean Daly, an authority on Cork labour history, believes that this was an employers' or masters' association, established to protect them against prosecution under the Combination Acts.[43] Because only freemen could become masters, this was also an exclusively Protestant body, whose members probably monopolised the meat stalls in the new Grand Parade Market, which opened for business the following year.

Following the repeal of the Combination Acts in 1824, which effectively meant the decriminalisation of trade societies and unions, the Cork butchers reappear in the records along with 26 other trades in June 1832 when they marched under a 'Cork Victuallers' banner, in a huge demonstration welcoming Daniel O'Connell to the city and

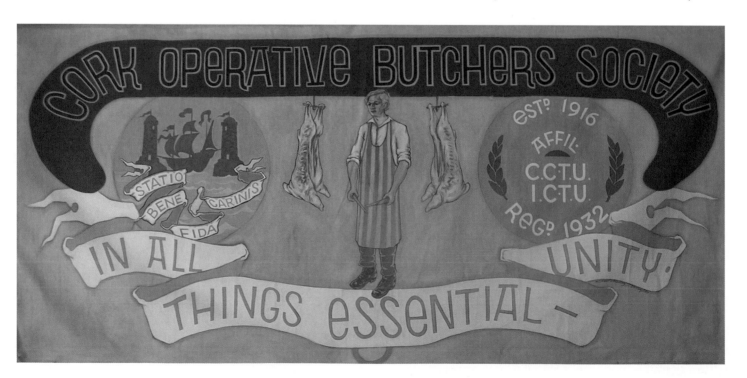

in support of repeal of the Act of Union.[44] It is likely that this body represented both Catholic and Protestant butchers, and perhaps both masters and journeymen. It functioned to regulate conditions within the trade, such as apprenticeships, to limit entry, and as a benefit or mortality society. The victuallers' body obviously went from strength to strength, as the following report from a Repeal procession in June 1845 indicates:

> Perhaps of all the trades the Victuallers formed the most imposing body, for number, appearance and decorations. All eyes were directed to the curious object by which they were proceeded – a noble bullock adorned with flowers and bound ready for sacrifice, was drawn in a waggon by a pair of horses; on each side stood an executioner dressed in the 'professional' garb of the craft. One bore a 'maul', the other a 'head axe'. The bullock's horns were gilded, and adorned with orange and green ribbons. Next came the trades banner, on which was a rich shield supported by a ram and bullock. The motto – 'Persevere and conquer – death before dishonour'.[45]

Because of the large number of butchers in the English Market, it provided the mainstay of the Victuallers' Society, a situation replicated in the twentieth century in both the workers' Cork Journeyman (later, Operative) Butchers' Society and the employers' Cork Master Victuallers' (later Butchers') Association. At a huge procession to mark the inauguration of the statue on St Patrick's Street of the 'apostle of temperance' Father Theobald Mathew in 1864, two of the Market's butchers headed the victuallers' group:

> Of all the trade societies which swelled the procession, none presented a more prosperous appearance than the victuallers. They numbered 75 members, and were headed by Messrs Henry

Below:
Advertisement from *Robert H. Laing's Cork Directory*, 1863.

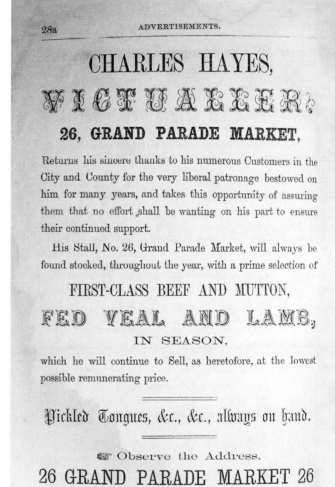

Bresnans – Michael Bresnan

Michael Bresnan and his sons, who run a butcher's stall, are the family with the longest unbroken presence in the Market. Michael's grandfather, also called Michael, was born in Herbertstown, County Limerick and moved to Cork when he was apprenticed to a butcher called Treacy in Castle Street. In March 1898 he took a stall in the Market and married Julia O'Callaghan, from Dripsey, County Cork, soon afterwards. In 1908 he bought a farm in Ballinlough, where he fattened cattle and operated a slaughterhouse. The eldest son, John, was born in 1900 and worked in the Market with his father from an early age. When Michael died in his early forties in 1921 his widow Julia took over the tenancy of the stall, passing it to John in 1928 and John's youngest brother, Patrick; two of his sisters, Sheila and Kitty, also worked in the business. John died in 1932 and Patrick ran the business until his retirement in 1974. His eldest son Michael was born in 1945 and began work in the Market in 1961 where he maintains the Bresnan presence, now in its third century.

In recalling his early years in the market Michael remembers that their customers were almost exclusively women who had a very set routine: they came into town for mass, then bought their meat and groceries before going home to have dinner ready for their husbands and families at one o'clock. Meat was cut as the customer requested it and pre-cut meat was distrusted. Beef and mutton sold in equal measure and fresh pork, bacon and ham were only available from pork butchers or provisions stalls. Like all other butchers, the Bresnans employed messenger boys who were usually aged between twelve and fourteen. Many came from poor backgrounds and Michael remembers his father sending them to D'Arcy's café in Oliver Plunkett Street for a breakfast of a bun and a glass of milk before they started work. In Michael's memory the 1970s and 1980s were busy years in the Market in spite of the high unemployment caused by the closure of many of Cork's traditional industries. People had to work hard to make their money stretch and the Market was the ideal place to forage for value.

Though regretting the decline in the number of butchers in the Market Michael welcomes the new food stalls. The range of stalls and produce now on offer reflects the new lifestyles and habits of the consumers and he feels the Market will survive as long as it continues to adapt in this way. Michael's sister, Katherine O'Mahony, has a Market stall and his sons, Daniel, Neil and Peter, now work with their father, the fourth generation of Bresnans to do so and custodians of a tradition begun by their great-grandfather over a century ago.

Above:
Advertisement from *Guy's Directory* for 1891.

Mahony and James Creedon. Their banner was of white silk, with crimson border, fringed with gold. The design was executed in transparent colours, and consisted of the arms of the society – a shield displaying a pig and the implements of the trade [hatchet, saw and cleaver], with a ram and a bull rampant on either side, and the mottoes 'death before dishonour' and 'persevere and conquer'. This banner was also a creditable production of the brush of Mr J. [John] O'Hea. The members of the trade wore blue sashes trimmed with white and carried wands tipped with white and gold.[46]

The growth of the bacon curing industry in Cork, Limerick and Waterford in the last quarter of the nineteenth century led to the formation in 1890 of the Amalgamated Society of Porkbutchers. In a successful strike in January-February of that year, they shut down the bacon curing factories in the three cities and won reduced working hours (down to under 60 hours a week!) and wages that brought them closer to those of the recognised skilled trades.[47] It would be another 26 years before the journeyman butchers who worked in the Market organised themselves into a separate union.

The assertiveness of the Market butchers who protested against the allocation of a stall to a woolcomber (of all things!), and the self-confidence they displayed in their public outings, reflected the strength of the trade. Their attendance at Catholic and nationalist occasions, such as those above, reflects the growing predominance of Catholics. By 1871, 92 per cent of Cork butchers were Catholic, increasing to 95 per cent a decade later, and 96 per cent by the end of the century.[48] Butchers were one of the top five employers among the trades in the city in the nineteenth century, just behind grocers and publicans and on a rough par with bootmakers and butter merchants.[49] Many of these butcher employers ran large (combined or multiple) stalls in the English Market. The journeymen

and apprentices not only worked cutting and serving on the stalls themselves, but also in the slaughterhouses run by these larger butchers. The smaller units were usually run by the lessee and his or her family. The tradition was quickly established, as indicated in the victuallers' protest letter of 1846, not only of a stalls passing on within families, but also of vacant stalls being secured for sons who had served their time in the trade. While there were exceptions, such as the latter case, this tradition continued, resulting in the creation of dominant Market families. Many of the stallholders were related and there was a high level of inter-marriage. The Tolls and Markets Committee made intermittent moves to open up the procedure of stall transfer, especially when availing of the opportunity of a vacancy to secure a rent increase. In 1872 it was ordered 'that whenever a tenant vacated a stall, it

at present the shopkeeper's best friend'.[56] In August 1847 a Cork magistrate lamented 'the condition of the respectable traders' across the city, particularly in the Grand Parade and St Patrick's Street area, whose doorways and passages were blocked by beggars. He demanded that these poor people be brought before him and promised to bring the full force of the law to bear: 'It is not in human nature to endure such an outrageous system of mendicant persecution, and it must be put an end to. The shopkeepers are really to be pitied, and I have at various times done my best to get them rid of this abomination.'[57]

Despite a downturn in trade, caused partly by 'mendicant persecution', the English Market remained open throughout the famine years, the constabulary and its own beadles minimising disruption from the hungry. Meat became 'very dear' in the Market and good meat scarce, especially mutton, but sufficient supplies were maintained.[58] The better off, who despite being hurt financially due to the economic downturn, exposed, in some cases, to the danger of typhus, and discommoded by the invasion of beggars, continued to live much as before. In May 1847, a month when almost 3,000 hungry 'vagrants' were driven from the city, the Horticultural Society held its summer show in Cork, where 'vegetables were particularly large and luxuriant, the greatest, if not the most important, rarity under this head being a sample of fine new Potatoes, perfectly free from the least taint of blight or murrain'.[59] In late June disease-free potatoes were on sale at high prices in the city's markets, and the press reported that 'great crowds' gathered to view the novelties and 'large quantities' were purchased.[60] By mid-July,

large quantities of Potatoes of the ash-leaved kidney and ... the round common white kind, were on sale ... in the Grand Parade Market. They were remarkably large, and some of them as fine as were seen during former years. They were perfectly free from disease, and were selling as low as from 1s.6d. to 2s. per weight of 21lbs.[61]

Relief and harvest work and access to affordable food lessened levels of distress and starvation, though disease and vagrancy continued to be a major problem in the city. Death and emigration saw the population of County Cork reduced by almost 24 per cent between 1841 and 1851, though inward migration resulted in a slight increase in the city's population.

It was not until the 1850s that the effects of the famine began to ease in the city, though its longer-term consequences were profound. At a general economic level, the lot of those who survived, especially the lower and upper middle classes, was improved. Average incomes almost trebled and living standards and consumption levels rose correspondingly. Increased commercialisation saw a growth in the retail sector, and increased specialisation within it, and large department stores developed in the city. The *Cork Constitution* noted in 1855 that '[a]mong the alterations which have occurred within the past few years, not the least remarkable is that produced by the opening of numerous stores in all parts of the city, where potatoes of first rate quality are disposed of in small quantities'. It mentioned that as many as 20 to 30 of these stores had been established, and while they were 'a great public convenience', their effect on the trade of the markets was great. The article also pointed out that butchers' shops were becoming far more common, especially on the outskirts of the city.[62]

Right:
The Cork and Muskerry Light Railway was one of a number of railways that revolutionised transport in the Cork area in the second half of the nineteenth century.

Besides the expanding city trade, transport improvements and higher incomes in the countryside led to an increase in rural dwellers shopping in the city. There was a growth in demand, supply and consumption of luxury items, including expensive foods, and improved transport allowed more extensive importation of a wider range of foods from further afield. Irish agriculture underwent a period of improvement: cattle improved in quality, with knock-on benefits for the meat trade. There was increased diversification of vegetables and other crops, and mechanisation helped to increase quantity and quality. The railway network increased the range and quantity of supply of produce to the city. The English Market was an obvious beneficiary of these trends, despite the increased competition from shops.

An investigation of municipal corporations in Ireland by a parliamentary commission in the 1830s had been highly critical of many aspects of Cork Corporation's work, especially in relation to its collection of tolls on goods brought into the city for sale in markets or at street standings. While improvements followed the Reform Act of 1840 another commission was established in the early 1850s to examine specifically the administration and functioning of markets and fairs in Ireland.[63] Its report again highlighted 'the gross abuses, the injustice, waste, and inconvenience which characterised the market system of the day' and it pointed out that 'the exaction of unreasonable tolls, not warranted by law, charter "or usage" has been complained of for a number of years'.[64]

The tolls charged in Cork were set out in a schedule of 1711, which was still being followed 140 years later. A small basket of cockles, for example, was charged ½d as was a basket of greens. 1d was charged for 'a basket of fish, brought on a man or woman's back'. 2d was paid for a cow, steer, ox or bull while the most expensive charge was 3s 4d for 'a pair of mill-stones carried over one or both bridges'![65] The collection of tolls had been let by auction prior to 1830 but from that year John Kemp oversaw their collection on behalf of the corporation. When questioned by the commission as to how and by whom tolls were collected Kemp replied: 'The collectors are most respectable men, who would not charge more than they were entitled to do, and they assess the tolls as well as they are able, without weighing the articles.' If, on weighing the articles in the market, it was subsequently found that too much was paid, a refund was given. Kemp also explained that not all tolls payable were collected, the collectors having a certain unspecified discretion in relation to the hundreds of items listed in the schedule.[66] The schedule also set out the rents payable for standings in and outside the various city markets. The English and St Peter's markets had stalls with fixed weekly rents, but only temporary standings were available at the other city markets and at specified places on the streets. Women usually held these standings and are variously termed tripe, butter, pudding, lemon or roasting pig women, depending on the items sold.

The Vegetable Seller – Eileen Ahern by Nell McCafferty

She was as fresh as the vegetables she sells and more deeply rooted. Eileen Ahern's mother worked there before her, her daughter Deirdre will work there after her, her sister Siobhán stands in a second stall alongside her in Cork's 'English Market'; a family tree offering sustenance and sweet succour to all who linger by their banked rows of nature's own produce.

She is a confident Cork presence in a cosmopolitan world of shiny brown dates from Saudi Arabia, cheeky tangerines from Spain, Indian peppers sweet and strong, courgettes, celery and carrots. Eileen is at home with them all. Spinach does not daunt her, salsify satisfies, cabbage red or green presents no problem. A potato is not necessarily a potato, there are yams – she points proudly – from America. Aubergines, artichokes, asparagus, broccoli, beetroots and beans, corn, courgettes or cucumber, parsnips, peas and Swedish turnips, the wealth and wonders of the natural world form a peaceful phalanx around a woman faced with gutted fish and sliced flesh in the marketplace.

All the same, she confided to me when I was first drawn to her, did you ever taste anything as nice as a pig's foot on a Saturday night? She was driving to Dublin on the Sunday for a hurling match. She invited me home to see the medals Deirdre had won for Irish dancing. I could swap Northern names with her husband, she said, who used to organise a yearly bus tour for Ulster people around the ambush spots of west Cork. Now he organises holidays for children of the North, from Shankill to the Falls.

She drew my attention to the fruit. Green apples, blueberries, yellow bananas, eponymous oranges, plumy plums, passion fruit – did they work or just grow on trees, like money – Eileen has no time for fantasy, though she wages merry war against reality, morning, noon and evening six days a week. When Cork Corporation wanted to remove the fountain that had not worked for ages she held out for an aesthetic that surpassed articulation. She sensed that it was lovely. The fountain, its song silenced, holds mute court still before her eyes.

An English visitor proferred a sterling pound note. Eileen sent him round the corner looking for punts. Her soul is not for sale; one link at least had been broken and she was glad to leave the chain gang.

I brought her a cutting from my spider plant; she met me in an ice-cream shop, pressed upon me reacquaintance with a melting Dream-boat in a glass dish; thereafter

The commission examined in detail the income and expenditure of the corporation for the year ending 27 August 1851 to assess the relative importance of the income from markets and tolls.[67] The net income of the corporation from all sources for that year was £7745 12s 6d, of which over £5000 came from tolls and markets. £1390 12s 5d, or over 18 per cent of the total, came from the English Market alone. In addition to the English Market there were nine other markets of varying size operating in the city. The combined net income of those other markets in the year examined was £440 15s 10d, less than one-third of that from the English Market and a further indication of the latter's significance as a market and revenue source for the city.

In the later 1850s there was a developing realisation within the corporation that its relative neglect of its leading market could be counterproductive, and conspicuous, in the light of urban renewal projects, overseen by it under the Improvement Clauses Act, 1847. In the early 1860s the first moves were made to restore its premier market to its former glory.

The Princes Street Market

In August 1861 a city councillor, Mr Julian, moved a motion at Council that steps for making a 'suitable entrance' and other improvements to the Root Market at the Princes Street end of the English Market be referred to the Markets Committee.[68] No action was taken until, following a letter of complaint to the *Cork Examiner* the following November, the mayor, Sir John Arnott, paid a visit to the Market. That letter, from 'G.P.W.', had asked the mayor why the public gas was not lit in the Market in the evenings, as was usually the case at that time of year, from 4pm until closure:

> It is an injustice to the parties doing business there, who I need not remind his Worship, are contributors to the public revenues of the city, and also an injustice to such of the public as to go to the market at a late hour in the evening, for being deprived of light they cannot be judges of the articles they purchase. I should like to know if the officers of the Market have received instructions from the Council to 'keep the market in the dark' or if it be done at the desire of any one individual. Such a state of things would not be permitted in any other Market in the kingdom.[69]

Arnott took note of the complaint, visited the Market at five o'clock in the evening, and was not impressed: '[I] should say that it was in a discreditable state. It was as dark as pitch, and no one could grope his way through it … That market yields us a large revenue and it is discreditable to leave it that way.' Blame was laid at the door of market superintendent, Rogers, whose duty it was to ensure the gas lighting was put on, and an order was issued for the immediate lighting of the market.[70] Arnott's visit convinced him of the need to extend improvements beyond mere lighting, and Julian's proposals of the previous August were finally taken up and extended.

The semi-covered Root Market was in a particularly poor state at the time, as captured in this description from the *Cork Constitution*:

> The scenes of confusion presented on a busy day ... the chaos in which the goods exposed for sale generally were, cannot easily escape the mind of one who, through a mass of people, over heaps of cabbage leaves and other refuse vegetables, and in wet weather through mud and slush, had to wend his way. Such a state of things was not only a great inconvenience to the purchasers but a loss to the sellers, owing to the confined and confused way in which their stalls were placed; and many a person has on a Saturday made a hasty retreat from the place rather than stem the torrent of people who from within its confined space were trying to make their exit through the ill-constructed and narrow entrances.[71]

In January 1862 a general plan of a new entrance and roofed interior for the Root Market was adopted. City engineer, the renowned architect Sir John Benson, was instructed to prepare plans and specifications, including for two houses or shops on either side of the entrance. As Benson was 'engaged in other works at the time', he was given permission to 'procure assistance', which he received from a Mr Walker Jnr., who was paid £20.[72] Benson has always been given the credit for the new Princes Street Market, and he doubtless approved the plans and perhaps amended them, but, clearly, a substantial part of the praise should go to Walker. On 1 March 1862 the Tolls and Markets Committee put out a call for proposals for the building of 'two houses with ornamental front and entrance to the Root market, Prince's-street. Also, erecting Galleries, and New Roofing the entire Root Market, in accordance with the drawings and specifications now lying for inspection at the office of the city Engineer.'[73] The tender of Thomas Walsh was accepted on 28 March. Work began in May and lasted for eight months. Discussions in August and September about the possibility of locating 'a Council Room and Corporate Offices', in other words, a city hall, over the Grand Parade Market led to no action.[74]

During the construction many of the 'vegetable women' of the Root Market were relocated to the peripheries of the adjoining Grand Parade Market, mainly to Pump Lane (now Market Avenue), which entered the market from George's (now Oliver Plunkett) Street. The 'fowl women' who had been dislocated had to take to the streets; when they requested permission to 'vend fowl at the west side of the Parade', the corporation, unable to give official permission, decided to turn a blind eye and ensure that 'no measures would be taken to remove the women off the streets' until the new market was ready. The vegetable women in Pump Lane were charged the same rent, 2s 2d per week for each standing, that

TO BUILDERS.

THE MARKET and TOLLS COMMITTEE of the Corporation will, on FRIDAY, the 21st Instant, receive Proposals from persons willing to contract for BUILDING TWO HOUSES, with ornamental front and entrance to the Root Market, Prince's-street.

Also, erecting Galleries and New Roofing the entire Root Market, in accordance with the Drawings and Specification now lying for inspection at the office of the City Engineer, No. 20, South Mall.

Sealed Proposals to be lodged in the tender box at the Office of the General Superintendent, City Court House, at or before Ten o'Clock, a.m., on the above day (Friday, March 21st, 1862), marked on the outside Tenders for New Entrance (and Houses) in Prince's street. By order,

JOHN FRANKLIN.

Cork, 1st March, 1862. (738)

they had paid in the Root Market. They sent a deputation to the corporation's Improvement Department in November complaining that it was 'a cold uncomfortable place – in fact they were in purgatory for several months in it', and seeking a rent exemption until the Princes Street Market was complete. Within weeks, their new accommodation was ready, and they reportedly 'cheered, danced, and sang at the prospect of their removal from their present contracted position to the roomy, handsome, and convenient market provided for them'.[75]

The new market occupied the same space as the old one, but, due to 'its well arranged construction' and the addition of a surrounding gallery (or balcony), allowed for almost double the number of stalls. The city's daily newspapers, the Catholic *Cork Examiner* and Protestant *Cork Constitution*, both carried lengthily technical and wonderfully effusive descriptions of the new market prior to its official opening. It was hailed as the finest market in the 'Kingdom', indeed as fine as any in the 'three kingdoms', and 'one of the greatest public improvements effected in this city for some time.' Both papers stressed the beauty of the façade and entrance gate, and the architectural achievement of the covered interior, with its improved layout and additional gallery space. The core objective of providing a protected space for dealers and customers was 'realised with the utmost regard to utility, and yet in the most perfect compliance with the rules of good taste and effect'. The only negative note related to the fact that the handsome front could not be fully appreciated due to the narrowness and busyness of Princes Street itself.

The new Princes Street Market was officially opened on 19 December 1862, amidst enthusiastic scenes. The *Examiner* reported that:

Opposite page [top]:
Advertisement from the
Cork Examiner, 5 March
1862.

[bottom]:
Women selling
vegetables at a street
standing.

> Some amusement was created today when the barriers were removed and the enthusiasm of the legitimate lords of the soil, consisting of the fish, fowl and vegetable women, took place. To say that their delight was rapturous would be to faintly depict it. The most favourite mode of giving vent to their emotions was by performing a wild dance around some prominent corporate officials, contributing very much to the awkwardness and timidity of the gentlemen selected. Singing and declaiming on the Mayor, Corporation and everybody 'generally' were also popular amusements and it was quite evident altogether that those most interested in the improvements to the market were perfectly satisfied with them. Our readers who have the opportunity will be repaid by taking a stroll through the market tomorrow.[76]

'A Citizen', in a letter to the *Constitution*, wrote that:

> The entrance to the Market in Prince's-street will be a credit to the city, and I do hope that the Corporation will now, at once, do the same by the entrance on the Parade. Let it be made to correspond with the Prince's-street entrance, and it will be both useful and ornamental.[77]

This 'Citizen's' advice was eventually heeded, but not until two decades later. In the meantime, traders and customers enjoyed their first Christmas in the new portion of the Market. The *Constitution* of 24 December reported that:

> Of vegetables there was a very large supply. They were ranged on the stalls provided for them in the New Prince's-street market. There was a very brisk demand for them during the day at the following prices:- early greens, 8d. a dozen, turnips, 2d. a bunch, parsnips, 4s. a cwt., carrots and celery, 8d. a dozen, drum cabbage, 1½d. a head, and onions, 6d. a dozen.

In the adjoining meat market, customers chose from a range of beef, mutton (from sheep of South Down breed), ham, bacon, pork, veal, chickens, turkeys and geese. In January 1863 the corporation advertised the letting of the two shops at the Princes Street entrance and in March, the letting of stalls for the sale of fruit and flowers in the completed gallery area.[78] The shops were let for the first year at the high cost of £90, but this had to be reduced to £40 the following year.[79]

NEW ENTRANCE TO PRINCE'S-STREET MARKET

The entrance to the new Prince's-street market ... will henceforth rank amongst the principal buildings in our city. It is certainly as handsome a structure as exists in the three kingdoms having the same object, and reflects the greatest credit on our city Architect who designed it, and superintended its construction, and on Mr Walsh, the builder, who carried out the design. The only fault that can be suggested, not in the immediate work itself, but in connection with it, is the difficulty of getting a good view of the front in its position, in a narrow street, which is also one of the busiest thoroughfares in Cork ...

The front is a well-designed and graceful structure which under any disadvantages of position must look well. In the centre is a lofty entrance or gateway, twenty feet high and ten feet broad. This being the main purpose of the erection is of course the part to which everything else is subservient. Use and profit, however, are not neglected in the accessories, which consist of two exceedingly handsome houses, especially designed for shops, one at either side of this entrance, the whole forming a large building designed artistically, and erected in a workmanlike manner. There is no particular style adhered to in the design, but in it a general resemblance to buildings built in brickwork after the Lombardo-Italian school, prevails. The front is chiefly constructed of red brick, tastefully varied however in several parts by other colours. For instance, the large arch over the entrance is in black and white brickwork, and the mouldings are of the limestone of this district. The whole building stands on a base of two feet and a half of handsomely cut limestone. The houses on each side are divided vertically on the lower storey into three divisions by two pillars, one division acting as a doorway, and the other two serving as windows. The second storey of each house is in four divisions created by three handsome pillars, and the top storey in five divided by pillars. Over the central arch is a large semi-circular light very ornamentally finished, and a little above this is a circular space for a clock, should it ever be deemed advisable to put one there. The whole is surmounted by a capping of limestone, consisted of a series of corbals, each carrying a semi-circular arch over it, the spaces under the arches being deeply cut, so as to throw a deep and effective shadow – an arrangement that must be noticed and admired by anyone looking at the front from Princes-street. The keystone of the large arch is of limestone. On the whole the front is one of striking beauty.

Passing in through the archway, the visitor stands in a corridor thirty feet deep, the shape of the arch, at each end of which there will be exceedingly handsome gates; inside the outer one will be an entrance from this long archway or corridor into the houses at either side. Inside the corridor lies the market. As is well known, the original object of the change in the market was to provide protection for the dealers carrying on their sales there of vegetables, fowl, fruit, fish, &c. That this object has been realised with the utmost regard to utility, and yet in the most perfect compliance with the rules of good taste and effect, will be evidenced to the most casual visitor to the market.

The roof is supported on two rows of cast iron pillars, and is constructed in the usual angular form, being supported, however, on wooden girders. In it is a continuous light from one end of the market to the other, consisting of fluted glass. Round the building are large and commodious galleries, the right one of which, being very spacious, has also a fluted glass light along the top. This gallery is destined for the lighter description of sales – such as fruit, flowers, some species of fowl, &c. In the large space under the galleries below, the large proportion of the traffic will be carried on. The front of the gallery is protected with ornamental iron work. The tops of the pillars are also decorated with ornamental iron spandrils. The centre of the roof is nearly forty feet from the ground; the length of the market is 179 feet; the breadth between the pillars is 35 feet; and the greatest breadth underneath the galleries is 75 feet. The pillars themselves are 25 feet high, resting on an octagonal cut limestone base. In the centre of the market a fountain will stand, serving both for the use of the market and an additional ornament to the building, already so handsome.

On the whole, while it is evident the purposes for which the construction was designed have been fully met – while the accommodation afforded is ample and well arranged – the beauty and neatness of the entire design are of an order sufficiently high to make this, as we have remarked, one of the principal structures in Cork. It seems pretty plain that on occasions of emergency the building may fitly be used for other purposes besides that for which it is designed – whether to hold public meetings, horticultural or other exhibitions, or for some of the many purposes to which a handsome and spacious building can be converted. The two houses in the front will be amongst the handsomest and best situated business premises in Cork, and we foresee great competition to obtain them. The rent they will bring, it is quite certain, will more than cover the interest on the money expended on the entire work, so that the citizens, while obtaining a most desirable addition to their public edifices, get it under circumstances of the greatest pecuniary advantage.

Cork Examiner, 1 November 1862

The Market at Christmas

The Market came into its own in Christmas week, when its annual exhibition of plenty was reported in the local press with classic Victorian hyperbole. While Christmas was clearly exceptional, these reports, which peaked in the 1860s and 1870s, give valuable glimpses into the range of products available in the later nineteenth-century Market, and the relative prices of the various foodstuffs. They also evoke Christmas in Cork city in an era of developing commercialisation and consumerism. The *Examiner* in 1860 described the scenes in the approach to 'the cheery season':

> In nearly all the provision shops through the city large bunches of mistletoe and holly appear in the windows and over the wares, while the streets are unusually crowded with persons of both sexes and all ages ... In the markets this bustle is especially evident. From a very early hour on Saturday morning till late in the evening the meat, fowl and vegetable markets of the city were scarcely passable with the vast numbers of persons thronging to them to make their Christmas purchases.

The *Constitution* waxed lyrical in 1874, adding a seasonal Dickensian sting in the tail:

> The old allurements which make Christmas welcome to all classes – children as well as grand-fathers, vegetarians and professed gourmands, cynics who despise the folly of youth, and youngsters who look on Noah's Arks as the greatest of earthly treasures – are to be witnessed throughout the city. Yesterday opened the Christmas week, during which everybody is supposed to go out of his or her way to purchase something that is not wanted, give out-of-place presents, and generally make a fool of one's self in endeavouring to obey the tyrannical etiquette of the season ... and there is everywhere proof that no lack exists in the expenditure of money ... Though we may joyfully stand before the shop windows, or the heavily laden market stalls, and gloat over the superfluity of all that can please the fancy or the palate, we should not forget the miserable ones, who, perhaps, shivering and shoeless at our side, cannot enjoy a hundredth part of the comfort we enjoy, or a thousandth part of that we anticipate for ourselves ...

A similar whiff of seasonal cynicism pervades the following year's offering:

> As the great festival approaches the city appears in its wonted state of busy preparation in the purchasing of all that is both needful and unnecessary, useful, ornamental, and stomachabable, together with the other multitude of wares and condiments that amuse or afflict us at this season ... But, as usual, the principal

throng is to the English Market, where are to be seen all the welcome things that to some associate Christmas with biliousness, over-feeding, and chronic headache, but to the many with most of the delights, and what are called the 'creature comforts' so much needed at this particular season.

The principal throng always seemed to be in the English Market, where variety was the spice. Thousands visited: the wealthy purchased and the poor gawped at 'the rich display' on offer, as the Market became 'a grand exhibition' of, for the majority, unattainable abundance. Stalls 'groaned under the supplies heaped upon them and hung from every available hook ... the eye met nothing but successive tiers of rich hind and fore quarters of beef and delicious looking mutton, flanked by hams and bacon that might tempt a Rabbi; together with very fine fowls of all kinds'. While vegetables were always plentiful, it was meat that dominated: 'the sight on Saturday', reported the *Constitution* in 1866, 'was one to delight the beef-eater or make the cold-blooded vegetarian rush in dismay from the market.'

'Every joint from the massive hind quarter and side of beef down to the tiny leg of mutton and shoulder' was available. Throughout the 1860s, reporters repeatedly remark on the shift away from the 'tremendously large, heavy animals that were formerly to be met with at this season at our markets', which yielded virtual 'joints of fat', to leaner 'well-finished, moderately-sized beasts, which are more suitable to the present taste and more profitable to the butcher', and better value for the purchaser. This reflected the improved husbandry techniques and the increase in pasture that characterised post-Famine Irish agriculture. The butchers were supplied by cattle and sheep breeders in County Cork, and also from the rich pastures of Counties Limerick, Waterford and Tipperary. The development of the rail network greatly facilitated this variety of supply. In 1858 roasting beef was available for 8d per pound. By the mid to late 1860s, beef averaged 10d per pound; corning pieces cost 6 to 7d, while roasting pieces were sold at a shilling (12d). By the mid 1870s, beef prices had risen to 1s.3d per pound for roasting beef and 8d to 9d for corning pieces. A reporter noted in 1876 that 'beef, now-a-days, is dear, and poor people, who were once able to obtain their supplies in even its finest condition at sixpence per pound, will require longer purses now that it can scarcely be had for double that amount. But', he continued:

even with the poor there appears to be no power of self-control when they visit our English Market and see the prime grass-fed beef and mutton so temptingly displayed, each haunch, joint, and quarter seeming as it were to struggle and crush themselves into notice. It is difficult under such circumstances for visitors to the English Market to pass along between the various rows of stalls and witness such a sight without experiencing tooth-watering sensations ...

Right:
A butchers advetisement showing prices of beef cuts taken from Guys 1891 *Directory of Cork Businesses.*

No. 1, Grand Parade Market Buildings.

C. MILLARD

Is constantly supplied with the primest of **Ox and Heifer Beef** and the choicest **Three Year Old Wether Mutton**. He is offering his Beef at very low prices, and all his meat is marked with figures, quoting the lowest prices for Cash.

PRICES AS FOLLOWS—

Roasting Beef	**9d.**
Corning do.	**6d. to 7d.**
Boiling do. ... ... from	**4d. to 6d.**
Steaks and Chops	**10d.**

Customers supplied all the year round at **9d.** per lb.

Mutton, ham, lamb and veal prices remained steady. A leg of mutton in 1863 cost 8d per pound; hams were 10d for the same weight, salt pork 4d to 6d and flitches (sides of bacon) 8d. Lamb and veal were less plentiful, but that which was available retailed at 6d to 9d per pound of veal and 7s 6d per quarter for lamb. None increased by more than a penny or two over the following decade.

Fowl was sold mainly by the pair: a couple of turkey cocks cost between 12s and 16s in the mid-1860s, turkey hens and geese cost 8s a pair (though geese were often down to a half-a-crown [2s 6d] each), while chickens were obtainable at 2s to 4s a couple. At Christmas 1874, William Kinmonth was stocking over 100 geese and 200 turkeys, with prices ranging from 18s to £1 for a pair of turkeys and geese at 10s a pair. Geese, at almost half the price of turkeys, provided for 'the artisan classes ... a repast in quantity and quality all that need be desired'. The squeamish vegetarian who rushed 'in dismay' from the bloody spectacle could find some solace among the Princes Street vegetable stalls, which in 1863 offered cauliflower at 1d a head, cabbage at 4d to 8d a dozen, celery at 8d a dozen, turnips at 2d a bunch and onions at 3d a dozen. Fish also featured, though it was dwarfed by the meats, and was relatively expensive. In 1863 the fish market had 'an immense supply of haak and cod ... taken principally by the Kinsale fishermen and forwarded by rail to Cork'. Cod cost up to 4s each, and hake up to a shilling. Ling was slightly cheaper at 10d. In 1874, however, the Christmas fish market was 'but sparsely supplied, and bore a strange contrast with its neighbour, the meat market'. The shortage was reflected in the prices: turbot at up to 14s each, sole 5s to 10s a pair, britt (small herrings) 4s to 5s each, oysters 18d per dozen, cod 4s to 6s each and scallops, 2s per dozen.

At this time, a skilled tradesman in Cork was earning £1 to £1.6s (20s to 26s) per week. The well-paid Market Inspector was receiving approximately 35s weekly, while the Market Watchmen were paid 15s. Unskilled labourers, the majority of the city's working population, brought home 10s per week in this period. A pair of turkeys in the Market at Christmas 1874 would thus have cost a skilled artisan the bulk of a week's wages; a couple of geese would have left a labourer with no change from his weekly pay packet. One cod in 1863 was almost a half week's wages for an unskilled worker, and a turbot in 1874 would have required him to go into debt. Clearly, then, the average citizen of Cork would not have been buying such items in the English Market, forced instead to rely on cheaper cuts and the wide variety of offal being sold in some of the less 'media-friendly' stalls, but more so in St Peter's and the other working-class markets, in the smaller, low cost butchers' and provision shops, and on the streets. More generally, the diet of the poor was based on cheaper alternatives like oatmeal and bread.

The Market's accessibility, the variety of its fare, and its enduring reputation for quality helped it to maintain its custom in the face of increasing competition from grocery, provisions, butchers' and fish shops, as well as the continuing presence on its peripheries and entrances of seasonal street sellers of poultry, fruit and vegetables. Here, the Royal Irish Constabulary and the corporation's Street Inspectors lent a hand by clearing them away.

Plans, changes and improvements

The 1870s was a decade of plans, changes and improvements. The new Princes Street Market gallery had not attracted sufficient numbers of fruit and flower sellers, and in the mid-1860s it was given over to fowl and tripe and drisheen dealers, who occupied separate sections. By the early 1870s, there are numerous references in the Tolls and Markets Committee minutes to the 'bad state' of the gallery and the need for refurbishment and improvement. At the same time, the committee was beginning to formalise the sale of fish and place the fish market on an improved and more permanent footing. The old 'unsightly' benches in the fish market, in the area of the Market closest to George's (now Oliver Plunkett) Street, were supplied with marble tops, while new marble tables were also fitted, at the considerable cost of £176.10.0. The fish stalls were also supplied with water jets. The number of fish stalls was increased, they were individually numbered, and rents increased. The old wall at the back of the fish market was demolished and every second column was removed in order to open up the space. Room was also created at the south-east end for the tripe and drisheen dealers who were transferred from the gallery. Florists were circularised to advertise the newly created space in the gallery. Sean Preston of Coburg Street took up residence, sharing the cost of erecting special stages for the display

INAUGURATION OF THE GRAND PARADE MARKET BUILDINGS

The new front of the Grand Parade Market was inaugurated yesterday, at twelve o'clock, by his worship the Mayor, accompanied by several members of Council, amongst whom were Ald. Jones, Ald. Geary, Mr. M. Daly, Mr. Corker, Mr. Kennedy, &c. The Mayor declared the name of the new structure to be that which is inscribed on the slab over the northern gate, that is to say, "The Grand Parade Market Buildings". A second slab is placed over the southern entrance which bears the following inscription:- "Erected in 1881. Daniel Vincent O'Sullivan, Mayor; M.J. McMullan, B.E., City Engineer; Terence O'Flynn, Builder". In order further to signalize the occasion, the Mayor, with his wonted hospitality, entertained the members of the Corporation at his residence, Currabinny. At half past one o'clock the party assembled on board the "Commissioner", which was lying at Anderson's quay, and then followed a most agreeable trip down the river and out to sea. The party landed at Currabinny about four o'clock and proceeded to the Mayor's residence, where a sumptuous repast was prepared. Over forty sat down, all being members of the Corporation except the High Sherriff (Mr. J.W. McMullan). The good things having been disposed of the usual formal toasts were proposed and most cordially received. The High Sherriff, in felicitous terms, responded to the toast of "Prosperity to Ireland", and the "Harbour Board" was spoken to by Mr. Cantillon. The health of Mr. Kennedy, as ex Mayor, was proposed, and acknowledged by that gentleman. Sir George Penrose gave the health of the Mayor, of whom he spoke in the most eulogistic terms, and bore testimony to the highly successful and satisfactory manner in which his worship was discharging all the duties of his position. The toast was received with great enthusiasm, and was acknowledged in grateful terms by the Mayor. The toast of the Lady Mayoress, proposed by Mr. Cantillon, was also most warmly received. "The Corporation", "The Officers", and other toasts followed. A number of excellent songs were given, and altogether a most agreeable evening was spent.

Cork Examiner, 15 July 1881

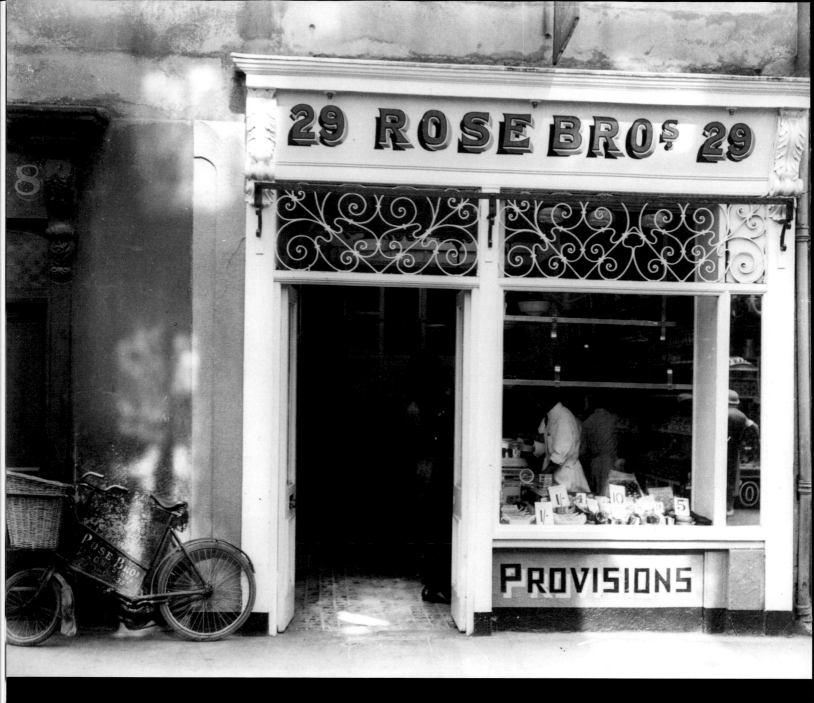

place to work, especially at a time when women did not generally wear trousers. At that time women were valued for the tidiness and efficiency they brought to a stall.

The first job of the day was to cut rashers but most meat was cut to the requirement of the customer. The Cork classics of bodice, skirts and kidneys were always popular and the more affluent customers bought pork steak and centre cuts of ham, especially at weekends. Shoulder and streaky bacon were also in demand. Mary recalls a very visible contrast between the well-off and those struggling at the other extreme of the economic and social scale.

As the 1970s advanced Mary saw the Market decline. Many stalls were left vacant as long-established traders left, retired or went out of business. The bleak economic conditions in the city were reflected in the Market and there was little optimism for the future. The rebuilding of the Princes Street Market following the fire of 1980 boosted confidence for a time but the arrival of the new traders in the mid-1990s brought a vibrancy and diversity to the Market that Mary sees as crucial to its survival. Mr Bell's, Iago, On the Pig's Back and the Real Olive Company, amongst others, attracted a new range of customers to the Market to the benefit of all.

Mary's father, John, died in 1994 and Mary continued trading in pork and bacon at the stall, but the demand for such products was falling and she decided to close the pork and bacon business and open a take-away coffee stall. Coffee Central opened for business in 2001 and has become a meeting place and a stopping point for both traders and customers. As her father did in 1963, Mary Rose has successfully met a challenge forced on her by changing habits and has created a new business catering to a new habit!

4 Market People 1830-1925

The inspector

In October 1830, following the Market's refurbishment and extension, the corporation decided to appoint a superintendent or inspector specifically for the Grand Parade and Princes Street Markets. An advertisement appeared in the local newspapers seeking a 'person competent to undertake the Superintendence of the Parade Markets – who must devote the entire of his time to the duties attendant thereon. Salary One Guinea per week'. A disgruntled 'Citizen' wrote to the *Cork Constitution* suggesting that two to three hours would be ample time to perform the necessary duties, and asking: 'does it not smell of a job – a rank job?' for 'some dependent or hanger-on'. On 6 November it was announced that 'Mr Robert Rogers has been appointed Superintendent and Assay Master to the Markets of this City. The appointment has given very special satisfaction as from Mr Rogers' well-known character, there can be not a doubt that the duties will be efficiently performed'.[1]

The inspector oversaw the day-to-day management of the Grand Parade and Princes Street Markets. He was answerable to the corporation's Tolls and Markets Committee, whose weekly meetings he was required to attend. He had an office in the Market and was provided with a uniform, described as 'a frock coat, vest and trousers of dark blue material, suitably braided' and a cap with a French peak and gold band. The inspector was expected to 'be continually in and about the markets, devoting his whole time to the situation, collecting the rents on Saturday and lodging the bank receipt for them with the Treasurer on the following Wednesday'.[2] He had a long working week, as the markets were open from 8am until 6pm, Monday to Friday, and until 11pm on Saturdays. The inspector's salary in the second half of the nineteenth century started at £90 per year, rising in annual increments of £5 to a maximum of £110. It stood at £130 per year in 1914 and had risen to £200 by 1919. While the corporation regarded his most important function as the collecting of rents and the keeping of accurate accounts, the inspector also supervised an assistant, scalesmen, sweepers and two beadles, or market constables, and had the power to discipline these employees by fining or suspending them. His management of personnel also extended to the traders in the Market, and he frequently had to resolve disputes between stallholders and pursue defaulting tenants for arrears of rent.

Robert Rogers was succeeded in 1838-9 by Thomas Rogers (probably his son) of 35 Warren's Place (now Parnell Place), who held the post until his death in January 1872. The Tolls and Markets Committee minutes suggest that his work never gave cause for complaint. Indeed, such was his devotion to duty that he lodged the full amount of rent due on stalls in the markets under his supervision even when some tenants were in arrears.[3] When he died in January 1872 it was noted that he left an elderly sister 'in straightened circumstances' and the residue of his year's salary was awarded to her.[4] The Committee's generosity did not, however, extend to the 'Widow Connors', whose husband, a toll collector, drowned while in the employ of the corporation. She was refused assistance on a number of occasions.

William O'Connell replaced Rogers in January 1872, and within six months it was reported that he had been 'most irregular in the discharge of his duties' through not making up the weekly accounts of the markets and missing a meeting of the Tolls and Markets Committee.[5] Although he assured the committee that he would be more attentive in future, O'Connell missed further meetings and repeatedly failed to lodge all monies collected. In August he was called on to resign 'in consequence of his general inefficiency to discharge the duties of his office',[6] but was given a reprieve on promise of improved behaviour. He soon lapsed again, however, and by March of 1873 he was £13 6s in arrears. O'Connell's situation was not helped by the conduct of his assistant, Eugene McSwiney, who was also frequently neglectful of his duties, due in part to his drink problem. He was jointly responsible with O'Connell for the collection and lodgement of Market rents, and O'Connell repeatedly complained McSwiney to the committee for neglect of duty and drunkenness. The situation had deteriorated to such an extent in 1874 that a sub-committee of four councillors reported that

> The Management of the Grand Parade Market is, in the opinion of your Committee, defective. There appears to be an absence of any proper supervision by the heads over subordinate employees, and the system of check is also deficient.

They also felt that the duties of the inspector and his assistant 'might be more efficiently performed' and reiterated the importance of proper accountability in the handling of rent collection and lodgment.[7] McSwiney was suspended twice in the succeeding

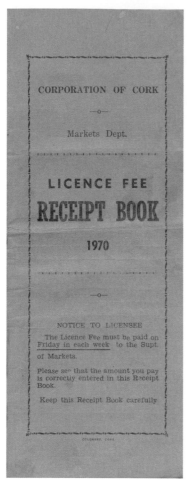

months and was eventually dismissed, but following a number of appeals by sympathetic Market traders, was given employment as a scalesman. Over the next two years O'Connell was suspended and reinstated a number of times, and eventually, in August 1876, his post was advertised.

The new inspector was appointed in September 1876. He was Felix Mullan, a commission agent with premises at 134 George's Street (now Oliver Plunkett Street). He lived in Monkstown and was a Justice of the Peace. Mullan was a pro-active inspector, with a strong puritanical streak, who immediately began suggesting improvements to the Market and made a number of recommendations to the committee regarding cleaning and the erection of additional stalls in the fish market. He also suggested a revision of rents and asked that the markets close an hour earlier, at 10pm, on Saturdays. Mullan did not tolerate bad language and in February 1878 complained William Dunlea, a trader in the Market, for using abusive language. Dunlea was summoned to appear before a magistrate and was fined.[8] Later that year Mullan reported 'the habitual use of bad language by stall holders in the Markets'. The committee decided to have a printed notice on the issue distributed to all tenants and warned that breaches of the regulation would result in immediate ejection.[9] Mullan's health began to fail in 1881 and while he was on extended sick leave during 1882 and 1883, his son, also Felix Mullan, substituted for him. On the death of Mullan senior in August, 1883, his son was appointed in his place.

Felix Mullan Jnr. inherited his father's intolerance of bad language and in October 1883 a scalesman in the Market was suspended on his recommendation because he 'had used insulting language towards him when required to sweep said market'.[10] The following year Mullan complained John Griffin, a Market trader, because he had 'abused and threatened' him and although Griffin was warned by the committee, the inspector reported that he 'had repeated his insubordinate conduct'.[11] Mullan's puritanism exceeded even his father's, and he often reported and disciplined his subordinates for being under the influence of alcohol while on duty. The number of offences noted in the first ten years of his tenure far exceeds that for previous or subsequent periods. The Tolls and Markets Committee minutes for the years 1883 to 1892 record fifteen instances of such reports by Mullan. He also abhorred smoking and in January 1887 he submitted a number of draft bye-laws for the improved regulation of the markets under his control to the Committee, including a total ban on smoking. All were accepted except the proposed smoking ban.

Relations between Mullan and the committee began to deteriorate in the late 1880s, and by the mid-1890s his position had become untenable. In 1889 he by-passed the committee and submitted a report directly to the Mayor and the corporation, stating that

> although I reported to your Council before, said report was not read, but immediately sent to the Tolls and Markets Committee, who at the time could not see its way to adopt any of my suggestions; and as to finance, it was useless to them, as they can see every week the exact state of the Market, its receipts and expenditure, so that I found it was only loss of time to go so completely into details as I had done.[12]

The high standards demanded by Mullan from others were not always evident in his own behaviour during the final five years of his tenure. He was often absent due to illness in 1892 and 1893 and consequently the accounts were occasionally late. The arrears of rent due from traders in the Grand Parade Market grew to over £30 by May 1895. The chairman of the Tolls and Markets Committee took to checking on Mullan in his place of work, and relations between the two men became increasingly strained, and the complaints increasingly petty. On 28 November 1894 the chairman complained that Mullan had not been wearing his uniform cap and he was asked to produce it at the following committee meeting.[13] In July of the following year he claimed that he had called to the Market and found Mullan absent. The committee ordered that he leave his office door open when he was inside and leave the Market report book outside when he was not present.[14] When the chairman next checked up on Mullan some days later, he found the inspector absent again and 'the vegetable Market in possession of the urchins of the city'. The office door was closed and the report book was not on display.[15] Two months later Mullan was reprimanded again for not wearing his cap and for refusing to accompany the chairman while on a visit to the Market. The committee ordered that the frosting on the glass of the Inspector's office be removed.[16] A week later the Committee's attention was drawn to a letter Mullan had written to a local newspaper complaining of this treatment and he was severely censured for 'commenting offensively on the manner in which the chairman thinks fit to conduct the business of the Committee'.[17] Relations seemed to improve after this, but 21 months later, in June 1897, Felix Mullan resigned after fourteen years of service. The committee approved a testimonial for him and his brother, J.C. Mullan, acted in his place until the vacancy was filled a month later.

Left:
The Princes Street Marke
in 1958. The inspector'
office can be seen on th
first-floor gallery.

A former city councillor, George D. O'Donnell from Western Road in Cork, succeeded Mullan. Shortly after he took up duty in July 1897, a new office was built for him in the gallery of the Princes Street Market and this was used by successive inspectors until the early 1970s. His handling of the accounts during his short two-and-a-half-year tenure was found satisfactory, especially in relation to the control of arrears of rent. When he died on 27 December 1899, the Mayor praised him as 'a straightforward and conscientious member of Council and for the past two or three years an efficient and courteous officer'.[18]

The O'Donnell family retained its hold on the post with the appointment of James C. O'Donnell in succession to his brother in March 1900, and he served as inspector until 1939. There was an early challenge to O'Donnell's authority when in January 1901 he called Ignatius O'Flynn, a Grand Parade Market trader, to task over the dirty condition of his stall. O'Flynn 'defied the Inspector to call the Committee's attention to it and questioned his authority to speak to him on the matter.' The matter was resolved in O'Donnell's favour.[19] Like previous inspectors, he occasionally had to deal with violent incidents involving traders and market employees. On 13 August 1902, for example, it is noted that Edward Lynch, tenant of Stall 69, had been drunk and disorderly in the market on two occasions and had assaulted another trader and the inspector. While the Tolls and Markets Committee was generally pleased with O'Donnell's work and awarded him his annual £5 increments, there were complaints from time to time. In May 1905 a Tolls and Markets sub-committee was 'taken by surprise' by the dirty state of the Grand Parade Market. They had visited following a report by a city public health officer who complained that the markets were in a filthy state. O'Donnell was ordered to be at work at 7am, an hour earlier than usual, and to be more vigilant in the discharge of his duties.[20] A month later the Committee expressed satisfaction with improvements in the general condition of the markets.

O'Donnell had reached his maximum annual salary of £110 by 1904 and ten years later it was raised to £130. The second decade of the twentieth century saw great upward pressure on wages due to the demands of organised labour and wartime wage inflation, and by 1919 his salary stood at £200 and rose to £250 in 1922. During 1923 the straitened economic circumstances of the newly established Free State began to have an impact at local government level. Expenditure on the Grand Parade Markets, for example, was £2,926 2s 4d, £87 0s 4d over income and this led to significant rent increases for market tenants. The auditor of the Free State's Department of Local Government felt that market staff numbers should be reduced and insisted that the markets not be a drain on limited resources. This austerity led to a reduction in O'Donnell's salary in 1924 from £250 to £237 10s. Cork Corporation was dissolved in October 1924 and the affairs of the city were run until 1929 by a commissioner, Philip Monahan, later to become City Manager. He was charged with running the administration of municipal affairs in a cost effective manner. The Tolls and Markets Committee ceased to function as Monahan streamlined the running of the markets. The corporation began to function again in 1929 with Monahan as City Manager, but by then the office of Inspector of the Grand Parade and Princes Street Markets had lost its previous status. The *Council Minutes* record Market affairs in subsequent years but in much reduced detail.

The next and final holder of the office of inspector was Jeremiah Buckley who took up duty in 1939 and served over 30 years. He worked from the office in the gallery of the Princes Street Market and presided over the markets through decades of decline. Buckley himself was not responsible in any way for this decline, which resulted from factors completely beyond his control. Cork's suburbs had grown and most people lived far from the city centre. The nature of food retailing changed and people relied less on markets for their requirements, which were increasingly met by suburban grocery and butchers' shops, and later by supermarkets. The Market failed to keep apace, and decline and apathy set in, often stifling attempts at improvement on the part of more progressive tenants. In the final years of Jeremiah Buckley's tenure as inspector the Market was becoming something of a curiosity and an article in the *Holly Bough* of 1968 remarked that 'in summer many foreigners sit outside his office looking down on the Fountain as they paint it.' This would not have been possible in earlier times, when the passages of bustled and all available space was occupied by traders.

The beadles

The corporation employed two beadles who acted as market policemen or constables and assisted the inspector in maintaining good order among traders and customers in the Market. From 1867, when the surviving records begin, until the 1920s there are frequent references in the minutes of the Tolls and Markets Committee to the activities of the market beadles. John Meagher (occasionally Maher) began work as a beadle in the 1840s and served 37 years in the position. For many of those years his companion beadle was Michael Murphy. In the 1860s they were earning 12s per week, a little more than the weighmasters or scalesmen and market sweepers. This rose to 13s in 1870 and by 1880 had risen to 15s In addition to their wages the beadles were supplied with uniforms. They received coats – variously called topcoats, overcoats or great coats – trousers, boots and caps. They had worn capes up to 1872.[21] The uniform colour was blue and the caps were marked 'Market Beadle'. In 1874 their coats were described as 'Chesterfield overcoats lined with fine woollen plaid', which were supplied by Patrick O'Connor of 79 North Main Street.[22] The overcoats cost £2 5s 0d each, the equivalent of three weeks' wages for a beadle, making the clothing and footwear allowances very valuable perks. The clothing provided had to be given back in case of dismissal.

Beadles Meagher and Murphy were often in trouble and frequently neglectful of their duties. In August 1867, for example, Murphy was fined 6d per week for ten weeks for unspecified negligence and the Market inspector, Rogers, was given full power to suspend him on his next offence.[23] In December of the same year Meagher was fined for an assault on one of the Market butchers.[24] Rogers complained the beadles to the Tolls and Markets Committee on many occasions and though they were fined, cautioned, suspended or threatened with dismissal for each misbehaviour, they managed to keep their jobs. In 1872, because of frequent absences from the markets and a 'general neglect of duty', the beadles were required to sign their names every half hour in a book provided for that purpose in the inspector's office.[25] The following month a sub-committee recommended that a system of fines be introduced for the wilful breach of any of the duties of the staff, including the beadles, and that three fines in any one year would earn dismissal.[26] The occasional misbehaviour continued, however, but was largely tolerated by the corporation.

Beadle Murphy died in December 1880 and was replaced initially by Myles O'Callaghan, a retired constable, who was declared to be 'unfit for the position' by the Market inspector two months after taking up duty.[27] The vacancy was re-advertised and Maurice Downey was appointed and served until his death in 1906. In 1883 Beadle Meagher fell ill and died. In recognition of his almost 40 years' service his widow, Ellen, was given £10 assistance 'to enable her to support herself and her children' and his son, also called John, was employed as a market sweeper.[28] Jeremiah Riordan joined Downey as the second market beadle, and during his eleven years service was reprimanded only once: he was suspended and fined £1 for being drunk before Christmas 1884.[29] Downey, on the other hand, was frequently in trouble for his excessive drinking and the committee minutes record numerous complaints against him, of which the following are but a sample: '[Downey] absented himself from duty 22nd inst., giving as an excuse that he had too much drink taken'; 'drunk on 23 and 24 Dec. – fined £1'; 'incapable due to drink'; Inspector 'has reason to believe Market Beadle Downey is at present addicted to drink'.[30] The committee eventually took action and dismissed him in 1894. A priest, Rev Father O'Leary, appeared before the committee to plead on Downey's behalf, 'as he had that day taken the Total Abstinence pledge ... and joined the League of the Cross'.[31] Downey was re-instated but was being complained again within a year for renewed drunkenness. In 1899 he was fined and reprimanded, along with a number of others, for selling back to a supplier the clothing provided by the corporation.[32] The following year he applied for a wage increase of 1s, which was first refused but granted three months later as 'he has been perfectly sober during this period'.[33] His remaining years in the Market appear to have passed without serious incident. Maurice Downey died in July 1906 after a two-year absence due to illness.

Following on Jeremiah Riordan's death in 1894, John Meagher, who had become a Market sweeper in 1883, was promoted to beadle, a position previously held by his late father. In December 1887 he was highly commended by the committee when he found £30 in his sweepings. It was restored to its owner and Meagher was rewarded with £3 for his honesty, the equivalent of two weeks' wages. No serious misbehaviour by him is recorded and his wage had risen to 20s per week by 1904. From 1908 he was unable to work and was paid half his weekly rate as sick pay from then until his death in 1922. Denis O'Brien was employed on a temporary basis in place of Meagher from 1908. In 1915 he joined the Irish Guards regiment of the British army and was killed three years later, six months before the end of the war.[34]

The last beadles to serve in the Market were Richard Scannell, appointed in 1906 to replace Maurice Downey, and Laurence Flaherty who replaced Denis O'Brien in 1915. They served until the mid-1920s, when they fell victim to city commissioner Phillip Monahan's re-organisation of municipal administration. Among the measures taken in pursuit of solvency was the sacking of 'superfluous staff' at the Market: the market beadles were no more.

The assistant

In the absence of complete records it is not possible to establish when this post was created, but it is probable that it followed the reform of the corporation in 1840. Eugene McSwiney became the assistant, sometimes deputy, Market inspector in 1863 and is the first and only holder of the position about whom any detail survives. His weekly wage of 18s in the 1870s was some 5s higher than that of the beadles and scalesmen and less than half that of the inspector. While his specific duties are not recorded, William O'Connell, the inspector, reported McSwiney for 'neglect of duty' in 1872 and complained him again in 1873 as he had to be sent for at 7.45am to open the Market, something he should have done at 7am.[35] The following month O'Connell reported him 'for not attending to open Market in the morning at the time appointed also for general neglect in the performance of his duty, and not reporting any misconduct in the Market or neglect of the other employees in the discharge of their duty'. McSwiney was ordered to make a daily report of the opening time of the Market.[36] He was eventually suspended from duty in the summer and was facing dismissal but for the intervention of a deputation of Market traders who successfully petitioned the Tolls and Markets Committee on his behalf. He was allowed back to work on 13 July but forfeited his wages for the period of his suspension and was to face dismissal in the event of further neglect of duty.[37] Within six weeks he was suspended again and was facing dismissal 'consequent on drunkenness'.[38] A group of women stallholders from the Princes Street Market attended the next committee meeting

Opposite page: Piotar Martyna working at the stall of Glenys Landon, Princes Street Market.

and requested that McSwiney be re-instated. He lost his job as assistant to the inspector but was re-employed as a scalesman on 23 December 1874.[39]

As McSwiney's position worsened in the second half of 1874, William O'Connell, the Market inspector, was himself frequently in trouble with the Tolls and Markets Committee and was suspended for mismanagement of the market accounts. It is quite possible that McSwiney was blamed for irregularities that were really the responsibility of the inspector and that his apparent drink problem made him more vulnerable. No assistant was appointed in succession to McSwiney.

Scalesmen

Up until 1896 there were two scales in the markets, one in the Grand Parade Market and the other in the Back, or Little, Market. These scales were manned by scalesmen, sometimes called weighmasters, who weighed carcasses or large cuts of meat when a delivery was made or when meat was traded between butchers. The butcher paid a small fee for each weighing but from 1872 a set amount was added to rents to cover weighing fees. Two scalesmen worked at the Grand Parade scales and a third worked in the Back Market until that was closed in 1896 when the premises was sold.

Patrick Murphy was already working in the Market as a scalesman when detailed records begin in 1867. He was dismissed in 1874 having been suspended a number of times for drunkenness.[40] A number of others are named as having served for short periods of time in the 1860s and 1870s – Denis Smith, Henry O'Sullivan, Thomas Ellis and John King. John Vaughan served for a little over three years and seems to typify the misery suffered by many working-class people in the nineteenth century and later. He was appointed in 1871 and within a year was absent due to illness. In 1873 the minutes of the Tolls and Markets Committee note: 'Complaint against Vaughan a scalesman for dirty appearance.'[41] A month later he was complained for 'being in a filthy condition and not competent for his office owing to ill health'. The committee ordered that he go to hospital and not be re-instated without its order.[42] The unfortunate Vaughan was dismissed two months later, 'not being fit for duty'.[43] He was replaced by Nicholas Daly, who in 1899, having served 25 years, was reported to be ill. He was 70 years old at this time and the committee proposed giving him some money to enable him join his daughter who lived in Australia.[44]

Eugene McSwiney became a scalesman following his dismissal as assistant inspector at the close of 1874. Within two months he was suspended for being 'drunk and incapable' and the committee, ever patient, allowed him back on a month's trial 'on condition that he takes the pledge'. He was to be dismissed on his next offence.[45] Ten years of apparent good behaviour followed until April 1885 when he was reported to

Above:
Bronze weights, dating to 1780, used by Cork Corporation officials in the city's markets. (Cork Public Museum)

the committee for being drunk in the Market. In July of that year he was suspended with the market sweeper John Meagher for renewed drunkenness.[46] McSwiney's misfortunes continued and three weeks later the committee noted that his wife had caused a great disturbance in the Market by attacking her husband.[47] He carried on drinking and was suspended in October, only to be re-instated on taking a further pledge not to drink.[48] In July 1887 William S. Perrier complained to the committee that McSwiney had called him 'an Orangeman' when he was passing through the Market. McSwiney was deemed to be 'under the influence' at the time and was suspended for a week.[49] Eugene McSwiney died in 1898 after 35 years of eventful service and was not replaced.

Daniel Cunningham was appointed scalesman in the Back Market in 1875 and was reprimanded only once, for drunkenness, in his 29 years of service. When the Back Market closed in 1896 he was given work of a general nature in the main market and took over as scalesman there on the death of Eugene McSwiney in 1898. He died in 1904.

In 1899 Nicholas Daly was succeeded as scalesman by John Creedon who died two years later. Charles Hayes was then appointed and after four years he was forced to resign due to ill health and the job was given to his son James. By now the strict demarcation between the duties of scalesman, sweeper and general worker in the Market was less defined and James Hayes, for example, is referred to separately as both scalesman and sweeper. Not unusually he was occasionally reprimanded for being absent from work due to drinking and was docked part of his wage. When this happened he was ordered to produce a certificate to show that he had taken a total abstinence pledge, something

K. Noonan Pork & Bacon – Kathleen Noonan

Kathleen Noonan was born in 1922 and grew up in Douglas Street on the south side of the city. Kathleen had her first stall in Cornmarket Street and in 1955 took a stall in the Market. She has traded as Kathleen Noonan Pork and Bacon for 50 years. Kathleen is now semi-retired and her daughter Pauline waits on their loyal clientele. The stall is unique in the Market as it is the only one that deals exclusively in pig meat, specialising in pig offal and offering a range of products that was the mainstay of the diet of the ordinary working people of Cork from early in the nineteenth century. Kathleen's daughter Pauline does not exaggerate when she says: 'We sell every part of the pig except his squeal!'

The stall displays crubeens, pig's tails, bodice, skirts, kidneys, loin bones, knuckles, hocks as well as rashers, collar bacon and other 'regular' cuts of pork and bacon. Pig's head is also sold but is not usually displayed as the supply is limited and regular customers have standing orders for every available head. The Noonans sell about 400 pig's tails per week and up to 600 crubeens. Pauline notices a surge in the sale of crubeens in the days before Cork play an important championship hurling match, cold crubeens being a favoured snack food to bring to a match or other sporting event. Bodice is also eaten on these occasions and maintains its popularity, mainly with older customers. While Pauline has seen a decline in business from her traditional Cork customer base since the 1980s, the stall is now benefiting from the custom of many of the immigrant population. Ukranians, for example, have a fondness for ham hocks and other nationalities see value and flavour in foods often avoided by indigenous Corkonians.

For the Noonans the pleasure of the Market is the relationship with the customers, the chat and banter with people whose mothers and grandmothers shopped at the stall over the past 60 years. Many customers go without rather than shopping elsewhere if what they want in unavailable. The Noonans are the sole representatives in the Market of a 200 year-old Cork love affair with pig offal and are modest custodians of a valuable, but not always valued, food tradition.

Opposite page:
Kathleen Noonan's daughters, Deirdre and Pauline.

This page:
Pauline and Kathleen Noonan.

129

George Martin

George Martin was born on 30 September 1946 in Chapel Lane on Cork's north side. He started work in the Market as a messenger boy for the butcher Jackie Waugh when he was fifteen. George's elder brother had been a messenger boy for Waugh's also. George worked six days per week with a half day on Wednesday and was paid £1 1s 8d. He gave £1 of that to his mother and kept the 1s 8d for himself. When this was spent he would often ask his mother for money and George remembers her reply – 'You give me £1 a week and then you look for £2 back!' George worked for Waugh's for about five years and then worked for Jimmy Dunlea, another butcher in the Market. In addition to making deliveries George helped in collecting and transporting the beef and mutton carcasses from the slaughterhouse to the Market and remembers feeling the heat of the freshly killed meat through his jacket as he carried it to the van. George is small in stature but had the strength to carry a side of beef on his shoulder, thereby earning the nickname 'the Bear', and to many he is still fondly known as Georgie Bear.

As a messenger boy George had to make deliveries throughout the city on his bicycle. The bicycles were usually kept in the Market, but if a late delivery had to be made, the messenger was allowed keep the bicycle at home overnight. This gave an opportunity for neighbouring children to have fun with the bicycle at a time when many children in working -class areas did not have bicycles or access to such play things. Many messenger boys cycled home at lunch time, or dinner time as it was known when most people ate their main meal about 1pm. Cork's north side is hilly and some of the principal thoroughfares, such as Shandon Street and Cathedral Road, are steep. After 'dinner', as the messenger boys returned for their afternoon's work, they often raced in groups down those streets back to the Market in the city centre. Wednesday was a half day in the Market and many of the messenger boys went to the cinema for the afternoon. When a screen character was shot or killed the shout often went up: 'Georgie! Remove the body!'

George Martin has worked in and about the Market for over forty years in various capacities and having observed the change and evolution over those decades he is most struck by the increased emphasis on hygiene in every aspect of the Market's operation. 'They're very choosey now. No sawdust and they'd nearly expect you to wear a bloody sink around your neck, you have to wash your hands so often,' he remarks.

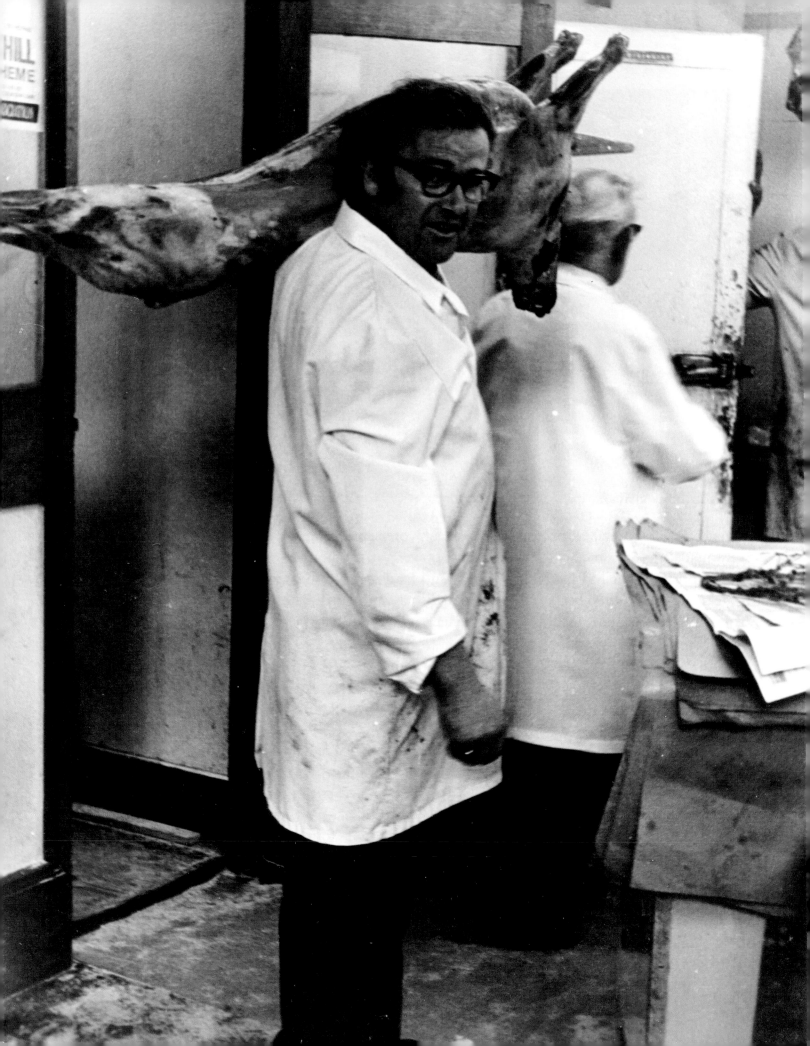

obstructed the free movement of people and traffic as they tried to compete with their more settled fellow traders inside. Certain sections of the markets were set aside for the sale of specific produce which led to competition between stallholders. This combination of circumstances, the consumption of alcohol and an apparent propensity towards argument, especially on the part of women, led to tension and occasional violence, which the minutes of the Tolls and Markets Committee record and newspaper correspondents complained of. Of the 55 instances of disorderly conduct in the markets recorded by the committee between 1869 and 1900, 37 involved women.

In 1855 a visitor to Cork wrote to the *Cork Constitution* to complain of the conduct of the vegetable women in the Market:

> Sir, - Will you allow me to enquire, through the medium of your columns, who are the proper authorities, or if there are *any*, for keeping order in the Cork Market? I am on a visit in Cork with a sick relative, and visiting the market this morning we were annoyed and insulted by the women in the Vegetable Market, so as to make it impossible ever to enter its precincts again. Not content with insulting us in their own domain some of them followed us into the street, repeating their annoyance, for which no kind of provocation was given, except that my friend begged the foremost of the party and the most offensive not to shout into her ears, as it distressed her. I looked around for a policeman on going into the street, but as usual none were visible ... [70]

In the same newspaper, three years later, a correspondent wrote of the obstruction caused by fruit sellers outside the Princes Street Market entrance. He wrote that the area

> is converted into a market for the sale of fruit and such like produce. The footways at both sides from Patrick-street to the market-gate are taken complete possession of, blocked up with baskets and 'standings', and made wholly impassable ...

This busy area attracted the attentions of pickpockets and the fruit sellers, all women, were accused by the correspondent of aiding these thieves in their work:

> The place has of late become one where theft flourishes and thieves find ready protection ... on not a few occasions pockets have been picked, and the thieves after a run captured, but nothing being found on them, and the gentle dames assembled there rather officiously and threateningly testifying to their innocence, the culprits have been let off, only, however, triumphantly to join their confreres and divide the booty, which had during the chase been cleverly dropped between the baskets, and recovered when the danger was past. On Saturday there was a very gross case

of interference on the part of these women to baffle the ends of justice. A fellow had been caught with his hand in a lady's pocket attempting to rob her, on which a gentleman who was near arrested him ... He was, however, immediately surrounded by several of those women, and although a person of determination ... he was so mobbed that he was compelled to allow the culprit to be dragged from him.[71]

In the nineteenth century the meat stalls in the Market were almost exclusively held by men. Some women had fish stalls but all the fruit, vegetables, fowl, butter and eggs were sold by women at stalls or at temporary standings or sittings. In 1869 Rogers, the inspector of the markets, reported two instances of misconduct by women traders: John Meagher, the Market beadle, was assaulted by a 'fruit woman', while two 'fowl women' were guilty of 'violent conduct'.[72] Julia Healy (or Haly), who sold vegetables, was cautioned by the Tolls and Markets Committee for fighting in the Market and one year later was in trouble again when, with Mrs Murray, she was found guilty of 'riotous conduct'.[73] Another vegetable woman, Hanora Sullivan, was fined 10s 6d when the Sub-sheriff of the county, Mr J. B. Johnson, complained that she had used obscene language to him in the Market.[74] Johanna Walsh was put out of the Market in August 1875 for disorderly conduct and although the minutes record that her application for return was rejected, she was apparently reinstated and was dismissed again the following month for being drunk and disorderly with another Market tenant called Cronin. On 6 October she appeared before the Tolls and Markets Committee to plead her case and brought a certificate to show she had joined a confraternity and mended her ways. The committee relented and she was allowed back. However she was suspended again three weeks later for 'misconducting herself'.[75] Johanna Walsh's association with the markets continued and in 1883 she was given a vacant fowl stall 'on condition that she be ejected the first time she misconducts herself'.[76]

Abbey Leahy was the tenant of a fish stall in the Grand Parade Market and her conduct led to her eventual ejection. In October 1897 the minutes record that she 'attacked a woman in the Market last Saturday night and that she has frequently given annoyance to other tenants and their customers by using bad language'. This resulted in a warning.[77] She misbehaved again one month later and was complained by another trader. No action was taken.[78] In August the following year the inspector reported her for selling bad fish and for using abusive language to the customer who complained. She was put out of the Market and the committee gave her notice to quit.[79] Three weeks later Abbey Leahy was still trading and although she was reported to be conducting her stall well, the committee refused to withdraw the notice to quit.[80] When a deputation of stallholders appeared before the committee and appealed on Abbey Leahy's behalf she was given a month's reprieve.[81] At the end of this trial period she had not paid her rent arrears of £1 12s 0d. and failed to appear before the committee to explain her case. As a result her stall was re-possessed.[82]

Mrs Margaret Lyster became a tenant of a vegetable stall in the Princes Street Market in 1897 and over the following 25 years became notorious for her misbehaviour. Within months of taking her stall George D. O'Donnell, the Market inspector, reported:

> Mrs Margaret Lyster and Mrs Margaret Lynch, tenants of Stalls No. 2 and 3 Princes Street Vegetable Market, were charged with ridiculing and abusing Mr and Mrs Goggin of Nos. 11 and 12 and that when he reprimanded them they only laughed at him.

The Tolls and Markets Committee demanded a written apology from the women.[83] Mrs Lynch complied but Mrs Lyster 'had not only not apologised, but had repeated the offence'. As a result she was given notice to quit.[84] A week later a letter of apology was sent to the committee but the notice to quit stood. On receipt of a further written apology Mrs Lyster was allowed remain.[85] She is next mentioned in the minutes six years later in August 1904 when she 'caused a disturbance' in the Market with another tenant.[86] Two years later she disturbed the Princes Street Market again when she became involved in a 'scolding match' and the committee again served her with a notice to quit.[87] The Lord Mayor and a number of stallholders wrote letters to the committee asking that she not be evicted. Their pleading worked and Mrs Lyster was let off with the warning that she would be evicted if she misbehaved again.[88]

Farmgate Café and Restaurant – Kay Harte

Kay Harte grew up in Youghal in east Cork and had no family connection with the Market before she opened the Farmgate with her sister Máróg O'Brien in 1994. Kay feels that this may have been an advantage in that she had no preconceived ideas about the place and was not unduly concerned by the pessimism expressed by many Market traders. Remarks like 'You won't sell a crumb!' still echo for her. Kay and Máróg viewed the gallery of the Princes Street Market as a unique space in Cork, overlooking and in close proximity to a range of stalls offering what was traditional, local and enduring, at a time when new food influences were beginning to be reflected in some of the newer stalls. The location embodied the basic elements of the food philosophy underlying the Farmgate enterprise. When Máróg opened the first Farmgate in Midleton, County Cork, in 1983 she sought to serve the best of locally produced food, cooked imaginatively yet simply and presented without fuss or undue preciousness. From the beginning it was Farmgate policy to court local custom and following on the success of the Midleton venture the Market offered the potential to take the ideas further, making a visible connection between the food served and that displayed at the stalls beneath.

Kay remembers the 1990s as a time when people were embracing new tastes and foods, while also becoming more concerned about how their food was produced and prepared. Simpler, traditional foods and dishes were rediscovered and it was seen that Ireland, and Cork in particular, had to offer could grace a table as well as any exotic fare. Farmgate attempts to balance these different factors and give due recognition to the local while adapting and adopting the best from outside.

Tripe is a regular on the Farmgate menu. Initially it was difficult to give customers exactly what they wanted as many of those ordering tripe in the restaurant were wishing to rediscover a taste from their youth and they wanted it to taste like the tripe their mothers had prepared. The tripe is boiled in milk with onions, salt and pepper for two hours and is served with white bread and butter or boiled potatoes in their jackets. Drisheen, Cork's unique blood sausage, is often served with the tripe in the traditional fashion. Farmgate has also revived interest in corned mutton, another virtually forgotten dish. Pat Murphy, the butcher who trades at the stall of P. Coughlan, supplies the meat, which is cured or corned in a salt pickle for a number of days. It is then boiled and served

with a caper sauce, a combination of the local and exotic that exemplifies the restaurant's approach to food. Corned beef and spiced beef are other old Cork favourites sourced at the stalls in the Market and served and eaten on the gallery above.

Kay Harte believes the Market can play a vital role in promoting the debate on food production and encouraging quality food producers. She shares the feelings of most traders that while visitors and tourists are welcome the Market should focus primarily on the day-to–day customers, local Cork people who are the bread and butter of the place, the people for whom the Market was first set up. To this end she holds that the Market is not merely a valuable piece of city-centre commercial real estate, but also an important social space that is integral to the regeneration of Cork. Mounting public concerns regarding healthy eating and a growing demand for fresh, seasonal and traceable food enable the Market to play its part in meeting these new challenges.

In 1909 she was in trouble with the committee again when she assaulted Mrs Ellen McKee, a tenant of the Market, in April and May of that year. She received a severe reprimand and was ordered to confine herself to her stall.[89] Within five months Mrs McKee was complaining that 'Lyster abuses her in such a way that unless strong action is taken she would have to give up her stall'. Lyster did not have the support of other tenants on this occasion and a number of stallholders supported McKee's case and informed the committee that 'unless stringent measures were taken with her [Lyster] she would destroy the reputation of the market'.[90] The committee deferred making a decision. Inaction like this on the part of the committee was not unusual in dealing with troublesome tenants. Threats of eviction were often made and warnings and reprimands were frequently given, but the final sanction was avoided except in extreme circumstances. Decisions taken by the committee were sometimes reversed by a vote of council or at the request of the Mayor. Mrs Lyster remained in the Market only to be 'seriously warned' six months later, in March 1910.[91] In April 1911 eviction notices were served on her and Mrs Ellen McKee for disorderly conduct in the Market. Their misconduct was reported by other stallholders, now obviously tiring of the ongoing difficulties, and they were to appear before the Police Court.[92] Yet again the committee reversed its decision and seven weeks later allowed Lyster and McKee back.[93]

In 1912 the pair were in arrears with their rent and as they still had not paid off the amount by March of the following year they were under notice to quit. Appeals and negotiations followed and they were allowed remain as they agreed to pay off their debt at the rate of 2d per week. The two women did not keep their agreement and the committee decided to proceed with repossession of their stalls.[94] The stalls were not repossessed and within three months Lyster and McKee were 'causing disturbance' in the Market and appeared before the Police Court. They were suspended from the Market, but were given 'a second chance' by the committee and allowed back in July 1913.[95] Mrs Ellen McKee finally lost her stall in May 1917 and her debts were written off as 'bad and irrecoverable'.[96] Mrs Margaret Lyster survived another five years. She is mentioned finally in June 1922 when the committee noted that they had had no communication from her, having enquired about her absence from the Market and her failure to pay rent.[97]

Men made up the majority of tenants in the markets and were almost exclusively butchers or victuallers. Their stalls were in the Grand Parade and Little, or Back, Markets and misconduct by these men is reported far less frequently than that by women. Men did misbehave, however. In 1884, for example, John Meagher, a Market beadle, complained 'of being beaten by tenants in the Market named Preston who are constantly fighting and disorderly'. As was usual in these circumstances they were given notice to quit but this was withdrawn the following month and they were reprimanded instead.[98] John Griffin, a tenant of the Little Market, was complained by Felix Mullan, the Market inspector, in May 1884 as he had 'abused and threatened him for closing the market at the hour fixed by the Corporation'. Griffin failed to appear before the committee and was given notice to quit.[99] He was given a reprieve when he expressed his regret and undertook to be well behaved, but 'had repeated his insubordinate conduct' to Mullan a week later. He was again ordered to quit the Market but a letter from his solicitor, Mr Arthur Julian, an apology and a promise to pay costs persuaded the committee to let him stay.[100]

In August 1885 Mullan reported a 'disgraceful disturbance' involving Market tenants Charles Hayes, his brother Edward and an employee of theirs named Carroll. All were summoned before a magistrate for disorderly conduct. The report also noted that the situation was not helped by the fact that Beadle Maurice Downey was 'incapable due to drink'.[101] Charles Hayes was in trouble again in 1887 when Mullan had him charged with drunkenness and disorderly conduct but an apology resulted in the charge being withdrawn.[102] In July 1900 John Ahern, the son of Mrs Anne Ahern of No 23 Grand Parade Market, was drunk and causing annoyance in the Market. The police were called to remove him. Three weeks later he was drunk again and forced his mother from her stall in an apparent attempt to take possession of it. The Tolls and Markets Committee met with Mrs Ahern and her sons but was unable to resolve the issue. Mrs Ahern subsequently wrote to the committee stating that she had no intention of giving up the stall. The committee agreed to let her stay if she kept her son John away and if he ceased causing annoyance.[103] John Ahern was back in the Market the following January, drunk and 'causing disturbance'. Mrs Ahern solved the problem by requesting that the stall be transferred to another son, Michael, 'with a view to keeping John out of the Market'.[104]

Edward Lynch became a tenant of Stall No 69 in the Grand Parade Market in December 1901, paying a rent of 6s per week. The following August the minutes note: 'Drunkenness, disorderly conduct and assault committed by Edward Lynch ... upon another stallholder, Ignatius O'Flynn, and upon himself (Inspector) on 19th July and 7th inst ... '. Lynch was to be prosecuted for the assault on the inspector.[105] Some three weeks later Lynch was again drunk and 'behaved in a violent and insolent manner in the market', yet the committee saw fit not to proceed with any prosecution but to serve him with a notice to quit should he re-offend.[106] Lynch wrote a letter of apology but offended again in October when he was drunk and disorderly in the Market. He assaulted John Meagher, the Market beadle, but refused to give up his stall when asked to do so by the inspector. He was served with a notice to quit but refused to go and was drunk in the Market again the following Saturday night.[107] Two weeks later, on 26 November, Lynch was still in possession of his stall and informed the committee that he wished to give it up and transfer the tenancy to Charles O'Flynn. His request was refused and he was ordered to give up the stall.[108] Although tenants were obliged to give up possession of their stalls

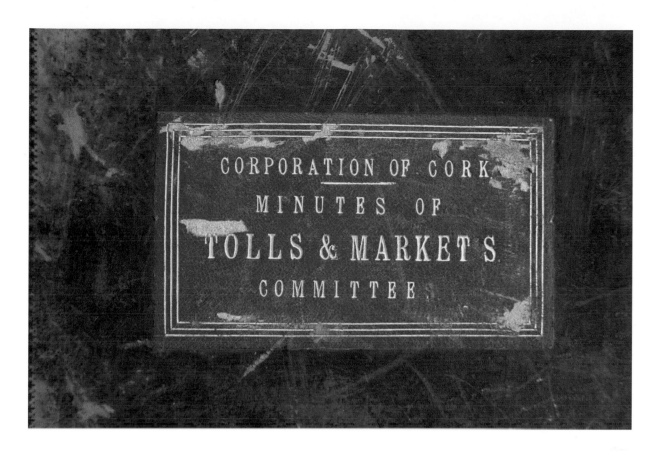

on receipt of one week's notice, Lynch still held his stall in December when he was reported for misconduct and ordered yet again to hand up his stall.[109] The committee was apparently successful on this occasion.

Amongst the more unusual incidents dealt with by the Tolls and Markets Committee was the case of Mrs Anne Conway. In April 1879 the minutes note:

> Mrs Conway, stall holder in Prince's Street market, applying for compensation for injury to her leg, alleged to have been caused by Denis Horgan, sweeper of the Market, having thrown a girl upon her, on the 19th November 1878.[110]

At its next meeting the committee heard from Mrs Conway, Denis Horgan and the unfortunate girl, Ellen Sheehan, but could not reach a conclusion as to the exact circumstances of the incident.[111] In June 1882 the committee investigated a case where a man's leg was broken in the Princes Street Market and the suggestion was made that the man had slipped on cabbage leaves thrown on the floor of the Market. The City Engineer investigated and reported that the accident was due 'to the man's own misconduct' and that market staff were not responsible.[112] In 1895 Mr William Hill, who lived at No 25 Grand Parade, next door to the Market entrance, sought damages from the Corporation when his mother 'was thrown down by a basket belonging to a fruit vendor' who had

Above:
The surviving minute books of the Tolls and Markets Committee are held in the Cork Archives Institute.

Chairman

Mr Mullan's accounts for Grand Parade and Prince's Street Markets, showing the following lodgments, viz:-

Week ended 22nd March, £32 : 12 : 10
  "   "   29th "   33 : 3 : 2

Mr O'Mahony's accounts for Tolls and Out Markets, showing the following lodgments, viz:-

Week ended 22nd March, 1879
  Tolls   £37 : 10 : 7
  Markets   7 : 17 : 10
  Bazaar   5 : 18 : 1

Week ended 29th March
  Tolls   £29 : 8 : 7
  Markets   7 : 14 : 7
  Bazaar   6 : 7 : 0

Account of Munster Iron Company for hardware goods supplied to Markets from July 6th, 1877, to July 8th, 1878

Margaret Barry again applying for a stall in Bazaar Market.

Ellen Spillane applying for salt meat stall in St Peter's Market.

as Superintendent obtains possession thereof, and present using the stall, to return to her own.

Mrs Conway, stallholder in Prince's Street Market, applying for compensation for injury to her leg, alleged to have been caused by Denis Horgan, Sweeper of the Market, having thrown a girl upon her, on the 19th November, 1878.

---

obstructed the street.[113] Mr William Hill's brother John, who had a shop at the same address, complained to the Tolls and Markets Committee on many occasions between 1881 and 1920 about the obstruction caused by the accumulation of fish baskets and boxes at the Grand Parade entrance to the markets that adjoined his premises. He also complained of 'the annoyance occasioned by men lounging idly, smoking and indulging in foul language near his shop door'.[114] Mr Hill and other Grand Parade traders made regular complaints like this. In 1894 they complained of 'the nuisance caused by wholesale dealing of fish on the street and at the entrance gate of the Fish Market' and in 1895 'the noise occasioned by women engaged in the sale of fish in the street' led to another letter to the committee.[115] In 1907 'the bad smell emitted from the entrance to the Fish Market' forced Mr Hill to write again and he continued to complain up to 1920, when his last complaint was recorded.

On 4 July 1917 John Fawcett MA, librarian at University College Cork, informed the committee that his wife had had a serious accident in the Grand Parade Market the previous month; she had fallen over a partition between the meat and the fish markets. The committee decided that a 'satisfactory settlement' should be arranged. In November of that year Mr Fawcett claimed £50 in compensation on behalf of his wife and the following February he settled for £40.[116] This was a significant amount, roughly the equivalent of twenty weeks wages' of the average Market employee.

Mr Hill's complaint about 'men lounging idly, smoking and indulging in foul language' was not unusual. In 1883, for example, a complaint was made about 'a crowd of men and women ... who squabble and use objectionable language' at the market entrance[117], in 1893 the committee was concerned about 'idlers lounging, smoking and spitting in the entrance to the market, Grand Parade',[118] and in 1897 the stallholders of the Princes Street Market were being annoyed 'by a number of idle lads frequenting the Gallery'.[119]

The markets were sometimes disturbed by other visitors. In October 1880 the *Cork Examiner* reported a disturbance in the Market caused by a drunken country policeman while on a visit to the city:

An occurrence took place yesterday in the English Market, which we chronicle with mingled feelings of awe and wonder, while regret also affects us. The Royal Irish Constabulary are noted for one great characteristic – they rise above the multitude into a region of morality so pure that lesser mortals scarce dream of. What then will be thought when we assert that one was drunk yesterday in the English market, as regular a case for 'five shillings or four days' as ever came before a bench? A fine, strong, able fellow, in the dreaded garb, including military shako, bayonet, &c., appeared early in the afternoon in our local mart for meat and vegetables, his gait unsteady, his features smiling – suddenly – tell it not in Gath – he staggered, and could not arrest himself in his erratic career. So he swayed from side to

Opposite page: Extract from the minutes of the Tolls and Markets Committee, 2 April, 1879.

Below:
The Onion Seller by Seamus Murphy, in Bishop Lucey Park, Cork.

side, first in the vegetable market, where he displayed a reckless disregard for cabbages &c. Then he became somewhat obstreperous among the meat stalls, not showing the slightest respect for even the best specimens of beef and mutton joints. Eventually it was considered that it would be just as well if the representative of law and order was removed, and three men who had come up with him from the country town where he is stationed, attempted to persuade him to leave. Morally weak, the 'peeler' proved himself physically strong, by gently knocking down his friendly advisers. Eventually some five stalwart policemen succeeded in removing their erring brother from the scene of his unhappy display, whilst some on-lookers seemed to take a vicious delight, no doubt caused by unpleasant memories of their own, at [illegible]'s falling away.[120]

Casual onion sellers were among the other unwanted visitors. The Grand Parade, Princes Street and the Market entrances were often obstructed by casual traders like these and rent-paying Market traders were quick to complain when they encroached on their territory. In 1892 the inspector reported '8 girls who constantly sell onions about the Market and refuse to keep out'. The committee recommended that two or three of them be prosecuted for trespass as a deterrent to the others.[121] In August it was reported that a girl had been prosecuted and fined but that there was 'serious recurrence'. The committee decided to have 'a half dozen girls so offending' prosecuted.[122] This did not deter the onion sellers as they were still causing a problem seven months later and the principal offenders were prosecuted at the committee's request.[123]

Part of the corporation's motivation in providing custom-built meat markets since the seventeenth century was to separate the slaughtering and retailing aspects of the meat trade and regulations forbade any killing at market stalls in the interests of public health. Market traders sometimes breached these rules. In 1875 a member of the committee reported that fowl were being killed 'to the injury of the cleanliness of the market'.[124] The following year a deputation of butchers complained of the nuisance caused by another Market trader, William Kinmonth, who was keeping live fowl at his stall and killing them there.[125] Kinmonth attended the next committee meeting and agreed to cease. The committee gave him a fowl stall in the gallery of the Princes Street Market, away from the butchers.[126] The practice continued, however, and is mentioned regularly in the minutes. In July 1893, for example, the committee decided that 'any person found killing or cleaning fowl ... will be expelled' and it also decreed that all live animals were to be excluded from the Market.[127] A month later a complaint was made that live calves were being brought into the Market and that dogs were being kept at their stalls by some tenants, and in March 1894 five kid goats were slaughtered at a stall. The committee asked that the regulations be strictly enforced.[128] The problem persisted and again in 1900 the committee ordered that that the killing and plucking of fowl cease. A sub-committee was set up to look into the ongoing problem and in June 1900 it recommended that an idle stall be covered and set aside in the Princes Street Market for the killing and plucking of fowl but that no killing was to take place after 3pm.[129]

Mr Bell's – Driss Belmajoub

Driss Belmajoub, a native of Morocco and a chef by trade, began selling Moroccan clothes and crafts in a small shop in Cork's Winthrop Arcade, which runs between Oliver Plunkett Street and Winthrop Street, in the mid-1970s. From his annual trips home he began to return with supplies of food not available in Ireland at the time – couscous, varieties of rice, herbs, spices, sauces. In the early 1980s he abandoned clothes selling and occupied a stall in the English Market, sublet by Mary Rose. Here, under the name 'Mr Bell's', he began selling herbs and spices, as well as frozen and home-cooked foods that brought unfamiliar, and not universally popular, aromas into the Market – curries and other spicy dishes as well as pasta dishes such as lasagne and canneloni. The response from the Cork public was underwhelming, and many took diversions in the Market to avoid his stall; complaints abounded about the 'weird' smells, and some would ostentatiously 'hold their noses' when passing by. He abandoned the experiment, transferred to another stall in the Princes Street Market and established Cork's first 'Oriental' foods outlet.

Cork taste buds were gradually diversifying, and Driss managed to stay in business in the Market. In the early 1990s, he moved to a new location, at the Princes Street end of the Grand Parade Market, which he subsequently expanded. In 1994, he took a further two stalls closer to the Grand Parade entrance to specialise in Chinese and Indian foods, while dedicating the older outlet to Italian and French delicatessan products.By this stage, however, the 'new generation' of stallholders was becoming established: others were now specialising in olives, pasta, cheeses, mustards, jams, beans and pulses, and so on, so both stalls became predominantly 'Oriental'. Added to the new internal competition is the growing external competition from the proliferation of 'ethnic' food shops which have sprung up in Cork in the opening years of the twenty-first century. Among their advantages is their flexible opening hours. While demand has steadily increased for his products, so too have alternative suppliers, while the costs of running his Market stalls have increased dramatically.

Now a Market stalwart, Driss Belmajoub was a pioneer who prepared the way for others. For the small number of non-nationals living in Cork in the 1980s, and the growing number of Corkonians whose tastes were becoming internationalised, Mr Bell's was a life-saver, the only supplier of products which are all supermarket standards today. Among his customers were some of those who went on to establish speciality stalls themselves. In more ways than one, then, Mr Bell rang in the new.

5 Market Trends 1900-2005

The English Market had been in business for 112 years as it faced into the new century. Despite various trials and tribulations, it remained Cork's flagship municipal market, as reflected in its two new handsome façades on the Grand Parade and Princes Street, and the fact that its annual income was almost double that of the other two main markets, St Peter's and the Bazaar, combined. The large income, however, was offset by the correspondingly high expenditure necessary to maintain cleanliness, appearance and efficiency. The improvement measures that marked the closing decade of the nineteenth century continued into the early years of the twentieth.

Improvements

More stalls were connected to the main sewers; zinc tops were fitted to the tripe and drisheen stalls; new tables or table tops, lights, skylights, sheeting and flooring were supplied. In some cases the corporation footed the entire bill, while in others the cost was shared, usually on a 50/50 basis. By 1905, this was the norm. In 1906 the corporation and larger stallholders co-funded the building of offices, heralding the era of the Market office-lady, often the wife or sister of the stallholder, who kept the accounts and often quietly exercised the real control of the business. The heyday of funded improvements ended in 1906; subsequently the corporation was far more selective in its expenditure, and most improvements had to be paid for in full by the stallholders themselves. The Tolls and Markets Committee and the Public Health Committee made repeated efforts to enforce the various hygiene regulations. The order banning the killing and plucking of fowl was reissued, butchers and fishmongers were banned from throwing offal on the floor, and stallholders were instructed to sweep out and maintain their own stalls. Market staff filled boxes of refuse which were removed twice daily by a contractor.

Problems persisted, however, and constant vigilance was necessary. A Sanitary Sub-Officer who visited the Market in May 1903 found it in 'a very filthy state';[1] tenants were not sweeping out their stalls and the place was littered with empty boxes and rubbish. The Tolls and Markets Committee ordered the inspector to go on duty at 7am instead of 8am in an effort to rectify the problem. 'Great improvement' in the general condition of the Market was noted by the following month, and another burst of activity followed: the entire building was painted for the first time in five years; new toilets were fitted, and the flagging in the fish market was altered to take the water to the back of the stalls instead of the centre of the passage, where it accumulated.[2]

While some stalls had connected individually to the electricity mains, the main lighting in the Market continued to be gas powered. Because of a strike in the gasworks in May 1901, the Market was plunged into darkness on a busy Saturday night, and emergency lighting had to be provided by eighteen oil lamps. The stallholders requested that electric lighting replace or supplement the gas. Additional gas lamps were installed, but it took until early 1908 for the committee to install fourteen new electric incandescent lamps, which increased illumination but cost 25 per cent less.[3] Electric lighting eventually replaced gas in the early 1930s, at the same time as the city's street lighting was similarly converted. The Committee was equally slow to accede to the Market butchers' demands for a proper collective cooling chamber for meat. When a decision was finally arrived at in June 1908, the project was deferred due to the objection of the fish stallholders to its erection in the passage running into the fish market. The records fail to record when the chamber was finally installed. Plans to 'spruce up' the roof of the Grand Parade Market by sheeting it with spruce timber, which would also do away with the inconvenience of constantly having to whitewash and plaster the roof, had to be abandoned in 1904 when only three stallholders agreed to pay an extra 3d a week onto their rents as a contribution to the cost of £269.[4]

Holidays, holy days and half days

The growing influence of Irish-Ireland, cultural nationalist ideas in the early twentieth century was evident in a number of decisions relating to the Market. In September 1901, for example, the corporation ordered a flag for the front of the Grand Parade Market 'which shall bear the Irish harp and shamrock in addition to the Cork Arms'. When the flag was damaged by high winds in 1908, a new one was ordered, with the stipulation that it 'be done as far as possible in the city of Cork, but entirely in Ireland'. In 1906 Andrew Dale surrendered one of his stalls because he was stopped from selling 'foreign meat'. A new clause was inserted into the tenancy agreements prohibiting the sale of 'any but Irish-fed beef, mutton or pork'.[5] Campaigning by the Gaelic League helped to establish St Patrick's Day as a holiday. It was officially made a bank holiday in 1903, but from the previous year the stallholders had agreed to close at 11am, while the inspector flew the new flag. The Market closed on Christmas Day, St Stephen's Day, and usually on 27 December also; it remained closed on Good Friday, until 1919, when it opened for the morning; on Easter Monday it remained open only until 10 or 11am, if at all; on other bank holidays it was usual to remain open until 11am. In an indication of the continuing compatibility between growing Irish national sentiment and loyalty to the British Crown, the tenants of the Market agreed to close for a half day on 20 May 1910, the day of King Edward VII's funeral.

All of Ireland was still a part of the United Kingdom at this stage, which brought occasional benefits. In 1912 the Liberal government under Herbert Asquith introduced the Shops Act as part of a raft of progressive legislation in the interests of workers in response to an upsurge in labour militancy, spearheaded in Ireland by James Larkin and the newly formed Irish Transport and General Workers' Union (ITGWU). In the interest of shop (and stall) workers, the Act enforced one half-day's closure each week. It was agreed in May 1912 to close the Market every Wednesday at 1pm. The fish stallholders objected, as 'it would seriously affect their trade', but agreed to close on Monday afternoons instead. To facilitate this arrangement, barriers had to be erected at the entrance to the fish section from the meat market, and two members of staff were kept on duty on Wednesday afternoons to prevent access to the other, closed markets.[6]

The decline of the 'Irish Market'

A similar cordoning-off of the fish section was undertaken in St Peter's Market, which, unlike its older sister, was in dire straits. Both it and the neighbouring Bazaar were suffering in the early twentieth century, bearing the brunt of competition from street traders. Indeed, the proliferation of vacant stalls in both these markets was directly related to traders abandoning them in favour of the freedom, in every sense, of the streets. The thoroughfares on either side of these markets, Cornmarket Street and North Main Street, were especially popular locations for street trading, much to the annoyance of those inside the markets as well as shopkeepers. At the beginning of 1905, 58 stalls in St Peter's and 43 in the Bazaar were vacant, St Peter's was running at a loss (its annual income in this period, amounting to less than £500, was over £200 less than in the mid-1880s), and various proposals were mooted as to the best way to remedy what was effectively a crisis. In November 1905 the Tolls and Markets Committee considered a proposal to convert St Peter's, which by then had 63 vacant stalls, into a wholesale market for the sale of fruit, vegetables, flowers, fish and poultry. The proposal, which was opposed by 30 councillors, and a petition of 140 residents and shopkeepers in the

Opposite page: Paddy McDonnell, trader in the Princes Street Market.

14 GRAND PARADE MARKET,

14 GRAND PARADE MARKET,

Cork, Dec 20 1941

Mr T. Murphy

Bought of **BRESNAN'S**

Victuallers

Guys, Cork

	Forward		53	15	0
	47	1/1	2	10	11
	59	1/0½	3	1	5½
	47	1/1	2	10	11
	7 Sheeps Tongues				7
	2 Mut Kidneys				6
	Ox - Tongue			3	0
19	3 Sheeps Liver	1/2 6		3	6
	3 Mut Kidneys				9
20	5½ Caul	5		2	3½
			62	8	11
	Less £				8½
			62	8	2½
	Week ending 13/12		65	15	2
			128	3	4

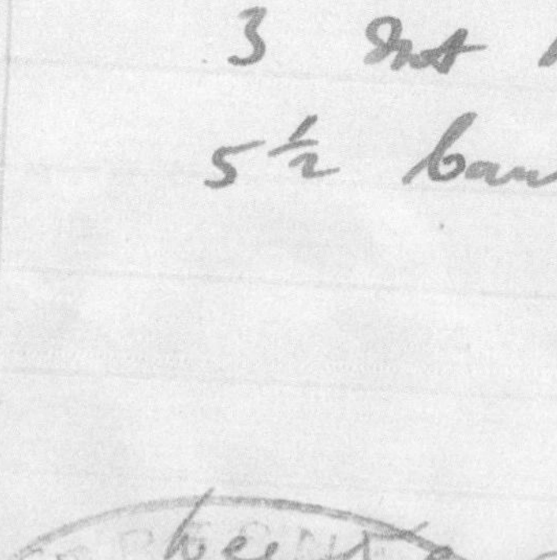

30-12-41

North Centre and Centre wards, was rejected. The Committee then suggested that the proposed market could be held on Cornmarket Street itself, 'under a glass or corrugated iron roof, supported on iron pillars, up to a certain hour, after which all commodities remaining unsold should be removed into St Peter's Market', a fascinating proposal that came to nought. In a context of increasing losses, the corporation decided in 1910 to close a portion of the market at the North Main Street end. In the meantime, a number of vacant stalls had been filled by the transfer of meat dealers from Cornmarket Street into St Peter's itself at reduced rents.[7] During the First World War, as we shall see, the greater part of the market was closed.

In time of war

'Rebel' Cork of 1919-22 would have been hard to imagine at the outbreak of the First World War in August 1914, as the city was engulfed by a wave of popular enthusiasm for the British war effort. Soldiers marched past cheering crowds and people flocked to recruitment rallies as the Catholic and Protestant churches, the city's newspapers, political parties, and its public bodies, led by the corporation, united in support of Britain's war. The Irish Volunteers, founded in 1913 as a nationalist response to the establishment of the Ulster Volunteer Force, which was pledged to resist Home Rule for Ireland by force of arms, split in September 1914, the vast majority going with the National Volunteers, who backed the Irish Parliamentary Party leader John Redmond's support for the war. Among them was Denis O'Brien from Fort Street, adjacent to the Elizabeth Fort British army barracks, who was employed as a beadle in the English Market. The National Volunteers put a nightly 'guard' on the city's bridges in the early months of the war, and in January 1915 O'Brien took up duty on the bridges; the Tolls and Markets Committee granted him leave on the days following his shifts. In April 1915, O'Brien became one of the over 6,000 Cork city men who went to war when he joined the Irish Guards regiment of the British army. He was granted leave of absence from his Market post, in line with the policy of Cork employers to keep the positions of volunteers open until their return. His wife, Theresa, was paid half his wages until her Separation Allowance came through, and thereafter such amount as made up his full pay of 20s per week. O'Brien never resumed his post; he was killed during a German offensive on the Western Front on 5 April 1918, three years almost to the day after he enlisted. He is buried in Doullens communal cemetery, near the Somme.[8]

The war years were a time of spiralling inflation, especially in food prices, which by the end of 1916 were 84 per cent above their pre-war level. This had an obvious impact on the Market, and in 1915 some vulnerable traders were granted rent reductions due to 'the present depression of trade'. In 1917 improvements, such as the fitting of

P. Coughlan – Paul Murphy

Paul Murphy was eleven when he started working in the Market and was a qualified butcher by the age of sixteen in 1950. Paul's maternal great-grandmother, Lizzie Coughlan, started the business over a century ago in Cornmarket Street and in the 1940s her son and grandson, Patsy and Pearse Coughlan, first took a stall in the Grand Parade Market. In the 1940s and 1950s the Grand Parade Market was still dominated by butchers' stalls and Paul recalls over 40 butchers trading there when he started work. This number has now fallen to eight and he sees this as the most notable change over his working life. While such a fall is regrettable, Paul knows that the Market would not have survived if it had not diversified and had continued to depend on butchers.

In his early years in the Market refrigeration was still something of a novelty and meat was delivered every day and kept cool and safe at night by being hung as high as possible above the stalls. In summer meat was brought by barrow to O'Sullivan's Cold Storage at the close of business, to be collected the following morning. Paul remarks that the Market customers came from across the full social spectrum, even though the popular perception is that the well off shopped elsewhere. He remembers the offal stall of Babe Anne Kane where pig's heads, crubeens, bodice and skirts were bought by both the working class and the more affluent professionals. The messenger boys' strike in the mid-1960s is another memory. Paul recalls a stand-off when the messenger boys of the city marched through the Market from the Grand Parade in pursuit of their demand for payment of 4s per day. The issue was resolved and good relations were re-established. Like many other Market traders, Paul Murphy misses the camaraderie of those more innocent years. He feels that the Market has lost its sense of fun as the pressures of rising costs, competition and fickle customer behaviour demand constant attention.

In the later 1970s Paul was one of the driving forces of the Market Traders' Association in their campaign to get security of tenure for stallholders. Traditionally tenants held their stalls on license, renewed weekly, and could theoretically lose their tenancy on receiving one week's notice. The association was successful and in 1978 traders were given 21-year leases with a rent review every five years. Paul has very strong views on what a market is and how it differs from the high street. He feels that rents should be much lower as stalls are not lock-up shops and tenants do not have access to their premises when the market is closed. Market trade is more dependent on personal service, on the relationship between the customer and trader. Paul is now serving the third and fourth generations of families as customers and he sees this continuity as key to the Market's survival. His son Alan is now a partner in the business and as the great-great-grandson of Lizzie Coughlan, is the fifth generation of his family in the meat trade.

'hopper' lights, were suspended until the war's end 'in consequence of the increased cost of such works'.[9] However, the English Market was strong enough to survive; indeed, the suspension of improvements meant that it recorded a surplus of income over expenditure in 1915-6, the first in a number of years. The 'Irish Market', St Peter's, however, became a casualty of war. In early April 1916 a Tolls and Markets sub-committee recommended that St Peter's be divided in two, with the south side cleared and let and all remaining traders moved to the north side. In the meantime, however, it transpired that the British government had allocated a national shell factory to Cork. Representatives of the Ministry of Munitions in Ireland had visited a number of potential sites, and decided that St Peter's would be ideal. A special meeting was convened by the Lord Mayor with trade and labour representatives, and it was unanimously agreed that the market be handed over to the Ministry. Provision was then made in the Bazaar for the displaced stallholders, and those with more than one stall in the Bazaar were asked to surrender all but one to accommodate the new arrivals.[10] A small portion of the market re-opened after the war.

Trade unions

The war years also saw another significant development: an explosion of trade unionism. Workers sought wage increases to keep pace with inflation, and as a wave of class consciousness spread through the workforce, the main body of employees in the Market helped to form the Cork Journeyman Butchers' Society (CJBS) in 1916. These assistant butchers had worked with little or no protection; they had little job security, were poorly paid, had no holidays, worked unregulated hours and received no overtime pay. Their situation was transformed with the creation of the union, which soon had the majority of journeymen in its ranks. The organised power of the workers was increased by the fact that they also worked in the butchers' slaughterhouses. Reduced and regulated working hours, significant wage increases and holidays all followed, and butchering in Cork took on the shape of a closed shop, where the union wielded significant power. While this limited the power of the butcher employers, it also worked to their advantage. The union operated as a type of labour exchange for butchers; a register of unemployed members was kept, and employers could call on the union to supply suitable labour when a temporary or permanent vacancy arose. Another mutually advantageous arrangement was the limitation of 'imported' meat from outside the city: only meat butchered by union members would be sold in the city, and as the slaughterhouses were mainly run by the master butchers themselves, this helped insulate them against outside competition.[11] The high concentration of butchers in the Market strengthened its ability to monitor the behaviour of the master butchers in relation to union rules. Throughout the remainder of the century the Market was a mainstay of the union, which was registered with the Irish Trade Union Congress in 1932 and changed its name to the Cork Operative Butchers' Society (COBS). Market butchers were always strongly represented on its executive.

The ITGWU was the fastest growing and largest union in the country. By 1918, at least, it had unionised much of the corporation workforce, including those in the Market. The union asserted and established workers' rights; in November, 1918, for example, it secured remuneration for Charles Crowley, Market Assistant, for having performed the duties of the weighmaster when he was on leave, extra work for which he would previously have received no extra pay. A succession of wage and salary increases in 1918-19 led the Tolls and Markets Committee to increase Market rents in early 1919, which yielded an additional £200 per annum in revenue. In May 1919 the corporation agreed a minimum wage of 50s per week for all corporate employees, which the union ensured was paid to its members in the Market.[12] In September 1919 the CJBS presented a list of demands to the master butchers, with a threat of strike if they were not met. They won a 12s weekly pay increase and improved rates for piece work. The strength of

Left:
The executive committee of the Cork Operative Butchers' Society in the mid-1930s. Christy Ring (back row, first on the left), John Howell (back row, third from left), and Jack Corkery (front row, first on the right) worked in the Market.

the union was being demonstrated to the masters at that very time. Lizzie Hayes, who had taken over her brother James Hayes' stall in the Market in 1914, was allowing a messenger boy do journeyman butchers' work. She was informed that this would not be tolerated and that the union would supply her with a 'Society man to kill and cut her stuff'. Having failed to have the boy accepted into the union, Hayes persisted, and was subjected to a union boycott. Any other butcher who had dealings with her was threatened with a withdrawal of union labour until he or she desisted. The case was eventually settled in September 1920, when the 'boy' was admitted into the union.[13] The union's muscle was increased with the gradual demise of the power of the police, the Royal Irish Constabulary (RIC), in the face of the success of the Irish revolutionary movement in Cork in 1919-20. Whereas previously picketing was restricted by the police,[14] the union was now able to picket individual stalls in the Market.

Rebel Cork

The trade union movement associated itself strongly with the growing separatist nationalist movement that developed in the aftermath of the 1916 Rising, in the context of the increasing unpopularity of the war and fading hopes of Home Rule. The walls of the CJBS office were adorned with portraits of 1916 heroes Padraig Pearse and James Connolly, and both they and the ITGWU joined a 30,000-strong Cork Trades and Labour Council demonstration against the British attempt to extend conscription to Ireland in April 1918, as part of a nationwide general strike. The leading role taken by Sinn Féin in the successful opposition to conscription laid the basis for its success in the general election of December 1918, which followed the end of the war. Its two candidates, Liam de Róiste and J.J. Walsh, won the two city seats, part of a Sinn Féin sweep across the country. The party then honoured its election pledge by establishing a secessionist parliament, Dáil Éireann, in Dublin and declaring an independent Irish Republic in January 1919. The British authorities at first refused to recognise, and subsequently outlawed the Dáil, and a situation of dual sovereignty emerged. Republicans developed a court system (which was utilised by the CJBS in July 1920, in a dispute with a Market butcher, Garrett Preston) and renamed the revived Irish Volunteers the Irish Republican Army (IRA). The remarkable shift from 'loyal' Cork to 'rebel' Cork was illustrated in July 1919 when the stallholders in the Market decided to remain open on the day of the Peace Treaty celebrations. There was huge disappointment at the failure of the treaty to recognise Irish independence, and all the other public buildings in Cork refused to close also; the Board of Guardians flew black flags from its offices, and a parade of regular and demobilised soldiers through the city was jeered, a stark contrast to the cheering crowds of a few years earlier.[15]

In the local elections of January 1920, Sinn Féin won control of Cork Corporation. The new corporation met on 9 January 1920 and passed a resolution recording its 'recognition of Dáil Éireann as the lawful legal and constitutional Parliament of the Irish Nation' and its executive as 'the lawful government of this country'.[16] This rebel body elected Tomás MacCurtain, who was also the commanding officer of the Cork IRA, Lord Mayor and the Irish tricolour was raised above the city hall. In the same month the IRA authorised open attacks on the Crown forces, and the war of independence began in earnest. The IRA quickly neutralised the RIC, leading to the introduction of reinforcements in the shape of the notorious Black and Tans and Auxiliaries, and a campaign of guerrilla warfare, terror and counter-terror, which continued until July 1921, ensued. Cork city and county were the storm centre of this violent upheaval.

The new Republican corporation appointed a Tolls and Markets Committee, which included Liam de Róiste TD. The extent to which this body attempted to carry on business as usual amidst the turmoil of revolution was remarkable, reflecting Sinn Féin's general policy of maintaining continuity as best it could, presenting itself as a respectable, reliable 'government'. Wages continued to rise under ITGWU pressure, and stall rents were increased. As the situation deteriorated throughout 1920, meetings of the committee became more difficult. In March Tomás MacCurtain was murdered by an RIC death squad; the Black and Tans had arrived in the city that month, followed by the Auxiliaries in October, and the level of tit-for-tat violence increased. The committee continued to attempt to meet, but as the situation deteriorated, it became less and less possible, and there was frequently no quorum. In July the inspector recommended that the Market close at 8pm on Saturdays because the city had been placed under a curfew by the military authorities. (In March 1921, the Market began to close daily at 4.30pm, due to curfew regulations.)[17] Terence MacSwiney, who had been elected both Lord Mayor and OC of the IRA's No. 1 Brigade in succession to MacCurtain, was arrested with other IRA officers in August. MacSwiney commenced a hunger strike in Brixton prison, and the committee twice adjourned in September in protest 'against the treatment to which the Lord Mayor and his fellow political prisoners' were being subjected.[18] He died on

Below:
Signature of Tomás MacCurtain from a Council Minute Book, 9 January 1920.

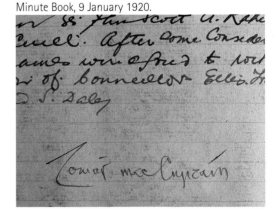

25 October after a 74 day fast. His protest and death received worldwide attention and sympathy for the Republican cause. The CJBS sent a note of condolence to the Lady Mayoress 'on the death of her heroic and Patriotic husband'.[19]

On 28 November, Tom Barry led his famous flying column in the Kilmichael ambush, which killed seventeen Auxiliaries. Martial law was declared in Cork, Limerick and Tipperary on 10 December 1920, and the following night the IRA ambushed an Auxiliary patrol in Dillon's Cross, close to the Victoria (now Collins) Barracks, killing one and wounding a further twelve. On this pretext, the Auxiliaries and Black and Tans went on a rampage of looting and burning. The city hall and nearby library were destroyed, as was most of St Patrick's Street and premises on many adjoining streets. The Market miraculously escaped the main brunt, but two stalls were burnt and the roof of the Princes Street Market was extensively damaged when fire spread from nearby Grant's department store, and stalls in the adjoining Market Lane were also destroyed. Perhaps it was the actions of three of the Market staff who were on duty that prevented further damage; they were each later granted double pay 'for services rendered on the occasion' of the fire.[20]

A new era: decline and survival

The war of independence ended with the truce of July 1921. Cork remained in the control of the Republicans, and a spate of burglaries in the Market in late 1921 was dealt with by the Irish Republican Police. Following the split in the Republican movement over the terms of the Anglo-Irish Treaty of December 1921, Cork became a Republican, anti-Treaty stronghold. It remained so during the civil war, which broke out in June 1922, and the anti-Treaty IRA remained in control of the city until it was taken by Free State troops in August 1922. The city returned to semi-normality following the end of the civil war in May 1923, but the effects of the four years of violence, trade disruption and destruction, not least the city fires of December 1920, had left it in a poor state. In 1923 a group of influential citizens formed the Cork Progressives Association to promote the revival of the city's fortunes. At its instigation, an Inspector of the Free State Government's Department of Local Government held a local enquiry into municipal affairs. The Inspector found that the corporation had been lax in discharging its duties in a range of areas. The corporation had been without a proper base since the burning of the city hall and little progress had been made on rebuilding the city centre. The city had a deficit of £75,000, and the markets had been operating at a loss for a number of years. The report highlighted the 'overstaffing' at the English Market and the need to reduce and 're-organise' the staff there.[21]

The government's remedy was drastic: the city council and its fifteen committees, including Tolls and Markets, were dissolved and their responsibilities were entrusted to one man, Phillip Monahan, who was appointed City Commissioner in October 1924. Monahan was an 'enforcer', a no-nonsense administrator who epitomised the Cumann na nGaedheal government's policy of fiscal rectitude and administrative ruthlessness. Monahan immediately sacked the 'superfluous staff' in the Market, marking the end of the era of the beadles, scalesmen and other assistants. Those who remained, such as sweepers, were subjected to severe wage cuts, along with all other corporation employees, as many of the wartime and postwar gains were rolled back. The Market went into profit, but this was not all due to Monahan, as is often assumed, as in 1923 the city council had already instigated sweeping rent increases to offset ongoing losses. Those rent increases yielded over £750 extra per year, over a quarter of the existing annual income from the Market. Direct competition was introduced in the allocation of stalls; the criteria became purely financial, and vacant stalls, of which there were increasing numbers in 1925-6, went to the highest bidder.[22] This resulted in a break in family and generational continuity, and also a reduction in the number of specialist butchers and the beginning of a proliferation of general 'provisions', eggs, butter and poultry, and tripe and drisheen stalls. There were also increasing numbers of 'mixed' stalls – selling vegetables together with tripe and

The Chicken Inn – Mary Mulcahy

The Chicken Inn occupies a large block of stalls in the Grand Parade Market and is run by Mary and Jack Mulcahy. Mary's father, John Lane, had a wholesale poultry business based in Tower Street in Cork and supplied a number of city shops though the bulk of his trade was in the export market. In the mid-1950s he took a stall in the Market, previously held by the Cuthbert family, and commenced business selling poultry, eggs and butter. Having this retail outlet enabled him to maximise profit as his wholesale firm supplied the stall. Supplies were sourced at country markets in towns like Millstreet and Macroom and directly from the farm also, where the farmer's wife usually ran the eggs and poultry side of the business. A government initiative had established a programme to encourage farmers' wives to raise poultry and training was given by poultry instructors to enable farm families diversify and increase their income.

Mary started working in the Market when seventeen at £4 per week. At that time all the produce sold at the stall was locally produced, the chickens and eggs were free-range and there was a seasonality in the trade. In spring and summer the supply of roasting fowl, young chickens raised specifically for their meat, greatly increased. Older hens that were past laying were available throughout the year as boiling fowl. Roast chicken was a relatively expensive meat and was regarded as a novelty or treat, often served for Sunday dinner. Boiled chicken was more commonly eaten and chicken broth was a popular food for the sick and old. Chickens were sold whole and were cleaned at the stall when purchased. Mary remembers that it was not until the 1980s that the practice of selling separate parts of the chicken became commonplace. Half chickens were first sold and later wings, breast fillets, legs and chicken pieces were offered. Today this range has increased further with an ever-changing variety of prepared meats and new and more intensive production has greatly increased the supply of chicken and brought it within the reach of all.

In reflecting on 50 years in the Market Mary recalls that in the past most customers were women and were very regular and predictable in their buying habits. Today an increasing number of customers are recent arrivals in the city, coming from Africa and Eastern Europe, and on Saturdays nearly half the customers at the Chicken-Inn are non-nationals. Their tastes are different and there is an impetus to cater for new demands, a development that Mary sees as exciting as the Market adapts to its changing customer base. The Market needs to appeal to a wide cross-section of people to survive and prosper, however, and Mary hopes that it will not change so much that the ordinary traditional customers will feel excluded.

drisheen, for example, and, as the 1930s progressed, an increasing number of fruit and vegetable stalls in the Grand Parade Market, which had originally been exclusively and later overwhelmingly a meat market. In 1929 Monahan was appointed city manager, the first in the country, and entrusted with extensive executive powers, including overseeing the markets, together with the town clerk. The corporation was revived in 1929, but its old power and status had gone.

The gradual decline in the status of the English Market from the mid-1920s was the result of a combination of historical factors. The disruption and economic impact of the World War, war of independence and civil war had all had an impact on Cork, its trade and administration. The Market became a casualty of post-war/post-independence restructuring, as well as the prolonged economic depression of the city. The emasculation of the once-proud and powerful corporation impacted on one of its prime creations and symbols. The dissolution of the Tolls and Markets Committee (tolls were abolished in 1927) and the abolition of the beadles with their tall hats and frock coats, together with the other trappings that made the Market more than just a commercial space, marked the end of an era. The reduction of the Irish Market, St Peter's, to a pale shadow of its former self, together with post-independence sensitivities, saw the decline of the usage of the term 'English Market'. Interestingly, it came back into vogue with the Market's revival in the 1990s, and its rediscovery by the bourgeoisie, though the phenomenon was probably driven from the front by marketing and the media. Although Cork was physically improved under

Monahan in the later 1920s and 1930s, unemployment and poverty remained high. The decline in trade linked to the self-sufficiency policy of the Fianna Fáil government which came to power in 1932, and especially the 'economic war' with Britain in the mid-1930s, impacted heavily on the port city of Cork. Over 40 per cent of the city's workforce was unemployed in 1936. The war years, 1939-45, saw real wages drop by 30 per cent and the cost of food rose to 67 per cent above its pre-war level by March 1944. Wartime emigration to Britain led to a decline in the city's population. The Market reflected this broader picture, as economic reality combined with its status decline to undermine its former 'upmarket' character. Although streamlining, rent increases and minimal expenditure kept the Market in profit, the surplus declined steadily through the mid-1930s.

It became an increasingly working-class market, and its fare reflected its altering customer base. The old divisions between the meat (Grand Parade), vegetables and fruit (Princes Street), and fish and tripe and disheen sections gradually broke down. A cluster of fruit and vegetable stalls emerged close to the Grand Parade entrance, in the area now occupied by Superfruit. Among those trading there in the 1940s was Gus Healy, who went on to become a famous local politician and Lord Mayor in 1964 and 1975. Despite its 'downmarket' trajectory, the Market retained a certain status, its future revival always a possibility. When the corporation's General Purposes Committee suggested a reduction in rents in 1941 in order to increase the number of traders, as up to a dozen stalls lay idle, Monahan responded that, in his opinion, this would not lead to an increase in occupied stalls, but would 'reduce the market to the level of that of Cornmarket Street'. He added

Opposite page:
Women shopping for tripe and drisheen at O'Reilly's stall.

Left:
Fish auction at Alfred Street, Cork, 1961.

169

that once building materials again became available at the end of the war, it would probably be necessary 'to reconstruct the market as a whole so that each tenant would have a lock-up shop'.[23] As usual, the perpetual plans for the Market remained unrealised, but it managed to keep going until, in the 1950s, new food hygiene regulations forced the hand of the manager.

Under the 1947 Health Act, the Minister for Health introduced statutory regulations in 1950 covering food hygiene and food premises. These specified that premises where food was sold had to be 'kept in a proper state of repair and in a clean and hygienic condition'. Regulations related to ventilation, lighting, water supply, the condition of table tops and equipment, refuse, storage, clothing, personal hygiene, etc., and food stalls were specifically included.[24] The manager noted that the regulations probably spelt the end for street trading of food, while the Bazaar and the remnant of St Peter's also seemed doomed. Only 71 of the Bazaar's 168 stalls were in daily use in January 1952, while only nine of the 34 stalls in St Peter's were let. These markets were operating at an annual loss of £300, and the manager began to consider alternative uses for the buildings. At the end of 1955 the stallholders in St Peter's were given notice to quit, and were given alternative

accommodation in the English Market, which had the added bonus of filling the vacant stalls there. Among the proposals considered for St Peter's was its conversion into a new city fire station and a basketball arena; both were eventually rejected, and both premises were leased,[25] though a portion of the Bazaar continued as a second-hand clothes market until the 1970s, while another section housed a fish auction.

Cleanliness and godliness

The economic stagnation and crisis of the 1950s, when unemployment and emigration reached record levels, was accompanied by widespread religious fervour, manifested especially by devotion to the Virgin Mary. In anticipation of the approaching Marian Year of 1954, a Market stallholders' committee, one of whose secretaries, John (Jackie Sam) O'Flynn was a Marian devotee, wrote to the corporation in May 1953 'suggesting that a picture or statue of the Blessed Virgin be placed in a prominent position either inside or outside the Grand Parade Market and that the name of the Market be changed to 'Our Lady's Market'. Even in Catholic Ireland of the 1950s, however, cleanliness came before godliness, and the matter was deferred as, according to the council minutes, 'the Corporation have under consideration the extensive renovation of the Markets' due to the new food hygiene regulations. The stallholders persisted, and in September 1954 sent a petition signed by 69 of them (the vast majority) supporting the name change. The application was rejected by the corporation's General Purposes Committee. Some of the stallholders, however, erected an altar to the Virgin Mary in the Princes Street gallery, which was now used mainly for storage, and Jackie Sam O'Flynn walked the aisles of the Market each day ringing a bell calling people to the rosary upstairs.[26]

In an interesting feature article in the *Cork Evening Echo* on 2 April 1958, the writer quoted a description of the Market as 'the barometer of the city':

When trade in the Market is good, it is a fair assumption that there is money in the pockets of the people, but when there is little demand for meat, or for the better cuts of it, the citizens in general are feeling the pinch of the times ... The Market, too, reflects the passage of the days of the week. Monday, the day of Sunday's joint cold or hashed, is the quietest day of the week. Saturday, the day for getting a joint of mutton or beef, used to be the busiest day but of latter years Friday has tended to see more buying and selling. One can only guess at the reasons – wider use of domestic refrigerators to keep the meat sweet under all conditions, and a possible shift of 'roasting day'. More motor cars on the road mean more drivers and families abroad on Sundays and less desire to have to cook a full meal on that day. Is it now a case of roast on Saturday and cold on Sunday?'

John O'Flynn & Sons
– Simon and Patrick O'Flynn

'Unless you lived through those times, you don't understand Dickens', says Simon O'Flynn, who worked in the Market from the late 1950s until 1980. The atmosphere, the range of produce sold and the customs and habits of the place were virtually unchanged since the nineteenth century. Simon remembers the sawdust, the office ladies with their high desks, ledgers and dip pens, the novelty of refrigeration, the drovers and messenger boys, conservative business practices, fights, obvious poverty, and the customers, mostly women, who shopped on tight budgets and often intimidated the butchers in their demand for value and quality.

Simon's father was John O'Flynn, more affectionately known as Jackie Sam. He was born in Cork in 1897 and died in 1983 at the age of 86. He lived in Bleasby Terrace in the north of the city and earned his money where and when he could, trading in sheep, cattle and pigs on a small scale, occasionally bringing animals to London where a higher price more than compensated for the expense of the journey. He sometimes kept animals in a small yard near his home at Bleasby Terrace and although surrounded by the houses of his neighbours, none complained of the smell or noise. Such activity was considered neither unusual nor abnormal in a residential area of the city in the early decades of the twentieth century. In 1927 Jackie Sam took Stall No. 50 in the Market and operated as a butcher for a short period before surrendering the stall within a few years. He married Sheila Bresnan in 1940 and they lived in Marble Hall Park in Ballinlough. Simon was born a year later. Sheila was a daughter of Michael Bresnan, who had traded successfully in the Market since 1898 and Simon feels the Bresnans were instrumental in his return there in 1944, when he recommenced business, this time at Stall No. 3 in the Princes Street Market. He was not very adept at the trade's finer skills and employed a butcher, Eddie Ring, to work with him.

Simon was attending secondary school and was within months of sitting his Leaving Certificate when his father fell ill and was unable to work. This unfortunate circumstance gave Simon an attractive opportunity and he left school to work in the Market. Eddie Ring taught him the trade and he worked at the family stall with both Eddie and his father, who had returned to work on his recovery. Simon remembers his first task as an apprentice was to skin and crack a sheep's head. These were bought to feed dogs and were also used as a base for soup. Simon's brother Patrick joined the business some time later and the brothers continued the business after the retirement of their father. They remember their father with affection as a frugal and religious man. He railed against the high cost of electricity and on receipt of what he considered to be a particularly costly bill, he immediately turned off the lights at their stall and forbade any use of electricity. In the Marian Year of 1954, Jackie Sam erected an altar to the Virgin Mary in the gallery of the Princes Street Market. At six o'clock every evening he walked the aisles of the market ringing a bell to call people to prayer and then led the Rosary at the altar. Simon and Patrick were greatly embarrassed by the fervour of their father and this embarrassment was made even more acute for Simon when he was given the task of walking the Market and ringing the bell.

In the 1950s and 1960s the practices of the butcher's trade were very much as they had been 100 years before. Butchers bought animals at fairs, which were regularly held in the country towns of County Cork and as many did not have the means of transporting the animals, drovers were given the task of walking the animals bought by a number of butchers back to the city. The animals were first marked with a raddle, a red waxy chalk, to distinguish which animals belonged to whom. Simon O'Flynn remembers a drover, Danny Tar, who often drove cattle from country fairs to the O'Reilly abattoir on the South Douglas Road. The O'Flynns and many other butchers killed their animals there. Most Market butchers sold an average of ten sheep and one or two beef cattle per week. Simon remembers mutton as outselling beef in those years. It was said at the time that 'a side and seven will feed a family' i.e. a butcher who sold a side of beef and the meat of seven sheep per week could earn an income sufficient to support a family.

Connie and Richie O'Neill supplied the sawdust for the butchers' stalls They acquired this at the Victoria Sawmill in Cork, bagged it and transported it to the Market with a donkey and cart where they sold it at 1s 6d per bag. Washing facilities were quite basic in Simon's early years in the Market and the fountain in the Princes Street Market served as a communal washing facility. It was not unusual to see dishes, cloths, ox tongues and even boots being washed there. Messenger boys were employed by almost all butchers up to the 1970s and Simon recalls the consternation in the butcher trade when a regulation was introduced obliging butchers to release messenger boys to attend school at least one day in the week. Further objections were raised when the butchers were forced to supply messenger boys with rainwear – 'Christ Almighty, they'll break us!', was the reaction. Mackesey's on Oliver Plunkett Street and Jimmy Ring's in Mutton Lane were favoured drinking places and many market traders would down a pint or two

at intervals through the day, often fuelling their bad humour and
leading to argument and discord between stalls.

For Simon and Patrick O'Flynn the Market was always
a village within the city: one's pedigree was known, traders and
customers were its population and it had character and characters,
rules and customs. In the early 1980s Simon and Patrick left the
'village' and now trade from a premises in Marlboro Street as John
O'Flynn & Sons, Master Butchers.

30 of the 74 stallholders at that time were butchers; 31 sold vegetables, fruit, butter and eggs, nine sold fish, five specialised in salt meat and five more specialised in tripe and drisheen. The Market opened at 8am, as it always had done, closed at 6pm on weekdays, except for the half day on Wednesday, and at 7pm on Saturdays. It had originally stayed open until 11pm on Saturday nights.

Around this time, a significant newcomer arrived. Bert Bagnall, a cockney, took a number of stalls near the Grand Parade gate (the area now occupied by Superfruit) and began selling fruit. Bagnall was a brash and dynamic trader who offered a wide variety of fruit at affordable prices. The stall became extremely popular very quickly, and, together with the improvements of the 1960s necessitated by the new hygiene regulations, helped to revitalise the Market, bringing a 'buzz', and many new customers, into the old place.

The necessary improvements to the Market were long fingered, until, in January 1959, the Department of Health began to apply pressure. The work was costed and planned, and it was estimated that to bring the Market to a satisfactory standard would require an outlay of approximately £7,500. This cost was recouped from stallholders by increasing the basic rent of 26s to 36s per week, with pro rata increases for other stalls. Work commenced in 1962, and two years later the Market had been painted, a new drainage system was fitted, each stall had its own water supply and sink, and the floor surfaces were cemented. All of this had cost £7,680; further work, such as the asphalting of the floors and repairs to stall partitions, cost approximately £2,000. The planned removal of the Princes Street Market fountain, which had been used for the washing of vegetables but was no longer necessary for that purpose, was halted following the objection of councillors, who argued for its

The old versus the new? The small trader against the speculator? ... What shall it be? A barren ultra-modern building devoid of atmosphere and sensitivity; or an entity with its own intrinsic values and credibility that has withstood the test of time for centuries'.[30]

Intensive lobbying of councillors by the MTA and public pressure saw the plans dropped and the old market lived to fight another day. The scare had awakened both the traders and the Cork public to the value of the Market and the need to ensure its survival, while the speculators withdrew temporarily to the long grass, awaiting the next opportunity. The traders, through the MTA, organised joint advertising and moved to improve hygiene in an attempt to improve trading and maintain custom in the face of increasing competition from the modern shopping centres and arcades that were beginning to emerge in the city centre, as well as proliferating in the suburbs. A suggestion for late-night opening, however, was voted down by a substantial majority. They also campaigned for investment in the Market; the rotting, leaking old roof was a particular concern.[31]

On the industrial relations front, COBS, the butchers' union, remained strong within the Market. In 1975 a new, more radical executive was elected and in 1976 COBS presented the Cork Master Butchers' Association (CMBA), which represented the butcher employers in the Market, with a claim for a group pension scheme, whereby CMBA would be treated as a single employer and a union member could freely transfer his employment among CMBA butchers without losing his pension benefits. The employers resisted and prevaricated, until, in April 1977, the union issued a strike notice, which would affect not only butchers' shops and stalls, but also the city's abattoirs. The strike began on 23 May 1977, when pickets were placed on abattoirs, shops, the Market entrance and individual butcher stalls. The strike lasted a week, and ended successfully. The CMBA agreed to the transferable group pension scheme, only the second of its kind in the state; the system has since become law under the 1990 Pensions Act. COBS struck briefly, and successfully, again in December 1986 in pursuit of a pay claim; two Market stalls, chosen at random, Tim O'Sullivan's and Paul Boyling's 'Best Meats', were picketed. [32]

The decay of the Market roof was a growing concern as the 1970s progressed, and in August 1977 the city council announced a £450,000 Market Development Scheme which made the re-roofing of the Grand Parade section a priority. The refurbishment was carried out over the following fifteen months; as well as a new roof, new flooring was put down and stalls were improved. The opportunity of the refurbishment was taken to instigate new trading arrangements. The traders felt vulnerable under the system whereby they held their stalls under a licence, which had to be renewed weekly. Their demand for improved security of tenure led to a new system of granting each stallholder a 21-year lease, with rent reviewed every five years. Each stall was also charged an annual rent on a square footage basis, and stallholders also had to pay service charges and rates.[33] The future of the Market seemed assured as the new decade dawned – then, disaster struck.

Fire! The Market 'stalls'

Shortly before 11.30pm on 19 June 1980 a gas explosion in the Princes Street Market caused a fire to engulf the building and, according to the account in the *Cork Examiner* of the following day, 'within minutes flames were leaping 30 feet into the air through the roof of the building and a short time later the roof of the old market collapsed. At the height of the blaze the flames could be seen to a radius of two miles'. Six units of the city's fire brigade fought the blaze and had the flames under control within 30 minutes but the Market was in ruins. The 120-year-old roof timbers, gallery and stalls had been consumed and the stallholders who gathered at the scene that night could do little more than comfort each other. The fire had been prevented from spreading to the adjoining Grand Parade Market, which had been re-roofed only a year before. Eleven traders lost their stalls and many felt that the straitened financial conditions of the time would make restoration unlikely. The fountain of the Princes Street Market symbolised for market traders, shoppers and passers-by the enduring quality of the place. Despite the devastation wrought by the fire the fountain survived, with minor damage, and seemed to physically embody the energy needed for the regeneration of the market buildings.

The Cork writer and columnist, Robert O'Donoghue, expressed poetically what Cork people felt about this icon.

Right:
Aerial view of Cork city centre 1980. The new roof of the Grand Parade Market and the burnt-out shell of the Princes Street Market are visible in the middle foreground.

IT WILL RISE AGAIN

by Robert O'Donoghue

Since the fire, I don't go through the English Market anymore. I cannot take the amputation. I wonder where now lies the fountain; it, at least, survived the inferno. Does it still stand in that charred place? I must check it out, not only for reasons of sentiment, but, also, aesthetic. It was taken very much for granted by the stall-holders and the passing citizenry – until there was an alleged threat to remove it and we saw it afresh, as it were.

I check with City Hall. I am informed: Yes, we are concerned that the fountain remain as part of our restoration plans. It may be a little further down than it originally was – we intended that without any fire. There was never any intention to remove it. Yes, it is still in Princes Street, but we are in the process of dismantling it piecemeal for the time being. But it will be absolutely restored and incorporated into the plan for rebuilding the destroyed section.

That, indeed, is good news. And I must say that Mr. McHugh [city manager] assured me on the telephone, on an earlier occasion, that at no time was it contemplated by City Hall that this unique fountain would be interfered with. I rest easier.

On the night of the flames it proved itself, as Ezra Pound might have remarked, unkillable. During the aftermath, water dripping cold from what remained of the roof, in the acrid smoke, wreckage everywhere, hoses crisscrossing, the vague shapes of the firemen, in the glow of their torches, I groped my way to the fountain: it was hot to the touch but still intact and for the first time I really felt its form, experienced empathy. It was a curious thrill, to feel these sculptings I could not see and know their marvellous eccentricities and complexities, devoid of their representational qualities.

At its height, the fire appeared all-consuming. When the roof went down and all about was flame, I thought, 'there goes the fountain'! At a cooler moment, back at the newsdesk, where we were trying to piece the story together – and rejigged the front page – I was more hopeful, reflecting on other infernos in which had survived other such artifacts, even when all else had gone down, to speak to the future. These are the durables from which we weave the stuff of history.

Not that but if all Cork and Ireland had gone down that night the fountain, had it survived, would hardly have been much value to the future historian of either living or art. It really has no significance to either. Like Shandon, it just happens to be one of our parochial quirks – though a fine example of art nouveau, if predating that peculiar category – to which we attach our own significance, a valid symbol in its place.

Its eventual, and guaranteed, return will now have the further dimension of the Phoenix, risen from the ashes, indestructible.

Cork Examiner, 29 July 1980

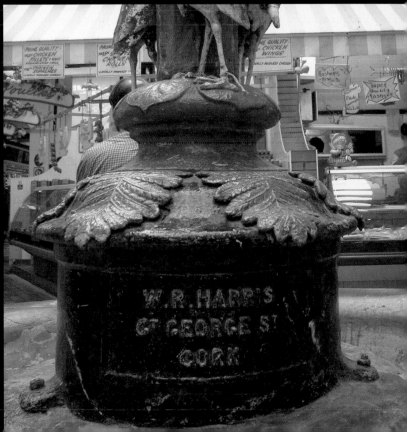

W.R. HARRIS
GT GEORGE ST
CORK

recognition of its contribution to the enhancement of Europe's architectural heritage. While the praise for the overall restoration was deserved, certain details of the work can be criticised. The ceramic floor tiles are of a scale and style more suited to a smaller space. The walls separating the stalls are built with modern concrete bricks, which do not harmonise with the other styles of brick used in the building and they project well beyond the cast iron pillars that support the gallery and roof. This obscures the impact of the elevations, breaking the vertical continuity from floor upwards. The continuous striped yellow and white awning, which projects above the stalls, also jars: it is too bright and spoils the effect of the structural features it partially hides. The uniform style used for the stallholders' names seems somewhat inappropriate in a market that celebrates variety and choice. These criticisms aside, the restored Market is a unique enclosed space in the city, and the architects and craftsmen who worked on the project 'achieved more with their limited resources than others who work with more benevolent bureaucracies'.[35]

There was renewed interest in the restored market but the economic recession of the 1980s had a profound effect on the city and all retail traders, including those in the English Market, suffered a fall in business. Unemployment was high in Cork and between 1983 and 1984, for example, three significant employers, Ford, Dunlop and Verolme, closed leaving over 2,500 workers idle. Many smaller concerns closed also, especially those in traditional manufacturing sectors, as they increasingly succumbed to foreign competition. Emigration increased during this decade and as well as losing the 'traditional' unskilled emigrants Ireland also saw the departure of thousands of third-level graduates and skilled workers. The city centre became less attractive to shoppers and an increasing air of pessimism pervaded business. The Market reflected this decline as the number of vacant stalls grew and falling trade persuaded some long-established traders to retire or relocate. The shopping centres in suburbs like Douglas and Wilton as well as other smaller suburban retail developments took trade that otherwise might have been done in the Market or elsewhere in the city.

The difficulties of the Market were compounded on 6 January 1986 when, as the *Cork Examiner* reported, 'shocked traders watched in disbelief last night as fire ripped through Cork city's award-winning Princes Street Market for the second time in six years'. The fire started in the gallery and destroyed four stalls there and another four on the ground floor below. A portion of the roof was also damaged but the prompt arrival of the fire services prevented further loss. Eight traders were put out of business temporarily and their anger and frustration was expressed by one who complained: 'We were told it would never happen again. We were told that the timber was fire-proof. The last fire already hit the business. Since then we have been barely existing.' Over £150,000 worth of damage was done but the repair work was not as extensive as after the previous fire and traders were able to resume business within a short time.

The Real Olive Company – Toby Simmonds

When a friend in Bantry asked Toby Simmonds if he knew where he could get olives for his shop, his life took an unexpected route. An acquaintance in Germany put him in contact with a European olive supplier, who suggested that he introduce olives to the Irish market, through its markets. He spent the summer of 1993 trying to gain access to the primary Irish food market, Cork's English Market. Eventually, with the support and encouragement of new and established traders, such as Anne-Marie Jaumaud and Martin Guillemot, Isabelle Sheridan and Mary Rose, he 'got in by the back door', securing a vacant stall from poultry dealer Gerry Moynihan in the Princes Street Market. Toby began with a basic range of olives, in twelve barrels, and for his first year was greeted with daily bemusement from shoppers who gazed at these exotic products in their truncated barrels, frequently being asked 'what class of grapes' he was selling!

The adventurous began to sample his distinctively prepared and dressed olives, word spread, Cork palates adapted and the business began to gain a foothold. In May 1994 he moved to a larger unit close to the Grand Parade entrance, and expanded his product range: additional varieties of olive, chillies, feta cheese, pickles, vine leaves, dried fruits, olive oils. He was soon selling from up to 40 barrels. In 1994 also Toby began to trade in outdoor markets in Bantry, Tralee, Galway, Limerick, Dublin's Temple Bar and elsewhere, something he has continued to do, with the help of a growing network of associates. Since 1999 the stall has been run by Toby's partner, Jenny Rose Clarke. In 2001, along with Rachel McCormack, she took over Sheehan's adjacent vacated fish stall, and established a successful sandwich and salad business. Toby now concentrates on importation and wholesaling, and trading in the outdoor day markets in Galway, Ennis, Bantry and Macroom, but his commitment to the Market, and the market ideal generally, is undimmed. From humble, and almost accidental beginnings, Toby Simmonds' Real Olive Company has become synonymous with the revitalisation of the English Market since the 1990s.

When Driss Belmajoub, trading as Mr Bell's, took his first stall in the English Market in the 1980s, he introduced foods and ingredients largely unfamiliar to the everyday shopper. Couscous, harissa paste, olives, bamboo shoots, spices, herbs and a host of other exotics from North Africa, the orient and elsewhere found a place in the Market and contrasted sharply with the familiar traditional foods that had been its mainstay for the previous two centuries. Driss also prepared and sold cooked dishes at his stall. Restaurant owners, foreign nationals and adventurous cooks and eaters were attracted into the Market and began a change that gained momentum in the early 1990s, transforming the Market over the following ten years.

Trading up

Following the debate in 1988 on the proposed redevelopment, an awareness grew among traders, corporation officials and many Cork people that the English Market had a significance that was not widely appreciated and a potential that could be exploited to the advantage of all stakeholders without compromising its integrity as a market. £1.5 million had been spent on the Market since the 1970s and the corporation wished to see a return for the city on that investment. A business strategy report was commissioned in 1989, which found that while there was a high pedestrian flow within the Market and on adjacent streets, both customers and traders focused on poor standards, lack of hygiene, the cold environment and bad management. The report favoured the full or partial privatisation of the Market but the corporation decided instead to contract out its management to a specialist retail property management company. In 1991 the contract for the day-to-day management of the English Market was given to Irish Estates Management Ltd. For the next five years or so Jim O'Shea managed the operation on behalf of that company and his brief was to promote the Market as a retail location, to improve services and maintenance, and to streamline general management. Overall control and ownership remained with the corporation. At this stage rent arrears were in the region of £70,000, many stalls were vacant and the gallery in the Princes Street Market was unused. The period of Irish Estates Management's stewardship coincided with an improvement in the fortunes of the English Market.

The early 1990s saw the first surge in economic growth that led to new self-confidence. With increasing affluence, foreign travel and a more open and adventurous outlook there were significant changes in patterns of food buying and eating as well as in many other areas of Irish life. Many influences from abroad were absorbed and the best of traditional Irish food was seen differently and valued by an increasing number of people willing and able to pay for what they considered to be the best. Consumers wanted to know more about what they were eating and were concerned about the growth in factory farming and the over-use of herbicides, pesticides and other farm chemicals. This led to an increased demand for naturally and locally produced foods. Influential food writers and broadcasters like Myrtle Allen, Darina Allen, John McKenna, Tom Doorley and others celebrated what was best in Irish produce and contributed to a new Irish food culture. Food historian Regina Sexton in her books and articles explored the heritage of Irish food, giving this new movement an historical foundation. For a growing number of people food had become more than just a source of necessary nourishment. Buying organically produced meat and vegetables, for example, is a way of sourcing safer food, partly a protest against unsavoury modern methods and sometimes a political act. Buying, preparing and eating food has become, for many, almost a fashion statement and price is often less important than the projection of a knowing image. The majority of people, unconcerned with fashion and often under pressure in providing for themselves and their children, continue to seek value, quality and convenience, untouched by the apparent sophistication of those with other priorities. The English Market succeeded in accommodating the needs of all those disparate groups, adapting and contributing to the new food culture as the decline of previous decades was reversed.

Local, national and foreign newspapers and magazines now featured the English Market as Cork's principal attraction, a food emporium combining all that is best in traditional and contemporary food, a place where the local and exotic can co-exist, an example to be followed. The headlines changed: 'Market a great symbol of Cork',

The Bandon Fish Store – Jack and Marian Burke

Jack Burke began to work full time at his father John's fish stall in the Market in 1970. John had been a fish seller who, since the 1940s, had travelled around the Bandon area, initially on a pony and trap, selling pollock, mackerel, herring and whiting, bought from the fishermen in Kinsale. Later, in the 1960s, with the advent of motorised transport, he was able to spread his net more widely, buying further afield in places such as Schull and Ballinskelligs, the first from Cork to buy in bulk directly at the ports, and supplying the Clayton Love fish auction on Cork's North Main Street (in the back portion of the old Bazaar Market). Towards the end of the decade, a vacant stall came up in the Market, and he took the plunge. His teenage son Jack would help him out at weekends, and could not wait to join his father full time, which he did at the age of sixteen. As Jack learnt the ropes, and showed himself capable of running the stall, John left him in charge and concentrated on his wholesaling business.

Jack remembers the vibrancy of the fish market in the 1970s, and the strong sense of community and camaraderie. Bill Kidney (his immediate neighbour, whose retirement in 1979 allowed Jack to double his stall), Pat Scannell, Bill O'Regan, Mrs O'Donovan, the Mulcahys, Vincey Nolan, the Murphys, the McCarthys, Mrs O'Leary, the Sheehans, Kay O'Connell and others all traded fish here in a bustling environment. (The fishmongers shared their space with three tripe stalls.) The older, experienced fishmongers such as Bill O'Regan and Pat Scannell were always on hand to offer advice to the young novice. In 1976 Jack married Marian Quinn, who joined him in the business.

Transport improvements meant that fishmongers were increasingly able to obtain their supplies directly from the fishing ports. This resulted in a decreasing reliance on the city's wholesale fish auctions, and their eventual demise. Jack and Marian's main fish supply comes from the port of Union Hall in west Cork. Marian attends the auction there at 6.30am each morning. Over three-quarters of their Irish stock comes from here, and the remainder from Castletownbere and Dingle, which are visited on a less regular basis. The fish is transported back to Cork in refrigerated vans, which are now compulsory.

In the past, when the boats from the Cork and Kerry fishing ports were unable to sail in bad weather, emergency supplies of fish were imported from England and Holland. Nowadays, wholesalers in Skibbereen, Union Hall and Ballycotton, with huge stocks in refrigerated containers, are availed of in emergencies. Approximately ten to fifteen per cent of Jack and Marian's trade since the 1990s is made up of new, more exotic fish such

as red snapper, bream, swordfish, tuna, marlin, octopus, halibut and anchovy. Some, like swordfish and tuna, are available in Irish waters in the warm summer months, but these mainly come from as far afield as the Caribbean. They are supplied via the huge Billingsgate fish market in London and supplies are flown to Cork several times a week. The increasing demand for these fish is one of the main changes that Jack has noticed in the trade. He also points out the decline in size, volume and variety of the Irish staples such as cod, whiting, sole and plaice since the 1970s as a result of overfishing, particularly by the large factory ships and the increased number of boats from abroad fishing Irish waters.

In terms of the Market itself, Jack has seen many changes since he first started there as a youth, some positive and others less so. He welcomes the improved levels of cleanliness and hygiene and the new type of customer that the arrival of the 'new generation' of stallholders has brought into the Market. However, he misses the *craic* and camaraderie of the early days, and regrets that he is only one of three fresh-fish traders left in a market that had thirteen when he first came. While they supply many of Cork's hotels and restaurants, the retail trade remains the mainstay. Jack is now supplying the grandchildren of customers he served when he started out, and it is this loyalty of custom and the personalised service from himself, Marian and their staff that has enabled the Bandon Fish Store to stay in business in the face of tough competition from within the Market and outside.

'Market trip is a cultural experience', 'The best of all worlds under the same roof', 'Old Cork Market thriving', 'The market blossoms into its third century', 'Market is still heart of the city' and the like, became the norm. Food and travel programmes on television featured the Market, and Rick Stein, Keith Floyd and other renowned food celebrities endorsed it as a place of unique significance, able to maintain its traditions while offering a wide range of foods to a broad cross-section of customers.

From offal to olives

In December 1991 Anne-Marie Jaumaud and Martin Guillemot took a stall in the English Market to sell their farm-made cheeses. They had a farm near Kealkil in west Cork and made a variety of cheeses with unpasteurised cows' and goats' milk in a strictly traditional fashion, avoiding the use of laboratory starters. Their Maughanaclea Farm Cheeses stall was the first dedicated cheese stall in the Market and very quickly drew a loyal and appreciative clientele. While consumers had been enjoying the fruits of the growing output of Irish farm cheeses for some years, Anne-Marie and Martin took the product further and created a more challenging range with an authentic farmhouse taste and look. Such was the demand

that they found it difficult to maintain a sufficient supply as newspaper and magazine food writers lavished praise on their enterprise and quality restaurants like Ballymaloe House and Arbutus Lodge showcased the cheeses. The stall brought new customers to the Market and, along with Driss Belmajoub's Mr Bell's, began a rebalancing whereby the traditional long-established meat, poultry, fruit and vegetable stalls were joined by new arrivals trading in foods that reflected new consumer demands and tastes.

Although Anne-Marie and Martin had great popular support, the food regulatory authorities were unhappy with their production methods and in April 1995 they closed their stall rather than comply with regulations, which would have effectively forced them to make factory-type cheeses. In a newspaper article at the time Darina Allen was quoted as saying: 'Without question Maughanaclea were one of the best cheesemakers in Ireland. The market will not be the same without them.' Declan Ryan of the Arbutus Lodge restaurant said: 'We are losing a huge asset because the bureaucrats who interpret EU regulations know nothing about making cheese.' Myrtle Allen of Ballymaloe House set up the Cork Free Choice Consumer Group, which gathered signatures and lobbied politicians and others in an effort to facilitate small-scale artisan food producers like Ann-Marie and Martin. The publicity generated by the controversy changed attitudes and in March 1996 Maughanaclea Farm Cheeses returned to the English Market when

Anne-Marie and Martin took a new stall and recommended business selling cheese, organic fruit and vegetables, pulses and a range of dried and candied fruits. In 1998 Donal O'Callaghan bought their farm in Leap, County Cork, to which they had moved from Kealkil, and also took over their stall in the Market where he continued to sell the organic produce of the farm. The difficulties of maintaining an organic farm and running the stall on a full-time basis proved impossible and Donal discontinued the farm work to concentrate on the Market business. Other organic producers now supply his stalls, which occupy the space held for decades by Eileen Ahern and her sister Siobhán, another example of change with continuity, which typifies the evolution of the English Market.

Mr Bell's and Maughanaclea Farm Cheeses were also instrumental in the development of On the Pig's Back, the stall of Isabelle Sheridan. When Isabelle moved from France to live in Cork in the late 1980s she came to the English Market to shop at Mr Bell's for foods she could not get anywhere else in the city. Later she shared space with Maughanaclea Farm Cheeses and sold charcuterie before eventually acquiring her own stall and developing a modern mixed food business with a strong European flavour that has contributed greatly to the new mix of the Market. Shortly after Isabelle started trading, Toby Simmonds brought the Real Olive Company to the Market and introduced more continental flavours to the increasingly adventurous palates of the Cork people. Mary Rose and Gerry Moynihan, two traders with a long Market pedigree, were among those who supported Toby in securing his stall, a practical demonstration of the traditional embracing the new in the interest of choice and diversity. At about the same time Seán Calder-Potts opened Iago, initially an award-winning sandwich bar, but later a stall selling Irish and continental cheeses, salamis, pasta and a range of other quality foods.

Mr Bell's, On the Pig's Back, Iago and the Real Olive Company have prospered for over ten years and form the core stalls that represent the new food culture in the English Market. The success of that new culture was reinforced with the opening of the Farmgate Restaurant in the gallery of the Princes Street Market in 1994 by Kay Harte and her sister Máróg O'Brien. The philosophy of this venture, serving the best of locally produced traditional food balanced by the adaptation of new influences, mirrored the evolving nature of the market beneath and the changing culinary landscape of the city outside. Café Paradiso, for example, a cutting-edge vegetarian restaurant of international repute, opened in the city in 1993, as did the eclectic Ivory Tower Restaurant. The change in the nature of the English Market was part of a greater movement driven by increased prosperity and a more adventurous attitude to food. The Market was now very receptive to changing tastes and demands in marked contrast to the situation that pertained in previous decades when it seemed immune to change, albeit in a far less prosperous climate.

The Alternative Bread Company, Bubble Brothers wine shop and others have since joined the other new ventures and have become part of the 'new tradition' of

the English Market. Mary Rose, who traded in pork and bacon at the stall she inherited from her father, changed the nature of her business completely in 2001 when she opened Coffee Central (Lárionad Caifé), another example of change with continuity within the market.

While the new stalls and new food ranges have reinvigorated trade, attracted increased numbers and a greater mix of customers, and drawn much positive media attention, the endurance of the older businesses and the loyalty of their clientele ensured the survival of the English Market through the later decades of the twentieth century. The stalls of Ken Barrett, Paul Boyling, Michael Bresnan, Tom Durcan, Stephen Landon, Paul Murphy, Kathleen Noonan, Ashley O'Neill, Katherine O'Mahony, Stephen O'Reilly and Tim O'Sullivan represent that enduring tradition in the meat trade. Jack and Mary Mulcahy, Gerry Moynihan and Glenys Landon continue to deal in poultry and buttered eggs. Paddy McDonnell now runs the fruit and vegetable business founded by his mother, Bridget, while Donal O'Callaghan has the other fruit and vegetable stall in the Princes Street Market, the Root Market of the late eighteenth and early nineteenth centuries. Michael Corrigan, Michael Murphy, Mark O'Mahony and Michael Herlihy sell fruit and vegetables in the Grand Parade Market. Jack and Marian Burke, William Martin, Frank Hederman and Pat and Paul O'Connell have the four fish stalls that remain of the fifteen that once traded in the fish market. Tom and Harry Smith, Henry O'Connor and Joe Hegarty sell cakes and Des Murray's flower stall

endures, 130 years after flowers were first sold in the Market. Michael McBarron sells kitchen utensils and next door, Joe Lingnane's novelty stall continues the 'fowl' tradition, catering for 'hen parties'. Niall Daly offers speciality chocolates and the Fruit Boost counter provides contemporary refreshment. Paul Mulvany champions the 'People's Republic of Cork' at his clothes stall and the cobbler, Paddy Joe Harrington, plies his ancient craft. Over 40 different businesses make the mix that is the English Market.

The potential of the unique city-centre location of the Market stimulates creativity, not only among traders, but also in the wider artistic community. Since the mid-1990s cultural events have been staged there, finally fulfilling the *Examiner*'s prediction of 1862 that the new Market space opened that year 'may fitly be used for other purposes besides that for which it is designed – whether to hold public meetings, horticultural or other exhibitions, or for some of the many purposes to which a handsome and spacious building can be converted'. Fashion shows and food fairs have been hosted, and the Farmgate has been the venue for a series of the Cork Film Festival's 'Grand Café Screenings' of silent classics with live musical accompaniment. The old gallery has hosted poetry readings, choral, operatic and traditional song recitals, and art exhibitions, while a theatre company has used the entire night-time Market as a stage. These developments have been positively received and add a new ingredient to what the Market offers.

Evolution, change, decline, rejuvenation, neglect, passion and endurance have created the Market as it is today. Its existence has an organic quality that ensures continuing change, the pace of which has quickened in line with developments in the wider world. Some Market changes have not met with universal approval. In December 2001, for example, a new unit opened for business, but the design and layout of the retail space was regarded by many as a break with the tradition of open stalls that typified the Market. The local *Evening Echo* of 20 December 2001 asked 'Is this shop an affront to the English Market?'. It was felt that the lock-up nature of the stall, with its security shutters, was more appropriate to the high street or shopping mall and not in keeping with the way of doing business in a market. The controversy led traders and others to consider and debate the nature of the interaction with customers in a market context. Should the customer make a request to be fulfilled by the trader, or should the customer be able to choose items and then bring them to a checkout? Is the communication between customer and trader essential to maintaining the integrity of a market? What is the precise definition of a stall? Such questions have raised an awareness of the importance

of arriving at universally accepted practices for the continued functioning of the English Market as a traditional food market. The presence of a number of non-food stalls is seen by some as again contrary to the spirit and tradition of how and what business should be carried on there.

While the Market is ultimately owned by Cork City Council, and the tenants have secure leases, the responsibility for day-to-day management currently belongs to a retail property management company, which views its work from a commercial perspective. Traders, customers and the citizens of Cork also share ownership of the Market and their perspectives, though often going beyond the purely commercial, have equal validity. The dovetailing and blending of the conflicting priorities of the different stakeholders is the constant challenge in ensuring the continuing health of the English Market.

Smoked and GREEN Rashers

Bacon Loin Rib

butchers Pride sausages

ROUGHTY

Don't Just Stand There BUY SOMETHING

②

Lárionad ☕ Caife

BEST MEATS

— THIS WEEK'S SPECIALS —

On the Pig's Back – Isabelle Sheridan

Frenchwoman and Cork citizen Isabelle Sheridan has been trading in the English Market since December 1992, and running On the Pig's Back since 1994. She first discovered the Market when she moved to Cork in the late 1980s, coming in to shop at Mr Bell's for products such as couscous and pasta that she found difficult to find elsewhere. In 1992 her compatriots Anne-Marie Jaumaud and Martin Guillemot gave her space at their Maughanaclea Farm Cheeses stall, where she sold imported French patés and meats. When the Guillemots closed their cheese stall in 1994, Isabelle took over the entire space and established On the Pig's Back. She expanded her range, selling French and Irish cheeses and Declan Ryan's famed Arbutus breads, as well as an increasing range of meat products, such as chorizos from Spain, French saucissons and saucisses seches, and Italian salami. She rented a kitchen space on nearby Princes Street and began making homemade patés and terrines from traditional French recipes that had been handed down through generations of her family. She also began branching out in the mid-1990s, selling her wares at outdoor markets in Bantry, Tralee, Limerick, Galway and Temple Bar in Dublin, along with fellow English Marketeer, Toby 'Olives' Simmonds, which she found economically necessary as the Market, though 'on the up', had not yet fully 'taken off'. In 1999 a large butcher's unit just inside the Princes Street end of the Grand Parade Market became vacant, and Isabelle took the plunge.

The move was successful, and business boomed with a better location and more space. She moved her kitchen on site, and began baking, cooking and selling quiches, vegetarian filo pastries, pizza, croissants and freshly-made sandwiches. Her Irish products, besides the aforementioned breads and farmhouse cheeses, include free range eggs, fresh sausages, locally-smoked bacon, homemade jams, sauces, dressings, chocolates and biscuits. She continues to import French farmhouse cheeses, as well as an extensive French epicerie range including foie gras, cassoulets, sauces, dried mushrooms, mustards, galettes from Brittany, and ready meals from a duck farm in Normandy. Although approximately 30 per cent of her produce comes from France, Isabelle does not feel that she is running a 'French' stall. She has carved out her own niche, combining local, traditional produce like bacon and brown bread with the best from French small producers: 'I am not in any sense imposing my culture', she says, 'but sharing it'. She believes her stall reflects the best elements of the Market as it has developed since the 1990s: the old alongside the new, the Irish and the international, the gourmet with the plain. Isabelle is proud to be part of the growing international 'Slow Food Movement', which promotes food and wine culture, and defends agricultural and food biodiversity, in the face of fast food homogenity.

THIS CLOCK WILL
NEVER BE STOLEN
...The Employees are
always watchin' it.

Price List

½ lb. TRIPE	90c
¼ lb. TRIPE	€1.35c
1 lb. TRIPE	€1.80
1¼ lb. "	€2.25
1½ lb. TRIPE	€2.70
1¾ lb. "	€3.15
2 lbs. TRIPE	€3.60
3 lbs. "	€5.40
4 lbs. TRIPE	€7.20
5 lbs. "	€9.00
6 lbs. TRIPE	€10.80
7 lbs. "	€12.60
8 lbs. TRIPE	€14.40
9 lbs. "	€16.20
10 lbs. "	€18.00

All rubbi
In bins

6 Traditional Foods of Cork[1]

The consumption of offal in Cork has declined in recent decades, but for many centuries beef and pig offal provided the poorer people of the city with a cheap and plentiful supply of protein. Up to the 1820s beef was the predominant meat processed in the city and consequently beef offal was most widely available. As beef processing declined and the processing of pigs in the city increased pig offal became more dominant in the diet of many as the better and more expensive cuts were exported or sold in more lucrative markets. The popularity of these offals in the city resulted in the development of a distinct regional diet in Cork characterised by foods like drisheen, tripe, bodice, skirts and crubeens. Other foods such as dried salted ling, buttered eggs and spiced beef are also part of that distinct diet and all are still available in the English Market.

Drisheen

The term drisheen comes from the Irish word *drisín*, a diminutive form of the word *dreasán,* which means a sheep entrail, and describes a type of blood sausage or pudding made with a mixture of sheep's and beef blood. The consumption of animal blood as a food is an ancient practice in Ireland and elsewhere, as is the making of blood sausage, and drisheen is Cork's unique contribution to that tradition. The food historian Regina Sexton believes it may have been eaten in Cork from as early as the eleventh century.[2] The popularity of drisheen has declined greatly and today the firm of A. O'Reilly & Sons, that trades in the Grand Parade Market, is the only manufacturer of drisheen left in the city.

Three types of drisheen were traditionally eaten in Cork: a drisheen made with sheep's blood only, another made with a mix of sheep's and beef blood, and a third made with either blood, flavoured with the herb tansy. Only the second type is now made. The warm bloods of sheep and cattle are mixed and left overnight to allow the separation of the blood serum and coagulated blood residue. Beef intestines are used as casings and are turned inside out and cleaned before being filled with the separated serum. These are tied at both ends and boiled for five minutes. The drisheen is then stored in water until sold.

Opposite page: Helen Morey selling tripe and drisheen at O'Reilly's stall.

217

It is prepared in a variety of ways but needs only to be heated through as it has already been cooked. It can be heated in water or milk, skinned and served with a simple white sauce, seasoned with pepper and eaten with bread and butter. Drisheen can also be sliced and fried. As it has quite a soft texture drisheen was traditionally regarded as an ideal and nourishing food for invalids, people with delicate stomachs and those with no teeth!

Tripe

Tripe is a feature of many cuisines and has been a characteristic Cork food from at least the seventeenth century when the growth of large-scale beef processing in the city made large quantities cheaply available. Beef tripe is the commonest type and is made with the first stomach or rumen of the animal. In Cork it is known as 'plain', 'blanket' or 'vein'. 'Honeycomb' is tripe made from the second stomach or reticulum but is not now generally available. In the past, two further varieties of tripe, known in Cork as 'book' and 'reed', which came from the third and fourth stomach chambers of cattle, were also eaten but have long since disappeared from butchers' shops. When tripe is sold it has a white appearance, which is achieved by a lengthy preparation involving washing, bleaching and boiling. In Cork tripe is traditionally prepared by cutting it into small pieces and cooking it in milk for up to two hours. It is served in a sauce made with milk and onions, well seasoned with salt and pepper. Drisheen is sometimes added to the sauce and served with the tripe.

Pig Offal

Bacon curing in Cork grew significantly during the nineteenth century and firms such as Lunhams and Dennys operated on an industrial scale serving the home and export markets. As a consequence large quantities of pig offal were readily available and affordable to the less well-off in the city and became an essential part of the traditional Cork urban diet. While the consumption of these has declined with increasing affluence, there is still a demand among older people for the foods and tastes that they associate with their native city. The number of outlets selling pig offal has also declined greatly but the stall of Kathleen Noonan and her family in the English Market is almost unique in selling the full traditional range.

Bodice is used to describe the rib-cage of the pig and it is usually sold cured or salted for boiling. Fresh ribs, roasted as spare ribs, are less popular traditionally. The skirt is the pig's diaphragm and is a long flat piece of meat which is attached to the rib-cage. It is usually eaten stewed with pig's kidneys. Crubeens are more widely known as trotters but in Ireland, and especially in Cork, crubeen is the favoured term, coming from the Irish word *crúibín*. They are boiled for up to three hours and are still popular as a snack food, often eaten cold at football or hurling matches or while

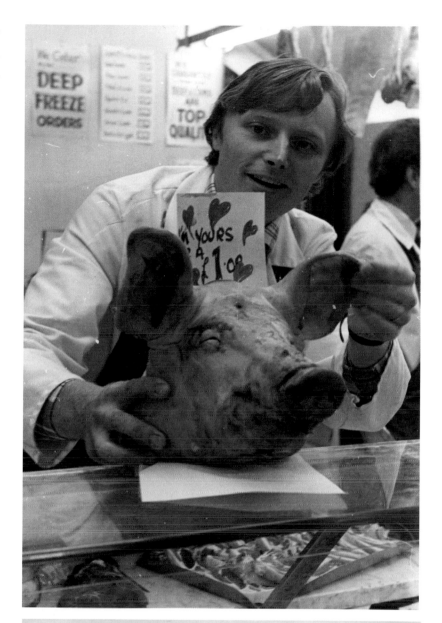

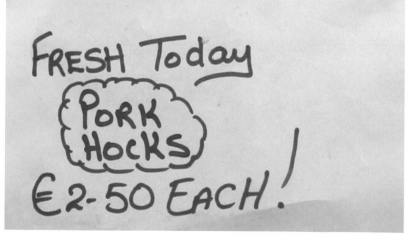

fishing. Other popular items of pig offal still sold in the Market but eaten by increasingly fewer people are pig's head, loin bones, tails, hocks and knuckles.

Spiced Beef

In Cork spiced beef is traditionally eaten at Christmas. Topside, tail-end or silverside of beef is marinated and cured in salt water with a mixture of herbs and spices such as allspice, cinnamon, nutmeg and ginger. When it is removed from the marinade it is coated with a dry mix of herbs, spices and seasonings and each individual producer uses his or her own unique mix and occasional secret ingredient. Though also produced and eaten elsewhere, spiced beef has been particularly associated with Cork since the late eighteenth century when the salt beef of the city's burgeoning beef processing plants was treated with the exotic spices and seasonings then becoming available in the city due to increasing trade with distant ports. Spiced beef is boiled in water, sometimes with an added bottle of stout, and, if preferred cold, is allowed to fully cool in the cooking liquid to absorb the full flavour of the spices. It is also eaten hot and can be roasted if a stronger flavour is desired. In the weeks leading up to Christmas every Market butcher has spiced beef on offer, but as the seasonality of food becomes increasingly less apparent, it is now offered for sale throughout the year by some.

Buttered Eggs

Before the advent of modern technologies, eggs were a seasonal food, plentiful in summer but scarcer and more expensive in winter. Eggs were not eaten during Lent and this often left a surplus to be preserved for eating on Easter Sunday and afterwards. Buttering was a traditional method of preserving eggs and keeping them fresh for up to six months and sometimes longer. The eggs are buttered soon after laying while they are still warm and they are rolled in fresh butter in the palms of the hand. The melted butter is absorbed by the porous shell and when cooled will harden and seal the egg keeping it airtight and fresh until it is used. The tradition survives today not out of necessity but because of the appeal of the buttery flavour of eggs preserved in that way. In the past a number of stalls in the Princes Street Market dealt solely in butter, eggs and buttered eggs, but today buttered eggs are only available at Moynihan's stall.

Battleboard

Battleboard is the name given to dried salted ling, a large Atlantic fish of the cod family, often a metre and more in length. In its preserved state it is stiff and hard and is often seen stacked like timber boards, hence the name. This was a cheap and plentiful food and was eaten by many during Lent and on Fridays when the eating of meat was forbidden for Catholics. Battleboard was also a traditional Christmas Eve dish in Cork and elsewhere. Its strong salty flavour and associations with abstinence and penance prevented the fish becoming a favourite and it is rarely eaten today. Before cooking the fish is soaked overnight to reduce the salt content and to re-hydrate the flesh. It is then boiled gently in water or milk and eaten with a milk and onion sauce. Battleboard can still be bought in the fish section of the English Market.

Seán Calder-Potts worked in Cork in the early 1990s as manager of a city-centre hostel. At six o'clock one morning a French guest, who was returning home that day, enquired where in the city he might buy a side of smoked salmon. Seán replied that he did not think it would be possible to make such a purchase that early in the morning. The Frenchman left to try his luck in the city and returned less than an hour later having succeeded in his quest. Seán asked where he had managed to buy smoked salmon at such an early hour and the man replied: 'Les Halles!', meaning the English Market. Not realising Cork had such a facility, Seán went to investigate and was surprised to find a busy food market like those he had seen abroad, in the heart of the city.

Seán Calder-Potts had traded at a stall as a *foirain* (occasional trader) in a market near La Rochelle in western France, selling nameplates for houses, and he saw the English Market as an attractive location in which to renew his love of market trading. He acquired a vacant stall and engaged architect Alex White of Monkstown to redesign it in an appropriate style. The new design revealed the original features of the stall, which had been hidden by successive renovations, and presented an open and well-lit food display area with good customer access. The new stall opened for business in August 1993 and the Royal Institute of the Architects of Ireland awarded Alex White's design one of its prestigious annual awards. Seán had been impressed by the approach of the Pret à Manger sandwich chain in England and his stall, styled Iago, began life selling coffee and sandwiches. The cheeses, salamis, sun-dried tomatoes and other sandwich ingredients used at the stall soon began to fill the display area and as customers began to buy these also, this new trade soon outweighed that of the café side of the business which was eventually closed. Iago now trades in Irish and continental cheeses, salamis, Parma ham, freshly made pastas, pizza dough, sauces and a variety of other foods that have become popular at Irish tables in the past decade.

Seán is passionate about the idea of a market. The relationship with the customer is closer than that in a normal shop or supermarket and dealing in a commodity as fundamental as food intensifies the bond. He sees the English Market as a civic amenity which should be maintained as a food market where traders pay lower rents in comparison to those paid by other city-centre traders, and he believes that, in return, market traders should give something back to the city, selling the best quality at the fairest price. Seán

says that market stalls have major advantages over shops and supermarket multiples in that they are not dependent on a central distribution system and do not need to rely on products with a long shelf life. They can respond very quickly to customer demand and profitably deal in smaller quantities of perishable items. A market stall, however, has a much higher staff/customer ratio compared to other retail outlets and the maintenance of a high level of personal service entails a higher wage bill.

The influence of newspaper and magazine food writers has benefited trade and a sudden rise in demand for a particular product on a Saturday morning is usually explained by an article in a weekend supplement. This media influence is so significant that Seán remarks, not entirely facetiously, 'If it's not mentioned in a magazine, don't try to sell it!'

Seán Calder-Potts, Josephine Kennedy and their staff run a stall whose product range reflects much of what is new in Irish eating habits since the early 1990s. Strong French and Italian influences are especially noticeable and their assimilation in the English Market mirrors parallel processes in the broader life of Cork and Irish society generally.

Above: Office area of Katherine O'Mahony's stall, Grand Parade Market.

EXTRA VIRGIN
OLIVE OIL

☐ EXTRA VIRGIN
☑ P.D.O. KOLYMVARI

Above: Toby Simmonds with his daughter Rosa

Stallholders 1845-2005

What follows is as definitive a list of stallholders as is possible with the available evidence. An indeterminite, though certainly a small minority, of stallholders have fallen through the documentary gap. Stall numbers were subject to constant change and re-ordering, stallholders often took numbers with them when they moved stall, and many stalls had rapid turnover of holders – all of which makes a complete listing impossible. In some cases, the stall is held in one name, but operated by another person whose name is not recorded. The lists for the 1950s - 1990s are not numbered because numbers were not available for all, so none are used to avoid confusion; also, they are not presented in any particular order. In general, all are butchers except where otherwise indicated.

1845

Grand Parade Market
(meat stalls only)

1	Richard Waugh
2	Richard Harrington
3	Letitia Stoke
6	John Ahern
7	John Ahern Jnr.
8	William Deeble
9	Denis Slattery
10	William Browne
12	William Corker
13	James Russell
15	James Ireton
16	Denis Smith
17	Edward Russell
18	Andrew Waugh
19	Edward Dale
20	Patrick Hennessy
21	Mathew Murley
23	Stephen Barry
26	John Geany
26B	Charles Hayes
27	John Duke
29	William Ford
31	R.G. Brown
32	John Daly
33	James Geany
34	Cornelius Murphy
35	James Hayes
36	Timothy Mahony
37	Patrick Buckley
38	John Looney
39	John Barry
40	John Cremen
41	Margaret Daly
42	Henry Mahony
43	James Sheehan
44	John Kearney
47	John Waugh
49	John Dale
50	William Cloake Jnr.
51	David McEnery
52	Michael Daly

56	Timothy Ahern
57	Denis Hallissay
58	John Preston
59	Jeremiah Ahern
61	Samuel Short
62	John McAuliffe
63	James Murley
64	John Mulcahy
65	George Cleary & William Shaughnessy
67	William Butler
68	John Fennell
69	John Morrison
70	Charles Hayes
71	John Key
72	Owen Connor
73	Jeremiah Connor
74	Denis Bradley
75	Ellen Hennessy
76	William Harrington
77	Thomas Shaughnessey
78	William O'Brien
79	James Lynch
81	Patrick O'Connell
82	Stephen Mintern
83	Richard Mintern
84	Daniel Gorman
85	John Burke

Source: *Slater's National Commercial Directory of Ireland* (London, 1846)

1856

'Corporation Market'
Fishmongers

10	James Hussey
12	James Marley
13	Michael Corcoran
14	Andrew Raynes
16	John Tehean
17	Thomas Leary
18	Mary McCarthy
27	Ellen Lynch
29	Ellen Manning
30	Eliza Collins
31	Laurence Flynn
32	Daniel Crowley

Butchers

6	John Ahern
8	John Ahern Jnr.
48	James Anglin
11	John Anglin
33	William Anglin
81	Patrick Barry
78	Michael Brien
45	William Browne
60	Michael Bryan
86	Michael Buckley
66	Michael Buckley
34	William Clancy
82	Jane Connell
21	Eugene Connor
22	Eugene Connor
59	Owen Connor
77	Owen Connor
12	William Cooke
28	James Creedon
30	James Creedon
39	John Cremen
49	John Dale
?	Andrew Daly
9	Michael Daly
44	Michael Daly
52	Michael Daly
27	John Duke
67	Michael Ellis
15	James Farrell
24	Michael Geany
25	Michael Geany
4	George Griffin
63	John Griffin
68	Samuel Griffin
67	Thomas Griffin
66	Charles Hayes
26	Charles Hayes

10	John Hayes
80	James Lynch
50	William McCormick
51	David McEnery
31	Henry Mahony
36	Timothy Mahony
5	James Manley
83	Richard Mintern
82	Stephen Mintern
69	John Morrison
64	John Mulcahy
21	Matthew Murley
34	Charles Murphy
34	Henry Murphy
56	Michael Nagle
37	Edward Naughton
38	Edward Naughton
62	James O'Brien
62	James O'Connor
2	James Power
3	James Power
58	Benjamin Preston
17	Edward Russell
86	Thomas Ryan
77	Thomas Shaughnessy
65	William Shaugnessy
32	James Sheehan
42	James Sheehan Jnr.
43	James Sheehan Jnr.
61	Samuel Short
89	Daniel Smith
14	Denis Smith
16	James Smith
55	John Smith
20	Daniel Sullivan
53	Daniel Swiney
7	Denis Twomey

Source: *Slater's Royal National Commercial Directory of Ireland* (London and Manchester, 1856)

Opposite page: Glenys Landon, Princes Street Market.

1857-1949: where the date of a new stallholder taking tenancy is <u>first noted</u> in the records, it is given in brackets

1857 – 1883

Grand Parade Market

90 vacant / taken by James Sheehan subsequently taken by Timothy Healy (1869)
89 Daniel Smith / Samuel Kincaid (1859)
88 Catherine Griffin
87 Mark Buckley / William Young (1871) / Richard Waugh / Charles Hayes & Sons (1875)
86 Denis Hallisy / Denis Bradley / Richard Waugh / Charles Hayes & Sons (1875)
5 Richard Waugh / vacant
6 James Power / Patrick Tracey (1868) / Timothy Healy (1873)
7 vacant / Charles Hayes / John Harrington (1861) / Hugh Looney (1868) / William Short (1869) / Samuel Kincaid (1887)
8 George Griffin / John Abraham Manley (1860) / Hugh Looney (1875)
9 John Abraham Manley / Hugh Looney (1875)
10 Michael Ahern / vacant (1864) / Richard Waugh (1874) / John Manley (1875)
11 Denis Twomey / William Dillon Jnr. (1864) / William Dillon (1874) / John Manley (1875)
12 John Ahern / Nicholas McCarthy (1864) / Hugh Looney (1874) / William Dillon (1875)
13 Michael Daly / William Dillon (1875)
14 John Hayes / John Manley (1874) / Nicholas McCarthy (1875)
15 John Anglin / John Callaghan (1868) / William Callaghan (1874) / Michael Daly (1875)
16 William Cooke / Robert O'Brien (1857) / John Hayes (1875)
17 James Russell / Daniel Leahy (after 1867) / John Callaghan (1875)
18 Denis Smith / Daniel Leahy (1861) / Nicholas McCarthy / Michael Barrett (1875)
19 vacant / Denis Hallisey (1861) / George Griffin (1866) / Michael Daly (1873) / James Russell (1875)
20 Denis Smith / John Creedon (1866) / Daniel Leahy (1867) / John Hayes / Denis Casey (1875)
21 Edward Russell / Michael Ahern (1864) / Mary Russell (1865) / John Callaghan / William Looney (1875)
22 John Morrison / Julia Morrison (1865) / Michael Barrett
23 Andrew Dale / James Russell / Michael Ahern (1875)
24 John Sullivan / Andrew Dale (1860) / Denis Casey / Mrs Morrison (1875)

25 Eugene Connor / Charles Hayes / William Looney
26 Eugene Connor / Charles Hayes / Daniel Leahy / George Griffin (1875)
27 INSPECTOR'S STORE / James Whelan (1863) / Michael Ahern / George Griffin (1875)
28 Michael Geany / Abigail Geany (1861) / William Foley / David McEnery (1875)
29 Michael Geany / Roger Morrison (1860) / Michael Daly (1875)
92 Roger Morrison
30 Charles Hayes (double stall) / George Griffin
31 John Duke / Maryanne Duke (1861)
32 John Duke / Maryanne Duke (1861) / David McEnery
33 John Duke / Maryann Duke (1861) / Michael Daly
34 James Creedon / Henry Mahony / Denis Twomey
35 Henry Mahony / vacant / Hannah Murphy (1875)
36 James Sheehan / Mary Sheehan / vacant
37 William Anglin / Eliza Anglin (1859) / William Anglin (1861) / vacant / Matthew Olden (1875)
38 Cornelius Murphy / Richard Daly (1860) / Cornelius Murphy (1861) / vacant / representative of Daniel Sullivan / James Riordan (1875)
39 William Clancy / Edmund Hayes (1860) / vacant / Hannah Murphy / Joseph Coffey (1875)
40 Timothy O'Mahony / Richard Daly (1861) / William Dunlea / vacant / James Creedon (1875)
41 Edward Naughton / Mark Buckley / Mathew Olden / James Creedon (1875)
42 Edward Naughton / Mark Buckley / James Riordan / James Hayes (1875)
43 John Cremin / Margaret Cronin (1861) / William Dunlea / Joseph Coffey / James Hayes (1875)
44 vacant / William Dunlea (1860) / James Creedon / Cornelius Millard / Mark Buckley (1875)
45 vacant / William Dunlea
46 James Sheehan / John Bowen / representative of James Hayes / William Dunlea (1875)
47 James Sheehan / Mary Sheehan / William Dunlea (1875)
48 Nicholas Daly / John Smith / Mark Buckley
49 William Browne / Mary Browne (1861) / William Dunlea / James Sheehan (1875)
50 John Waugh / Andrew Waugh (1857) / William Dunlea / John Bowen (1875)
51 John Waugh / William Browne (1875)
52 Samuel Anglin / representative of Andrew Dale

53 John Dale / Edward Dale (1860) / George Griffin / representative of James Sheehan
54 William McCormick / George Griffin (1860) / John Bowen
55 Daniel McEnery / David McEnery (1861) / William Browne / Andrew Dale (1875)
56 Michael Daly / Andrew Waugh / Andrew Dale (1875)
57 Denis Twomey / John Waugh / Charles Hayes & Sons (1875)
58 Denis Twomey / vacant
59 vacant / William Joyce (1857) / Patrick Vaughan (1860) / vacant / Andew Dale / Charles Hayes & Sons (1875)
60 ('SHOP') vacant / Daniel Leahy (1859) / William Dillon (1861) / Joseph Coffey / Charles Hayes & Sons (1875)
61 Daniel Sullivan / Charles Hayes & Sons / Margaret Duke (1875)
62 Hannah Murphy / John Leary / Margaret Duke (1875)
63 Owen Connor / Rebecca Connor (1860) / vacant / Charles Hayes & Sons / Margaret Duke (1875)
64 Nicholas Breen / vacant (1860) / Matthew Olden
65 Clara Short / vacant (1859) / John Griffin (1861) / James Riordan / Frank Duke
66 Jeremiah O'Connell / Jeremiah O'Connor (1860) / vacant / James Sheehan (1875)
67 vacant / Thomas Jones (1857) / James Sheehan Jnr. (1857) / James Creedon
68 vacant / Rachel Smith (1859) / James Sheehan Jnr. (1860) / Jeremiah Cambridge (1875) / Mrs Cambridge / Maurice O'Keeffe (1877)
69 vacant / Nicholas Ellis
70 Charles Hayes / William Dunlea (1875)
71 Nicholas Ellis

'Public Fish Market & Open Standings' (no names given)

Little Market
60 Catherine Leary / Michael O'Brien (1861) / Catherine O'Brien
61 Samuel Short / Clara Short (1861) / Samuel Short (1875)
62 James O'Brien / John Griffin
63 John Griffin
64 John Mulcahy / Henry Mahony (1875)
65 William Shaughnessy / Ellen Shaugnessy / Henry Mahony (1875)
66 Terence Ahern / Michael Ahern (1875) / Bridget Ahern
67 Thomas Griffin / Thomas Shaughnessy / Stephen Whelan (1875)
68 William Butler / Patrick Griffin (1875)
69 Cornelius Noonan / Mrs Noonan (1875)
57 Richard Mintern / Robert Millard (1875)

Opposite page: Advertisement for William Dunlea Victuallers from *Guy's Directory 1883.*

58 William Preston / Thomas Crocket (1857) / John Geany (1875) / Robert Millard (1875)
59 William Harrington / Denis Bradley (1875) / Timothy Moore (1880)
70 Marcus Goulding / Michael O'Brien / vacant / William Preston
71 James Whelan / Patrick Sweeney (1870)
72 James Lynch / Michael Preston / William Preston (1875)
73 Patrick Barrett
74 Patrick O'Connell / Patrick Barrett (1875)
75 Stephen Mintern / John Ellard (1875)
76 vacant / Daniel Murphy (1857) / William Preston (1875)
77 Mrs Harrington (1875)
80 James Lynch (1875)
81 Stephen Barry (1875)
82 Hannah Mintern (1875) / Mary Anne Ellard (1878)
83 John Mintern (1875)
85 vacant / David Manning (1857) / John Finn (1875) / Daniel Murphy
86 David Manning (1875)

Princes Street – Fruit and Vegetable Market and Open Standings (no names given)

Source: Valuation Books, Valuation Office, Dublin; *Guy's Directory* (1875-6); Cork Corporation Tolls and Markets Committee Minute Books, 1867-83, Cork Archives Institute.

Note: A list of Grand Parade Market stallholders appeared in the *Cork Examiner* on 28 May 1858. Names that appeared there but not in the list above are:
Patrick Barry
John [O'] Brien
Jane Connell
Michael Connell
William Cremen
Edward Dale
Nicholas Daly
John Dineen
Garrett Fitzgerald
Samuel Griffin
Joseph Hussey
John King
John Morrison
Roger Morrison
Eugene O'Connor
William Short
Denis Sweeney

Additional stallholders (unnumbered)
These are the names of stallholders which appear in the Tolls and Markets Committee Minute Books but not in the other records. The dates show when the stallholder is mentioned in the Minute Books.

Grand Parade Market
Denis Hayes (1870)
James Donovan (1871)
M. Creedon (1871)
M. Connor (1871)
P. Mulcahy (1871)
Thomas Conway (1872)
Robert Miller (1873)
A. Burke (1873)
Mrs Coffey (1873)
Margaret Hannigan (pre-1878)
Mary Long (1878)
James Clancy (1878)
Catherine Roche (1879, 1892)
John Hurley (1879)
Ellen Desmond (1880)
Mary Hurley (1880)
Poultry
James Lundy (1880)
Edward Ahern (1881)
Ellen Hinchin (1882, 1900): *tripe*
Edward Clarke (1882)
John Halloran (1883)
John Short (1883)
Fish
Michael Coakley (1872)
Corcoran (1872)
Mrs H. Reardon (1873)
Mannix & Son (1873) / Margaret Brown (1883)
O'Leary (1875)
Mary Hurley (1876)
Johanna Sheehan (1878)
Ellen Corcoran (1879)
May Welstead (1879)
Daniel Buckley (pre-1880)
Hannah Dennehy (1883) / Ellen Sheehan (1883)

Princes Street Market
Unspecified
Mrs Lyons standing (1874)
Mary Connor (1878)
Anne Conway (1879)
Hannah Brady (1883)
Ellen Dineen (1883)
Mrs Patrick Desmond (1883)
Fowl
Hanora Buckley (1838)
Mary Desmond (1868)
Hanora Burns (1872, 1884)
Johanna Walsh (1872 , 1875)
Johanna Connor (1873)
Wm Kinmonth (1874)
O'Keeffe (1875)
Mary Lynch (1883)
Catherine White (1883)
Vegetables
Hanora Sullivan (1869)
Mrs Haly (1872)
Mrs Murray (1872)
Mrs Manning (1875)

Catherine Cogan (1878), (1882)
Bridget Riordan (pre-1883)
Butter and eggs
Ann Barry (1872)
Mrs Moynihan (1874)
Norah Kelleher (pre-1880)
Ellen Swiney (1880)
Flowers (gallery)
S. Preston (1874)
Unknown
(Grand Parade, Little or Princes Street Market)
Mrs Harrison, (1874)
John Austin, (1877)
Johanna Reardon (pre 1877)
Hannah Gandon (1877)
Mrs Dillon (pre-1881): *tripe*

1884 – 1893

Note: The *'public fish market and open standings'* disappear following the creation of the formal fish market in the 1870s. Instead we have a numbered listing for *'Grand Parade Market – fish stalls'*.

Grand Parade Market
72 William Smiddy
73 Representative of Daniel Murphy / Mrs Murphy (1886) / William Smiddy (1893)
74 Representative of Daniel Murphy / Felix Mullen/ Mrs Murphy (1886) / David Walsh (1893)
75 Mark Buckley / William Smiddy (1890) / Hannah Murphy (1893)
76 Mark Buckley / Mary Daly (1890) / William Smiddy (1893)
85 John Finn / Honora Finn (1890)
86 Charles Hayes & Sons
87 Charles Hayes & Sons
2 Timothy Healy (1884-8)
3 Sarah Kincaid / William McNamara (1886)
4 vacant / James Kinnealy (1886) / William McNamara (1893)
5 vacant / John Sullivan (1890) / Maurice Coughlan (1890) / Anne Coughlan (1892)
6 Richard Waugh / John O'Sullivan (1886) / William Dillon (1886) / vacant (1890) / Anne Coughlan (1892)
7 Richard Waugh / William Dillon (1886) / Timothy Buckley (1886)
8 Hugh Looney / John Murphy
9 Hugh Looney
10 John Manley
11 John Manley
12 William Dillon
13 William Dillon
14 Nicholas McCarthy / John Nolan (1889)

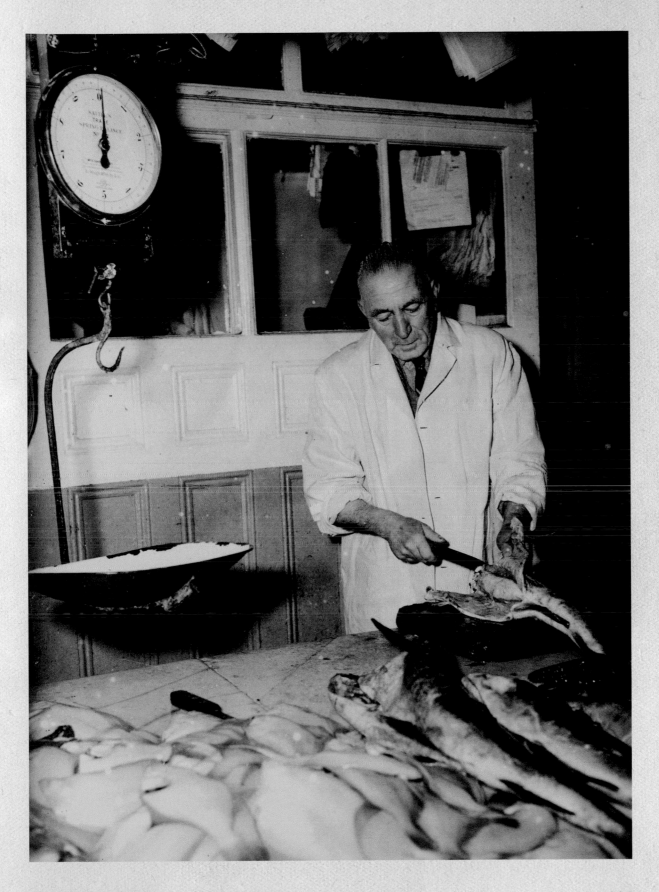

Above: John 'Bunny' Sheehan, Grand Parade Fish Market.

15 Michael Daly / Edmond Murphy (1890) /
   John Hayes (1886)
16 John Hayes / vacant (1890)
17 John Callaghan
18 Michael Barrett / Bridget Ahern (1886) /
   John Lisson (1891)
19 James Russell / vacant (1890) /
   John Lisson (1891)
20 Denis Casey / William Looney (1886) /
   vacant (1889)
21 William Looney
22 Daniel Leahy (1886)
23 Michael Ahern
24 William Foley
25 WEIGHING SCALES
26 George Griffin
27 George Griffin
28 Davis McEnery / George Griffin (1886)
29 Michael Daly / Mrs McCarthy (1886) /
   Edmond Murphy (1890)
30 Denis Twomey / vacant (1890) /
   Vincent Twomey (1893)
31 vacant / William Dillon (1886) / Joshua
   Manley (1887) / Johanna Manley (1890)
32 vacant / Charles Manley
33 vacant / Charles Manley
34 Representative of Daniel Sullivan / Mrs
   Dillon (1886) / William Dillon (1886) /
   Vincent Twomey (1891)
35 Hannah Murphy
36 vacant / William Dunlea (1886) /
   John Murphy (1886)
37 Matthew Olden
38 James Riordan or Rearden /
   Thomas Griffin (1889)
39 Joseph Coffey / William Dunlea (1886) /
   Francis Coffey (1890)
40 James Creedon / William Dunlea (1886) /
   Cornelius Millard (1886)
41 James Creedon / William Dunlea (1886) /
   John Treacy (1886)
42 Representative of James Hayes / Daniel
   Donovan (1886) / John Treacy (1893)
43 Representative of James Hayes /
   Daniel Donovan (1889)
44 Mark Buckley / John Buckley (1886)
45 William Dunlea / Daniel Donovan (1886)
   / David Walsh (1893)
46 William Dunlea / Ignatius O'Flynn (1890)
47 William Dunlea / Ignatius O'Flynn /
   vacant (1890)
48 Representative of Richard Daly /
   Humphrey Geany (1886) /
   Mary Geany (1889)
49 Representative of James Sheehan / Mary
   Ahern (1889) / Mary Sheehan (1891)
50 John Bowen / Mary Bowen (1886) /
   Joseph Hayes (1890)
51 William Brown / Mrs Brown (1886) /
   Denis Callaghan (1889) / Hannah Brown
   (1890) / Denis O'Callaghan (1893)
52 Andrew Waugh / Denis O'Callaghan

(1886) / William Kelly (1893)
53 John Waugh / Anne Waugh (1886)
54 John Waugh / Anne Waugh (1890)
55 Andrew Dale
56 Andrew Dale
57 Charles Hayes & Sons
58 John Leary / Charles Hayes & Sons (1889)
59 Charles Hayes & Sons
60 Charles Hayes & Sons
61 Frank Duke
62 Frank Duke
63 Frank Duke
64 Henry Mahony / Michael Barrett (1886)
65 Henry Mahony / William Kinmonth
   (1886) / Michael Barrett (1886)
   / Michael Barret & Peter Spillane Jnr.
   (1893)
66 Representative of James Sheehan /
   Mary Sheehan (1890)
67 vacant / Patrick McAuliffe (1886) /
   vacant (1890)
68 Jeremiah Cambridge / Maurice O'Keeffe
   (1890)
70 William Dunlea
71 William Smiddy

Little Market
60 Catherine [O] Brien / Catherine Griffin
   (1890)
61 Clara Short / vacant (1890) /
   Mary Mintern (1892)
62 John Griffin
63 John Griffin
64 John Mulcahy / David Mulcahy (1887) /
   vacant (1889)
65 Ellen Shaughnessy
66 Bridget Ahern / vacant (1890)
67 ('SHOP') Stephen Whelan /
   George Griffin (1888) / vacant (1890)
68 Patrick Griffin / Catherine Griffin (1890)
69 Cornelius Noonan / Mary Noonan (1890)
57 Robert Millard / George Paul (1890)
58 Robert Millard / George Paul (1890)
59 Denis Bradley / Timothy Moore (1890)
70 William Preston / vacant (1890) /
   Daniel Donovan (1893)
71 Patrick Sweeney / Mrs Sweeney (1875) /
   A. Sweeney (1890)
72 Michael Preston / Catherine Ahern (1890)
73 Patrick Barrett / Margaret Barrett /
   Samuel Dillon (1888)
74 Patrick Barrett / Margaret Barrett /
   Samuel Dillon (1888)
75 John Ellard / vacant (1890)
76 William Preston / vacant (1890)
77 William Harrington / vacant (1890)
78 James Whelan
79 James Whelan
80 James Lynch / Denis Kelleher (1890)
81 Mrs Morrison / vacant (1890) /
   John Mintern (1891)

82 Catherine Mintern / vacant (1890) /
   John Mintern (1891)
83 John Mintern / vacant (1890)
84 Daniel Murphy / vacant (1890)
85 David Manning

Grand Parade Market – fish stalls
1 Michael Sheehan
2 Michael Sheehan
3 Jeremiah Sugrue / Mrs Sugrue (1893)
4 James Carroll / Joseph Carroll (1890)
5 Cornelius Geary
6 Patrick O'Leary / Anne O'Leary (1893)
7 Patrick O'Leary / Anne O'Leary (1893)
8 Ellen Sheehan
9 P. Browne
10 John O'Connor
11 P. Browne
12 P. Browne
13 James Sheehan / Ellen Corcoran (1890)
14 Bartholomew Brown
15 Bartholomew Brown
16 Abbey Leahy

Additional Grand Parade Market fishmonger
listed in *Guy's Directory* (1891): James Quain

Princes Street – Fruit and Vegetable Market
and Open Standings
   (stalls not listed – see below)

Source: Valuation Books, Valuation Office,
Dublin; *Guy's Directory* (1886, 1891 and
1893); Cork Corporation Tolls and Markets
Committee Minute Books, 1884-1893.

Additional stallholders (unnumbered)

Dates shown are those when the stallholder
is mentioned in the Tolls and Markets
Committee Minute Books.

Grand Parade Market
   Bridget Murphy, Maria Fitgerald and
   Kate Sullivan (1884): *tripe*
   Kate Sullivan (1892-96): *tripe and drisheen*
   Hanorah O'Neill (1885): *butter*
   Mary Anne Hurley (1885): *butter*
   Kate Cogan (1886)
   Frederick Russell (pre-1886)
   Patrick Russell (1886)
   John Sisson (1887)
   Mrs O'Neill (pre-1887)
   Timothy Curtin (1893, 1896)

Little Market
   John McAuliffe (1892)
   Bessie O'Shaughnessy (1892)
   Annie O'Shaughnessy (1892)
   Catherine Lombard (pre-1893)

Princes Street Market
Unspecified
David Summer (1886)
Bridget Sullivan (1887)
Thomas Walsh (1887)
Mrs Walsh (1887)
Nora Murphy (1893)
Norah Burke (1893)
Fowl Gallery
M. Twomey (1884)
Catherine White (1885, 1887)
Mary Desmond (1885)
Ellen Kelly (1886, 1899)
Vegetables
(1885: minutes mention 23 vegetable
stallholders in the market)
Mrs Dunlea (1884)
Mrs Dineen (1884)
Ellen Desmond (1884-97)
O'Brien (1885)
Ellen McCarthy (1887, 1892, 1903)
Anne Sullivan (1887)
Margaret Dunlea (1887)
Anne Halloran (1887)

1894 – 1907

Note: The Little Market is sold to Alexander
Grant & Co. in 1896. Five of the fourteen
stallholders took up new stalls in the Princes
Street Market and several others transferred to
the main Grand Parade Market.

Grand Parade Market
71   William Smiddy
72   William Smiddy
73   Hannah Murphy / Hanora Murphy /
       C. Duggan (1902)
74   Felix Mullen
75   Hannah Murphy / William Smiddy
76   Mary Daly / William Smiddy
85   Honora Finn
86   Charles Hayes & Sons (part stall)
88   Charles Hayes & Sons (part stall)
3   William McNamara
4   William McNamara
5   Mrs M. Coughlan / P.J. Power (1894) /
       Andrew Dale (1906)
6   vacant / John Fitzgerald (1903): *tripe* /
       Denis O'Connell (1907)
7   Timothy Buckley / John Fitzgerald (1903):
       tripe / Denis O'Connell (1907)
8   John Murphy / Hugh Looney (1907)
9   Hugh Looney
10   John Manley
11   John Manley
12   William Dillon
13   William Dillon
14   John Nolan / Mrs Nolan (1894)

15   Edmond Murphy / James Hayes (1907)
16   vacant / James Hayes (1907)
17   John Callaghan / George Griffin (1907)
18   Bridget Ahern / John Lisson (1907)
19   vacant / John Lisson (1907)
20   vacant / Daniel Leahy (1907)
21   William Looney / Ellen Looney (1907)
22   Daniel Leahy
23   Michael Ahern / Denis Ahern (1907)
24   William Foley
25   WEIGHING SCALES
26   George Griffin
27   George Griffin
28   George Griffin
29   Edmond Murphy
30   vacant
31   Johanna Manley / Charles Manley (1907)
32   Charles Manley
33   Charles Manley
34   William Dillon
35   Hannah Murphy / John McDonnell
       (1894) / John Murphy (1907)
36   John Murphy
37   Matthew Olden
38   Thomas Griffin
39   Francis Coffey
40   Cornelius Millard
41   John Tracey
42   Daniel Donovan
43   Daniel Donovan
44   John Buckley
45   William Dunlea
46   Ignatius O'Flynn
47   vacant / Ignatius O'Flynn (1907)
48   Mary Geany
49   vacant / Joseph Spillane (1907)
50   Joseph Hayes
51   Hannah Browne
52   Denis O'Callaghan
53   Anne Waugh
54   Anne Waugh
55   Andrew Dale / Maria Cox (1906) /
       George Griffin (1906)
56   Andrew Dale / Maria Cox (1906) /
       George Griffin (1906)
57   Charles Hayes & Sons
58   Charles Hayes & Sons
59   Charles Hayes & Sons
60   Charles Hayes & Sons
61   Frank Duke
62   Frank Duke
63   Frank Duke
64   Michael Barrett
65   Michael Barrett
66   Mary Sheehan / Frank Duke (1907)
67   vacant
68   Maurice O'Keeffe / Cornelius O'Flynn
       (1907)
69   Denis Fitzgerald
70   William Dunlea

Little Market:
(All Cancelled 1897 – 'Taken by Grant & Co.')
4   Catherine Griffin
5   vacant
6   John Griffin
7   John Griffin
8   vacant
9   Ellen Shaughnessy
10   vacant
11   vacant
12   Catherine Griffin
13   Mary Noonan
1   George Paul
2   George Paul
3   Timothy Moore / Michael Noonan (1896)
14   vacant
15   A. Sweeney
16   Catherine Ahern / William Dillon (1893)
17   Samuel Dillon
18   Samuel Dillon
19   vacant
20   vacant
21   vacant
22   James Whelan
23   James Whelan
24   Denis Kelleher
25   John Mintern / vacant
26   John Mintern
27   Margaret Murphy / Samuel Dillon
28   vacant
29   David Manning

Grand Parade Market – fish stalls
1   Michael Sheehan
2   Michael Sheehan
3   John Sugrue / Patrick Sugrue (1902) /
       James Carroll (1905)
4   Joseph Carroll / Mrs Carroll (1900) /
       James Carroll (1902)
5   Cornelius Geany / Bridget Geany (1905)
6   Patrick O'Leary Jnr.
7   Patrick O'Leary Jnr.
8   Ellen Sheehan / Hanora Broderick (1897)
9   James Quain
10   John O'Connor
11   P. Brown / Bartholomew Donovan (1905)
12   P. Brown / William Quain (1905)
13   Ellen Corcoran
14   Bartholomew Brown / Hannah Brown
       (1895)
15   Bartholomew Brown / Hannah Brown
       (1895) / William Kinmonth (1899) /
       Patrick Sugrue (1900) / Michael Sheehan
       (1902)
16   Abbey Leahy / Mary Clancy (1902)
17   Thomas O'Sullivan (1899) /
       Patrick Sugrue (1899) / void (1900)

1897

Princes Street Market
(transfers from Little Market, 1896)
Meat
1   George Paul
2   Samuel Dillon
3   Samuel Dillon
4   John Griffin
5   Catherine Griffin
6   James Whelan / Patrick Whelan (1907)
(also mentioned, 1896, Mrs C. Higgins)
Vegetable, fruit, egg, butter and poultry stalls
not listed numerically
(see below for partial, unnumbered listing)

Source: Valuation Books, Valuation Office,
Dublin; *Guy's Directory* (1893, 1907); Cork
Corporation Tolls and Markets Committee
Minute Books, 1894-1907.

Additional stallholders (unnumbered)
Dates shown are those when the stallholder
is mentioned in the Tolls and Markets
Committee Minute Books.
Grand Parade Market
   Michael Hinchin (1900-07): *tripe*
   Bridget Griffin (1903): *tripe*
   James Heelan (1904-5)
   Frank Long (1907)

Fish
   Mrs Kelly (1901)
   Margaret Brown (1905)

Little Market
   Daniel Buckley (1895)
   Mary Manning (1897: transfer to GPM)

Princes Street Market
Unspecified – probably vegetables and/or fruit
   Abigail Barry (1894)
   M. O'Callaghan (1894)
   Maragret Chadwick (1894)
   Ellen Scannell (1895)
   Robert Cox (entrance) (1895)
   Mrs Scannell (1896)
   Bridget Canty (transfer to GPM, 1897)
   Margaret Shinkwin (1901)
   Ellen Daly (1903)
   Mary Long (pre-1903)
   Hannah Riordan (1903)
   Margaret Whelan (1906)
   James Dwane (1906)
   Eugene Cross (1907)
Vegetables
   Ellen O'Brien (1857) – transfer to GPM
    (1897)
   Margaret Lynch (1894)
   Hannah Murphy (1895)
   Catherine Goggin (1897)
   Mary O'Connor (1897)

   Catherine Leahy (1897)
   Margaret Lyster (1897)
   Catherine Sheehan (1897)
Flowers
   Eleanor Hardwick (1894): *(and gold fish)*
   E.J. Barton (1894)
Fruit
   Bridget Barrett and Mary Coughlan (1895)
   William Hosford (1894)

Fowl Gallery
   Catherine Riordan (1894)
   Stephen Sullivan (1897)
   Abby Twomey (1900)
   Eliza Harrison (1903)
   Ellen Kelly (1903. 1907)
   John Hartnett (1903)
Butter and eggs
   1896: minutes mention that the Princes
   Street Market has four butter stalls.

1908 – 1933

Grand Parade Market
1   Thomas J. Murphy (1912 - 28): *eggs,
    poultry and provisions* / Bridget Dee
    (1928) / Mary Savage (1928) /
    Denis Desmond (1931 -): *provisions*
2   Thomas J. Murphy (1912 - 28): *eggs,
    poultry and provisions* / Bridget Dee
    (1928) / Mary Savage (1928) /
    Denis Desmond (1931 -): *provisions*
3   William McNamara
4   William McNamara
5   Maurice Coughlan / vacant (1911) /
    Denis Nolan (1912-20) / John O'Neill
    (1922) / Margaret Cussen (1925) / Mary
    Corbett (1927) / Martin Collins (1928) /
    May Magner (1931 - 33)
6   vacant / Denis O'Connell (1911) /
    Hanora Barrett (1913): *tripe* /
    Monica McGuire (1922): *tripe*
7   Timothy Buckley / Denis O'Connell (1911)
    / Hanora Barrett (1913): *tripe* /
    Monica McGuire (1922): *tripe*
8   John Murphy / Hugh Looney (1911) /
    John Looncy (1922)
9   Hugh Looney / John Looney (1922)
10 John Manley / James Ryan / Michael
    Ryan (1911) / William Buckley (1914) /
    Denis Hawkes (1919) /
    Maria Dineen (1925): *butter and eggs*
11 John Manley / James Ryan (1908) /
    James Spillane (1914)
12 William Dillon / James Spillane (1911)
13 William Dillon / Michael Bresnan (1911) /
    Julia Bresnan (1921) / John Bresnan (1928)
14 Mrs Nolan / Michael Bresnan (1911) /
    Julia Bresnan (1921) / John Bresnan (1928)
15 Edmond Murphy / James Humphreys

    (1908) / James Walsh (1914) / Phillip
    Hussey (1915) / Michael Bresnan (1917)
    / Miss Julia Ryan (1920): *butter and eggs*
    / James Ryan (1923) /
    Dominic O'Brien (1924) /
    Mary C. Dwane (1930): *butter and eggs*
16 James Hayes / Miss Lizzie Hayes (1914)
17 John Callaghan / William Looney (1908)
    / Miss Jane Looney (1917) / William
    Hayes (1926) / William Finn (1927)
18 Bridget Ahern / John Finn (1910) / John
    Lisson (1911) / Wilfred Lisson (1924)
19 John Lisson / Daniel O'Sullivan (1923) /
    Wilfred Lisson (1924)
20 John Lisson / Ellen O'Flynn / Secretary,
    Blind Asylum (1910): *baskets* / Helena
    Corcoran (1920) / Madge O'Leary
    (1923): *butter and eggs* / vacant (1929) /
    Norah Healy, 'The Lily Dairy' (1928)
21 William Looney / Mary Anne Foley
    (1911-16) / Henry Drury (1920) / Roger
    O'Donnell (1920) / P. Dwane (1922)
    / Frank Lawton (1922): *'provisions'* /
    Ellen Crowley, 'The Lily Dairy' (1924) /
    Roger O'Donnell (1928) / vacant (1930)
    / A. Horgan (1931 -): *grocer*
22 David Leahy / Mary Leahy / Annie Leahy
    (1911) / Denis Ahern (1927)
23 Michael Ahern / Denis Ahern (1911) /
    Michael Foley (1926) / William Foley
    (1929)
24 William Foley / Mary Anne Foley (1911) /
    Michael Foley (1924) /
    William Foley (1927)
25 *WEIGHING SCALES* / John J. O'Neill
    (1929)
26 George Griffin / Patrick Sheridan (1908) /
    Timothy Morrissey (1917)
27 George Griffin / Patrick Sheridan (1908) /
    Timothy Morrissey (1917)
28 George Griffin / Timothy Morrissey (1908)
    / Margaret Cussen (1918) / 'Macroom
    Dairy' (1919) / Catherine Cash (1924)
29 Edmond Murphy / Sarah Murphy (1911)
    / Thomas Murphy (1928)
30 vacant /Vincent Twomey (1911)
31 Johanna Manley / Arthur Russell (1910):
    flowers, fruit and vegetables / vacant
    (1911) / vacant (1915) / John O'Flynn
    (1918): *butter and eggs* / Nicholas
    Tarrant, 'The Combine' (1919) / vacant
    (1920) / Patrick Mullane (1921): *butter
    and eggs* / Mary Mullane (1927)
32 Charles Manley / Arthur Russell (1910):
    flowers, fruit and vegetables / vacant
    (1911) / vacant (1915) / John O'Flynn
    (1918): *butter and eggs* / Nicholas
    Tarrant, 'The Combine' (1919) / Norah
    Wallace (1921) / John Long (1922) /
    Patrick Mullane (1924): *butter and eggs*
    / Peg Mullane (1926) / Michael Lucey
    (1927) / T. O'Shea, 'Farm Products' (1933)

33 Charles Manley / Cornelius Curtin (pre 1908) / Arthur Russell (1910): *flowers, fruit and vegetables* / vacant (1911) / vacant (1915) / John O'Shea (1917)

34 William Dillon / David Walsh (1911) / James McPherson (1927) / Augustine O'Flynn (1927) / Augustine O'Flynn (1932): *fruit*

35 Hannah Murphy / John Murphy (1911)

36 John Murphy

37 Matthew Olden / Katherine Olden (1919-) / Miss K. Quinlan (1932 -): *Butter and eggs)*

38 Thomas Griffin / Garrett Preston (1911) / Cornelius Cremen (1924) / Denis Nolan (1925)

39 Francis Coffey / Garrett Preston (1911) / Cornelius Cremen (1924) / Denis Nolan (1925)

40A Miss Murphy (1924): *butter and eggs* / void (1925)

40 Cornelius Millard / John Treacy (1911) / Norah Healy (1920): *butter and eggs* / Nan Murphy (1921): *butter and eggs* / Mary Keane (1925): *butter and eggs* / Augustine O'Flynn (1931): *fruit* / Miss C. O'Halloran (1932): *fruit*

41 John Treacy

42 Daniel Donovan / John Tracey (1911)

43 Daniel Donovan / William Smiddy (1909) / Thomas Murphy (1914) / vacant (1919) / John Murphy (1918) / Kate McGeoghegan (1921) / Mary Sullivan (1920) / J. Sullivan (1922) / Edward Lynch (1923) / Bartholomew Donovan (1924) / James McPherson (1926) / Patrick Buckley (1927) / Anne Buckley (1931): *fruit*

44 John Buckley / Anne Buckley (1908): *fowl and lamb & tripe and drisheen*

45 William Dunlea / David Walsh (1910) / David Walsh (1932): *fruit, etc.* / Augustine O'Flynn (1933): *fruit, etc.*

46 Ignatius O'Flynn / Timothy Morrissey (1913 -16) / Cornelius O'Flynn (1916) / Mary Clancy or Canty (1919) / Katherine Spillane (1925) / John Riordan (1930) / (1931): *butter and eggs*

47 vacant / Iganatious O'Flynn (1911) / Timothy Morrissey (1913 -16) / Cornelius O'Flynn (1916) / vacant (1919) / Kitty O'Donovan (1920): *butter and eggs*

48 Bridget Geany / Margaret Kennedy (1910): *fowl and lamb & tripe and drisheen* / Katherine Spillane / Joseph Spillane (1915)

49 vacant / Katherine Spillane (1908) / void (1922-29) / Joseph Spillane (1930)

50 Joseph Hayes / Jeremiah Barrett / William Buckley (1910) / Jeremiah Barrett (1917): *tripe* / Miss Buckley (1924): *butter* / William Buckley (1925): *butter* / Michael O'Sullivan (1927) / John O'Flynn (1927-) / Joseph Spillane (1932)

51 Hannah Browne / Denis O'Callaghan (1911) / Mrs Cronin (1931): *butter and eggs* / Mrs A. Hennessy (1932): *butter and eggs*

52 Denis O'Callaghan / F. Ashbourne (1931): *vegetables* / vacant (1932) / Miss K. Caulfield (1933): *fruit*

53 Anne Waugh / John Waugh (1911)

54 Anne Waugh / John Waugh (1911)

55 George Griffin / Annie Griffin (1915)

56 George Griffin / John Waugh (1908)

57 Charles Hayes & Sons / Timothy Coughlan (1908-): *tripe* / Jeremiah Coughlan (1915-): *tripe* / Timothy Coughlan (1919): *tripe*

58   Charles Hayes & Sons / Jeremiah Hayes
      (1911) / Timothy Coughlan (1919)
58a   Hannah Coughlan (1916) / Charlotte
      Cremar (1923): 'provisions' / James
      Rattigan (1926) / Norah O'Keeffe (1928)
      / Mary O'Brien (1928)
59   Charles Hayes & Sons /
      John V. Barrett (1911)
60   Charles Hayes & Sons /
      John V. Barrett (1911)
61   Frank Duke / Jane Duke (1908)
62   Frank Duke / Jane Duke (1908)
63   Frank Duke / Jane Duke (1908)
64   Michael Barrett
65   Michael Barrett
66   Mary A. Sheehan / Denis O'Flynn (1911)
      / Cornelius O'Flynn (1917) /
      John O'Flynn (1925) /
      Cornelius O'Flynn (1927)
67   Mary Spillane (1908) /
      Peter Spillane (1920)
68   Maurice O'Keeffe / Cornelius O'Flynn
      (1910) / James Condon (1918) /
      John Condon (1925) / Hugh Buckley
      (1926) / Hugh Looney (1929)
69   Denis Fitzgerald / James Condon (1911) /
      John Condon (1925) /
      Michael Ahern (1925)
70   William Dunlea / Ignatiious O'Flynn
      (1911) / Ellen O'Flynn (1912)
71   William Smiddy / Joseph Flynn (1924)
      / Augustine O'Flynn (1925) /
      J.B. O'Flynn (1931 -)
71a   Michael Connery (1924)
72   William Smiddy / Patrick Sheridan (1924)
      / Augustine O'Flynn (1928) /
      Christina Connery (1930)
73   Hannah Murphy / William Smiddy (1909)
      / Honora Murphy (1911) /
      Thomas McNamara (1911)
74   Felix Mullen / Cornelius Duggan (1910) /
      Thomas Murphy (1920) /
      Mary Dullea (1926 -): butter and eggs
75   Hannah Murphy / Cornelius Duggan (1910)
      / Thomas Murphy (1924)
76   Mary Daly / William Smiddy (1911) /
      Mrs McCarthy, 'The Bantry Fish Store'
      (1921) / Augustine O'Flynn (1924)
77   Honora Finn / Mary Finn (1909) /
      John Finn (1910) / Annie O'Flynn (1913)
      / Phillip Hussey (1916) /
      Nancy McCarthy (1920)
78   Charles Hayes & Sons / Mary Finn (1909)
      / John Finn (1910)

Grand Parade Market
Fish stalls
1   Michael Sheehan /
     Michael and Edward Sheehan (1911)
2   Michael Sheehan /
     Michael and Edward Sheehan (1911)

3   Patrick Sugrue / James Carroll (1911) /
     Michael and Edward Sheehan (1915) /
     John and James Sheehan (1920)
4   Joseph Carroll / James Carroll (1911) /
     Michael and Edward Sheehan (1915) /
     John and James Sheehan (1920)
5   Cornelius Geary /
     Patrick O'Leary Jnr. (1911)
6   Patrick O'Leary Jnr./ Hannah O'Leary
     (1911) / John Waugh (1916) /
     Caroline Coughlan (1921) /
     Lena O'Connell (1924)
7   Patrick O'Leary Jnr. / Hannah O'Leary
     (1911) / John Finn (1915): meat /
     Caroline Coughlan (1921)
8   Ellen Sheehan / Hannah Kelly (1911) /
     Michael O'Donoghue (1924) /
     C.P. Corbett (1933)
9   Patrick Sugrue (1908) / Gerald Griffin
     (1912) / Maurice O'Reilly (1915)
10   John O'Connor /
     Agnes O'Reilly (1920): tripe
11   P. Brown /
     Bartholomew O'Donovan (1911)
12   James Quain / James Quain Jnr. (1923) /
     Ernest Walsh (1926)
13   Ellen Corcoran /
     Michael and Edward Sheehan (1911)
14   Bartholomew Brown / Maggie Murphy
     (1910) / Hannah Brown (1911) /
     Michael and Edward Sheehan (1915)
15   Patrick Sugrue (1908) / vacant (1911) /
     Michael and Edward Sheehan (1915)
16   Mary Clancy / vacant (1911-) /
     Michael and Edward Sheehan (1918) /
     Nancy McCarthy (1926)

Princes Street Market
Meat
1   George Paul / Kate Paul
2   Samuel Dillon
3   Samuel Dillon
4   John Griffin / Samuel Dillon (1911)
5   Catherine Griffin / Catherine Whelan
     (1911) / Catherine Griffin (1915) /
     Patrick Griffin (1918)
6   James Whelan / Margaret Whelan (1911)

Former vegetable stalls, converted to meat
6   William Dillon (1930) / J. Gleeson (1934)
7   William Dillon (1930) / J. Gleeson (1934)
8   Jeremiah Hayes (1917): meat, tripe and
     vegetables / Mark Buckley (1924-29)
9   Jeremiah Hayes (1917): meat, tripe and
     vegetables / Mark Buckley (1924-29)
10   Jeremiah Hayes (1917): meat, tripe and
     vegetables / John Waugh (1926)
11   John Waugh (1926)
12   John Waugh (1926)
17   W. Murphy (1930)
18   W. Murphy (1930)

Poultry, butter and eggs
1   John Hartnett (1912): poultry /
     Bridget Lucey (1923) / vacant (1929)
2   John Hartnett (1912): poultry /
     Bridget Lucey (1923-25) / vacant (1929)
3   Norah Lane (1916) / Norah Kelly (1929) /
     vacant (1931) / W. Lane (1933): poultry
4   Norah Lane (1916) / vacant (1920) /
     Norah Kelly (1929) / vacant (1931 -) /
     W. Lane (1934): poultry
6   Ellen Kelly (1912): poultry / vacant (1920 -)
     / Kate Murphy (1921) / Mary Mulcahy
     (1922) / John Hartigan (1924): meat
7   Ellen Kelly (1912): poultry / vacant (1929)
8   Ellen Kelly (1912): poultry / vacant (1930)
9   Richard Cross (1908) / Mrs J. Cross (1912)
     / Lizzie Dorgan (1913-28): poultry /
     void (1929)
10   Richard Cross (1908) / Mrs J. Cross (1912)
     / Lizzie Dorgan (1913-28): poultry /
     vacant (1929)
11   Richard Cross (1908) / Mrs J. Cross (1912)
     / Lizzie Dorgan (1913): poultry
13   Mary J. Scannell (1911): butter and eggs
14   Mary J. Scannell (1916): butter and eggs
15   Mary Hurley (pre-1916) /
     Lillie Hurley (1918 -): butter and eggs
16   Catherine Moynihan (1916) /
     Mary Lynch (1926) /
     Miss B. O'Connor (1933): butter and eggs

Vegetables and fruit
1   Ellen Kelly (1909) / Ellen McKee (1909) /
     James F. O'Leary (1918 -): tripe, etc.
2   Margaret Lyster (1909) /
     James F. O'Leary (1918): tripe, etc.
3   Ellen Daly (pre-1916) / vacant (1919)
     / Margaret Lyster (1920) / Margaret
     Joyce (1922) / Bridget Joyce (1925)
4   Abina Hyde (1916)
5   Abina Hyde (1916) /
     Bridget Connell (1929)
6   Lizzie Kelleher (1911) / Bridget Connell
     (1916) / Patrick Sheridan (1927) / 1930:
     becomes meat stall (see above)
7   Ellen McCarthy (pre-1910) / Bridget
     Connell (1910) / Patrick Sheridan (1927)
     / 1930: becomes meat stall (see above)
8   Catherine Sheehan / Jeremiah Hayes (1918)
     / Anna Flood (1930): fruit and vegetables
9   Catherine Sheehan / Jeremiah Hayes (1918)
     / Bridget Troy (1923) /
     Anna Flood (1930): fruit and vegetables
10   Mary O'Connor / Catherine Desmond
     (1917) / vacant (1925) / 1926: becomes
     meat stall (see above)
11   Catherine Goggin (1897-): 1926: becomes
     meat stall (see above)
12   Catherine Goggin (1897-): 1926: becomes
     meat stall (see above)

17 Jeremiah Riordan (1914) / vacant (1917) / Mary J. Scannell (1918) / Miss Christina Barry (1919) / Margaret O'Connor (1920) / Peg Duggan (1922) / Maragret Kiely (1928) / vacant (1929) / *1930: becomes meat stall (see above)*

18 Jeremiah Riordan (1914) / vacant (1917) / Mary J. Scannell (1918) / Miss Christina Barry (1919) / Margaret O'Connor (1920) / Peg Duggan (1922) / Anne Cadogan (1926) / Margaret Kiely (1928) / vacant (1929) / *1930: becomes meat stall (see above)*

19 Bridget Hayes (pre-1909) / Catherine Hayes (1909) / Thomas J. Murphy (1911) / Catherine Coughlan (1913) / Margaret Kiely (1919) / Miss Christina Barry (1920) / Peg Duggan (1921) / Daniel O'Sullivan (1923) / Anne Cadogan (1926)

Source: Valuation Books, Valuation Office, Dublin; *Guy's Directory* (1910-33); *Purcell's Directory* (1918); Cork Corporation Tolls and Markets Committee Minute Books, 1908-1928.

1934 – 1949

Grand Parade Market

1 Denis Desmond: *provisions*
2 Denis Desmond: *provisions*
3 William McNamara / Mrs B. McNamara (1935-) / Sean O'Flynn (1943)
4 William McNamara / Mrs B. McNamara (1935-) / Sean O'Flynn (1943)
5 Mrs Lynch: *butter and eggs* / Miss Francis (1935): *butter and eggs* / Miss Finn (1938): *butter and eggs* / Francis Finn (1949)
6 Denis O'Connell / Denis O'Connell Jnr. (1938): *butter and eggs* / vacant (1943) / Francis Finn (1949)
7 Denis O'Connell / Denis O'Connell Jnr. (1938): *butter and eggs* / vacant (1943) / Mathew Ahern (1949)
8 John Looney
9 John Looney
10 Maria Dineen: *butter and eggs*
11 James Spillane
12 James Spillane
13 J. Bresnan / Miss S. Bresnan (1935)
14 J. Bresnan / Miss S. Bresnan (1935)
15 Mary C. Dwane: *butter and eggs* / vacant (1938) / P. Bresnan (1941)
16 Miss Lizzie Hayes
17 William Finn / vacant (1935-) / W. Lisson (1940) / Patrick Looney (1945)
18 W. Lisson / P. Dwane (1940) / vacant (1942) / John Nagle & Son (1943)

19 W. Lisson / P. Dwane (1940) / vacant (1942) / John Nagle & Son (1943)
20 Norah Healy, The Lily Dairy / vacant (1935-) / Daniel Kelly (1940)
21 A. Horgan: *grocer*
22 Denis Ahern / Mrs K. Ahern (1940)
23 William Foley / M. Foley (1935)
24 William Foley / M. Foley (1935)
25 John J. O'Neill
26 Timothy Morrissey
27 Timothy Morrissey
28 Macroom Dairy – Mrs Cussen
29 Thomas Murphy
30 Vincent Twomey / vacant (1942) / P. Bresnan (1944)
31 Mary Mullane / Mrs C. Mullane (1940): *butter and eggs* Mrs Lomabrd (1941): *butter and eggs* / Miss M. Donovan (1944): *fruit and vegetables*
32 Miss Daly: *butter and eggs* / vacant (1940)
33 John O'Shea / James Spillane (1935) / vacant (1938)
34 Augustine O'Flynn: *fruit* / Gus Healy (1938): *fruit*
35 John Murphy / vacant (1942)
36 John Murphy / vacant (1942)
37 vacant / M. O'Mahony (1941) / A. Lynch (1942)
38 Denis Nolan / vacant (1935) / Miss Lynch (1938): *fruit and vegetables* / John Lynch (1940): *fruit* / vacant (1942) / Michael Ahern (1944)
39 Denis Nolan / vacant (1935) / Miss Lynch (1938): *fruit and vegetables* / John Lynch (1940): *fruit* / vacant (1942) / Mrs Lombard (1944): *butter and eggs*
40 Miss C. O'Halloran: *fruit* / W. Mack (1935): *fruit* / vacant (1940)
41 John Treacy / vacant (1942)
42 John Treacy / vacant (1942) / M. O'Flaherty (1944)
43 Anne Buckley: *fruit* / vacant (1938) / Mrs E. Brady (1944): *vegetables and provisions*
44 Anne Buckley / vacant (1938)
45 Augustine O'Flynn: *fruit, etc.* / Mrs N. O'Flynn (1935): *fruit* / vacant (1938) / Gus Healy (1940): *fruit*
46 John Riordan: *butter and eggs*
47 K. O'Donovan: *butter and eggs* / vacant (1940)
48 Joseph Spillane / Peter Spillane (1937) / vacant (1940)
49 Joseph Spillane / Peter Spillane (1937) / Miss C. Spillane (1940) / William Richard (1944)
50 Joseph Spillane / Mrs A. Hennessy (*butter and eggs* (1935)
51 Mrs A. Hennessy: *butter and eggs* / vacant (1935-)

52 C. O'Herlihy: *fruit* / vacant (1935) / Miss E. Looney (1940): *fruit* / vacant (1944)
53 John Waugh
54 John Waugh
55 Annie Griffin / L. Griffin (1935) / N. Griffin (1938) / Leo Griffin (1940)
56 John Waugh
57 Timothy Coughlan: *tripe* / vacant (1935) / Mrs C. O'Sullivan (1940): *tripe*
58 Timothy Coughlan / Mrs M. Cronin (1935) / vacant (1940)
58a Mary O'Brien / vacant (1938) / vacant (1940)
58b Mary O'Brien (1937) / vacant (1942)
59 John V. Barrett
60 John V. Barrett
61 Jane Duke / Frank Duke (1935)
62 Jane Duke / vacant (1935) / Frank Duke (1940)
63 Jane Duke / vacant (1935) / John Waugh (1940) / vacant (1942)
64 Michael Barrett / Joe Barrett (1940)
65 Michael Barrett / Joe Barrett (1940)
66 Cornelius O'Flynn / P. O'Flynn (1935)
67 Peter Spillane / vacant (1937) / P. O'Flynn (1940)
68 Hugh Looney
69 Michael Ahern / vacant (1944)
70 Ellen O'Flynn / Ben O'Flynn (1937)
71 J.B. O'Flynn / Michael Connery (1935)
71a Michael Connery / void (1935)
72 Christina Connery
73 Thomas McNamara
74 Mary Dullea: *butter and eggs* / Mrs C. Bannon (1935): *butter and eggs* / Mrs Bannon (1940): *fruit*
75 Thomas Murphy
76 The Bantry Fish Store / J.B. O'Flynn (1935) / vacant (1938) / J.B O'Flynn (1942)
77 John Finn / Mrs N. McCarthy (1935-): *fish*
78 John Finn
3 Thomas Daly (1942)
4 B. Walsh (1942)
5 B. Walsh (1942)
6 vacant (1942)
7 vacant (1942)

Grand Parade Market – fish stalls
1 Michael and Edward Sheehan / John Sheehan (1935)
2 Michael and Edward Sheehan / John Sheehan (1935)
3 John Sheehan / William Kidney (1935)
4 John Sheehan / William Kidney (1939)
5 Patrick O'Leary Jnr.
6 Lena O'Connell
7 John Finn
8 C.B. Corbett / Ellen Corbett (1942)
9 Maurice O'Reilly: *tripe and drisheen*
10 Agnes O'Reilly: *tripe and drisheen*

11 Bartholomew O'Donovan / vacant (1938)
/ E.F. Sheehan (1939)
12 Ernest Walsh / D. Donovan (1935)
13 Michael and Edward Sheehan / vacant
(1935) / William O' Regan (1944)
14 Michael and Edward Sheehan / vacant
(1935) / Denis Mortell (1940) /
John Sheehan (1944)
15 Michael and Edward Sheehan / vacant
(1935) / P. Scanlon (1944)
16 Michael and Edward Sheehan / P. Scanlon
(1935)
18 J. Finn (1935) / vacant (1937) /
J. Finn (1942)

Princes Street Market
Meat
1 George Paul / Kate Paul / void (1939)
2 Samuel Dillon
3 Samuel Dillon / Mrs J. Murphy (1939)
4 Samuel Dillon / Patrick Griffin (1939) /
Daniel O'Sullivan (1942): *poultry*
5 Patrick Griffin / Francis Dillon (1939)
6 Margaret Whelan / Mrs Julia Murphy
(1935) / Francis Dillon (1939)
8 Kate Paul (1939) / Tom Paul (1943)
- J. O'Flynn (1943)
Former vegetable stalls, converted to meat
6 J. Gleeson / void (1939)
7 J. Gleeson / Francis Dillon (1939)
10 John Waugh
11 John Waugh
12 John Waugh
17 W. Murphy / vacant (1942)
18 W. Murphy / vacant (1942)
Poultry, butter and eggs
8 W. Lane: *poultry*
9 W. Lane: *poultry*
9 J.J. O'Neill (1935): *poultry*
10 Lizzie Dorgan: *poultry* / void (1939)
19 Daniel O'Sullivan (1939): *poultry*
13 Mary J. Scannell: *butter and eggs*
14 Mary J. Scannell: *butter and eggs*
15 Lillie Hurley: *butter and eggs*
16 Miss B. O'Connor: *butter and eggs* / Miss
M. Murray (1945): *butter and eggs*
Vegetables
1 J.F. O'Leary: *tripe, etc.*
2 J.F. O'Leary: *tripe, etc.*
3 Bridget Joyce / Mrs M. Crowley (1939)
4 Abina Hyde / Mrs A. Lombard (1939) /
vacant (1942) / Miss E. Looney (1944)
5 Bridget Connell / G. Murphy (1942) /
Miss N. Hannigan (1943)
6 vacant / Miss M. Moynihan (1939): *fruit*
/ (1944): *poultry and eggs*
7 vacant / Miss M. Moynihan (1939): *fruit*
/ (1944): *poultry and eggs*
8 Anna Flood: *fruit, etc.* / vacant (1935)
/ Miss C. O'Sullivan (1939): *fruit* / (1943):
poultry and eggs

9 Anna Flood: *fruit, etc.* / vacant (1935)
/ Miss C. O'Sullivan (1939): *fruit* /
(1943): *poultry and eggs*
- M.J. Crowley (1938)

Gallery
4 Mrs N. Kelly (1939): *poultry*
9 J.J. O'Neill (1939): *sausages*

Source: Valuation Books, Valuation Office,
Dublin; *Guy's Directory* (1934-45).

Note: information for the the 1950s-
1990s comes from assorted newspapaer
advertisements and articles, and the
recollections of individuals associated with
the Market, especially Simon O'Flynn, Paul
Murphy, Jim Cosgrave, Noel Murphy, Mary
Rose, Jack Burke, and William Martin.

1950s

Grand Parade
– Denis Desmond: *provisions*
– John O'Flynn
– Mathew Ahern
– Denis Ahern
– Hughie Ahern
– John Looney
– Maria Dineen: *butter and eggs*
– James Spillane
– Patrick Bresnan
– Lizzie Hayes / Paddy O'Sullivan
– Patrick Looney
– John Nagle & Son
– Daniel Kelly
– A. Horgan: *grocer*
– Mrs K. Ahern
– Michael Foley
– John J. O'Neill
– Timothy Morrissey
– Macroom Dairy – Mrs Cussen
– Thomas Murphy
– Miss M. Donovan: *fruit and vegetables*
– A. Lynch
– Michael Ahern
– Mrs Lombard: *butter and eggs*
– M. O'Flaherty
– Mrs E. Brady: *vegetables and provisions*
– John Riordan: *butter and eggs*
– Billy Richard
– Mrs A. Hennessy: *butter and eggs*
– John Waugh
– Leo Griffin
– John V. Barrett
– Frank Duke
– Joe Barrett
– P. O'Flynn
– Hugh Looney
– Benny O'Flynn

– Michael Connery / Christina Connery /
Liam Connery
– Thomas McNamara
– Patsy Coughlan
– Mrs Bannon: *fruit*
– Thomas Murphy
– James B. O'Flynn
– Mrs N. McCarthy: *fish*
– John Finn
– Thomas Daly
– A. Walsh
– Richard Short & Sons
– Kathleen Noonan: *pork and bacon*
– W. Collins: *bacon and hams*
– Bert Bagnall: *fruit*
– Redmond Roche: *bacon, eggs, butter*
– M. and J. O'Connor: *fruit, vegetables,
flowers*
– John Lane ('Chicken Inn'): *poultry*
– Babe Ann Kane: *pig offal*
– Peggy O'Regan: *tripe and drisheen*

Fish Market
– Michael and Edward (M. & E.) Sheehan
– William Kidney
– Patrick O'Leary Jnr.
– Lena O'Connell
– Francis & John Finn: *butchers*
– Ellen Corbett
– Maurice O'Reilly: *tripe and drisheen*
– Agnes O'Reilly: *tripe and drisheen*
– Denis O'Donovan
– Bill O'Regan
– J. & J. Sheehan
– Pat Scannell
– Crotty: 'Baltimore Fish'

Princes Street
– Mrs Ahern: *fruit and vegetables*
– Samuel Dillon
– Francis Dillon
– Mrs J. Murphy
– Chrissie, Danny & Aggie O'Sullivan:
poultry
– Tom Paul
– J. O'Flynn
– J.J. O'Neill: *poultry*
– Mary J. Scannell: *butter and eggs*
– Lillie Hurley: *butter and eggs*
– Nan Murray: *butter and eggs*
– J.F. O'Leary: *tripe, etc.*
– Mrs M. Crowley: *fruit and vegetables*
– Miss E. Looney: *fruit and vegetables*
– Miss N. Hannigan: *fruit and vegetables*
– Miss M. Moynihan: *poultry and eggs*
– M.J. Crowley

Gallery
– Mrs N. Kelly: *poultry*
– John J. O'Neill: *sausages*

Above: William Martin, Grand Parade Fish Market.

1960s

Grand Parade
- Stephen O'Reilly: *tripe and drisheen*
- Patrick Rose
- John Rose
- Richard Rose
- Byrnes: *pork butchers*
- Patrick Bresnan
- Paddy O'Sullivan / Tim O'Sullivan
- Stephen Coughlan
- Patrick Looney
- Hugh Looney
- John Nagle & Son
- Leo Griffin / T.V. (Vincey) Nolan
- John Waugh
- Patsy Coughlan / Pearse Coughlan
- John V. Barrett
- Frank Duke
- John O'Flynn & Sons
- Benny O'Flynn
- Mathew Ahern
- Denis Ahern
- Hughie Ahern
- Michael Ahern
- Thomas McNamara
- Liam Connery
- Kathleen Noonan: *pork and bacon*
- John J. O'Neill
- Thomas Murphy
- P. O'Flynn
- Hennessy
- John Lane: 'The Chicken Inn'
- Bert Bagnall: *fruit*
- Thomas McNamara
- Maria Dineen: *butter and eggs*
- James Spillane
- Michael Foley
- Billy Richard
- Richard Short & Sons
- Redmond Roche: *bacon, eggs, butter*
- M. and J. O'Connor: *fruit, vegetables, flowers*
- Macroom Dairy
- Mrs Bannon: *fruit*
- Babe Ann Kane: *pig offal*
- Peggy O'Regan: *tripe and drisheen*

Fish Market
- M. & E. Sheehan
- William Kidney
- Patrick O'Leary Jnr.
- Kathleen O'Connell
- Francis & John Finn: *butchers*
- Ellen Corbett
- Maurice O'Reilly: *tripe and drisheen*
- Denis O'Donovan
- Bill O'Regan
- J. & J. Sheehan
- Pat Scannell
- Vincey Nolan

- Willie Mulcahy
- Crotty: 'Baltimore Fish'

Princes Street
- Eileen Ahern
- Siobhan Ahern
- Tom Paul
- Samuel Dillon
- Francis Dillon
- Chrissie, Danny & Aggie O'Sullivan: *poultry*
- Nan Murray: *butter and eggs*
- Bridget McDonnell: *fruit and vegetables*
- Gawsworth: *poultry, eggs, garden produce*
- Redmond Roche: *bacon, eggs, butter*

1970s

Grand Parade
- Stephen O'Reilly: *tripe and drisheen*
- Patrick Rose / Michael O'Donoghue
- Byrne's: *pork butchers*
- Noel Lucey
- Michael Bresnan & Sons
- Tim O'Sullivan
- Stephen Coughlan
- Mary O'Connor
- Mrs K. O'Reilly
- Denis Ahern
- Mary O'Neill
- John Lane / Mary Mulcahy: 'The Chicken Inn'
- Phillip Murphy
- Mrs E. Treacy
- Timmy Coughlan
- Peter Hegarty
- Bert Bagnall: *fruit*
- Paul Boyling
- W.F. Murphy: *fruit*
- Kathleen Noonan: *pork and bacon*
- Paddy Short
- Mrs P. Murphy
- John Rose
- John Coughlan
- T.V. (Vincey) Nolan / Barry Collins
- Pearse Coughlan / Paul Murphy
- Margaret O'Regan
- John V. Barrett / Denis O'Sullivan & Tom Morgan
- Jackie Buckley
- Harrington's Cakes
- Gerald O'Flynn
- D. Fitzpatrick
- F. McNamara
- Bridget Desmond
- Peggy O'Regan: *tripe and drisheen*

- Babe Ann Kane: *pig offal*
- M. Nagle
- K. O'Callaghan
- Thomas Murphy / Katherine O'Mahony
- Thomas McNamara / Ashley O'Neill
- Ken Barrett

Fish Market
- Francis and John Finn: *butchers*
- Willie Mulcahy
- Vincey Nolan
- M. O'Reilly: *tripe and drisheen*
- M.& S. O'Reilly: *tripe and drisheen*
- M. & E. Sheehan
- J. & J. Sheehan
- Mrs B. O' Donovan:
- Bill O'Regan
- Kathleen O'Connell
- Pat Scannell
- John Burke / Jack and Marian Burke
- William Kidney
- W. Murphy
- Mrs O'Leary

Princes Street
- Eileen (Ahern) Kearns: *fruit and vegetables*
- Siobhan (Ahern) O'Connor: *fruit and vegetables*
- Gertrude Casey: *fruit and vegtables*
- Bridget McDonnell: *fruit and vegetables*
- Gerry Moynihan: *poultry*
- Nan Murray / Pat & Eileen Kelleher
- Dick Rose
- Florence O'Mahony
- Chrissy O'Sullivan / James Landers
- John O'Flynn
- Don O'Hare / Donal O'Hare
- 'Farmhouse Cakes'

1980s

Grand Parade
- Stephen O'Reilly: *tripe and drisheen*
- Michael O'Donoghue
- Byrne's Pork Butchers
- Noel Lucey
- Michael Bresnan & Sons
- Tim O'Sullivan
- Paul Mulvany: 'Dazzle'/'Sonic' (Rave Cave)
- Patrick O'Connor
- Mrs K. O'Reilly
- Denis Ahern
- Mary and Jack Mulcahy: 'The Chicken Inn'

- Driss Belmajoub: 'Mr Bell's'
- Michael Corrigan: 'Superfruit'
- Michael Herlihy: 'The Farmer'
- Phillip Murphy
- 'MK Cakes'
- Mrs E. Treacy
- Peter Hegarty
- Paul Boyling
- Michael Murphy: *fruit*
- Kathleen Noonan: *pork and bacon*
- Paddy Short
- Mrs P. Murphy
- T.V. Nolan / Barry Collins
- John Rose / Mary Rose
- Paul Murphy
- Margaret O'Regan
- Johnson Buckley
- Gerald O'Flynn
- D. Fitzpatrick
- Peggy O'Regan: *tripe and drisheen*
- M. Nagle
- K. O'Callaghan
- William Beechinor
- Katherine O'Mahony
- Ashley O'Neill
- Ken Barrett
- Bridget Desmond
- Paddy Joe Harrington: *cobbler*

Fish Market
- Francis and John Finn: *butchers*
- Willie Mulcahy / Cornelius Mulcahy
- M. O'Reilly: *tripe and drisheen*
- M.& S. O'Reilly: *tripe and drisheen*
- M.& E. Sheehan
- J. & J. Sheehan
- Mrs B. O' Donovan
- Bill O'Regan
- Kathleen O'Connell
- Pat Scannell
- Jack and Marian Burke
- William Martin

Princes Street
- Eileen (Ahern) Kearns/ Deirdre Kearns: *fruit and vegetables*
- Siobhan (Ahern) O'Connor: *fruit and vegetables*
- Gertrude Casey: *fruit and vegetables*
- Bridget & Paddy McDonnell: *fruit and vegetables*
- Gerry Moynihan: *poultry*
- Dick Rose
- Florence O'Mahony
- James Landers
- John O'Flynn
- Tom Durcan
- Don O'Hare / 'Old Mill Confectionery'

Gallery
- Sutcliffe Catering Company
- Martin Murray
- Máire Hanley

1990s

Grand Parade
- Stephen O'Reilly: *tripe and drisheen*
- Des Murray: 'Central Florists'
- Byrne's: *pork butchers*
- Joe Lingnane: *joke shop*
- Michael Bresnan & Sons
- Tim O'Sullivan
- Mary O'Connor
- Paul Mulvany: 'Sonic' (Rave Cave)
- Jack and Mary Mulcahy: 'The Chicken Inn'
- Driss Belmajoub: 'Mr Bell's'
- Philip Murphy
- Michael Corrigan: 'Superfruit'
- Paul Boyling
- Michael Murphy: *fruit*
- Kathleen Noonan: *pork and bacon*
- 'MK Cakes'
- Paddy Short
- Mrs P. Murphy
- Barry Collins / Isabelle Sheridan: 'On the Pig's Back'
- John Rose / Mary Rose
- Paddy Joe Harrington: *cobbler*
- Paul Murphy
- Johnson Buckley
- Harrington's Cakes
- Gerald O'Flynn / Toby Simmonds: 'Real Olive Company'
- William Beechinor
- Katherine O'Mahony
- Ashley O'Neill
- Ken Barrett
- Anne-Marie Jaumaud and Martin Guillemot: 'Maughanaclea Farm Cheeses'
- Michael and Susan Silke: *crêpes* / Joe Hegarty: 'Heaven's Cake'
- Mairead McCorley: 'Plato's': *pitta, hummus, etc.*
- 'The Kitchen Pot'
- 'Alternative Bread Company'

Fish Market
- Cornelius Mulcahy / Sean Calder-Potts: 'Iago'
- M. & E. Sheehan
- Kathleen O'Connell
- Jack and Marian Burke
- William Martin
- Shane Johnson and Greg Dowling: 'Fish Records'

Princes Street
- Eileen (Ahern) Kearns/ Deirdre Kearns: *fruit and vegetables* / Donnacha O'Callaghan: 'The Organic Garden'
- Siobhan (Ahern) O'Connor: *fruit and vegetables* / Donnacha O'Callaghan
- Paddy McDonnell: *fruit and vegetables*
- Gerry Moynihan: *poultry*
- Florence O'Mahony / 'Boys' Bakery' (Fr Rock)
- James Landers
- 'Old Mill Confectionery'
- Tom Durcan
- Stephen Landon
- Glenys Landon

Gallery
- Kay Harte and Máróg O'Brien: 'Farmgate Café and Restaurant'

2005

Princes Street
1 Donal O'Callaghan
2 Donal O'Callaghan: *organic produce*
3 Gerry Moynihan (storage)
4 Paddy McDonnell: *fruit and vegetables*
6 Gerry Moynihan
7 Gerry Moynihan: *poultry and eggs*
8 Stephen Landon: *pork and bacon*
9 Niall Daly: 'The Chocolate Shop'
10 Glenys Landon
11 Tom Durcan
12 'Old Mill Confectionary'
19 Kay Harte & Máróg O'Brien: 'Farmgate Café and Restaurant'

Grand Parade
1 Stephen O'Reilly: *tripe and drisheen*
2 Des Murray: 'Central Florists'
3 Joe Lingnane: *joke shop*
4A Michael McBarron: 'Pots and Pans'
4C 'Bubble Brothers': *wines*
5 Michael Bresnan & Sons
6 Tim O'Sullivan
7 Tim O'Sullivan
8 Tim O'Sullivan
9 Paul Mulvany
10 Paul Mulvany: 'Sonic': *clothes*
11 Isabelle Sheridan: 'On the Pig's Back'
12/24 Jack and Mary Mulcahy: 'The Chicken Inn'
14 'Fruit Boost': *juice bar*
15 Driss Belmajoub: 'Mr Bell's'
16 Ken Barret
17 Michael Corrigan
18 Michael Corrigan
19 Michael Corrigan: 'Superfruit'
20 Michael Murphy: 'The Roughty Fruit King'

21 Kathleen Noonan: *pork and bacon*
22 'Alternative Bread Company'
25 Driss Belmajoub: 'Mr Bell's'
27 Mary Rose Daly: 'Coffee Central'
28 Mark O'Mahony: 'The Organic Shop'
29 Mark O'Mahony: *organic meat*
30 Michael Herlihy: 'The Farmer'
30A Joe Hegarty: 'Heaven's Cake'
31 Paul Murphy
32 'MK Cakes'
33 Jenny Rose Clarke: 'Real Olive Company'
34 Paul Boyling
38 Paul Boyling
35 Ashley O'Neill
36 Ashley O'Neill
37 Katherine O'Mahony
39 Jenny Rose Clarke & Rachel McCormack: *salad and sandwich bar*
40 Jack and Marian Burke: 'Bandon Fish Store'
41 William Martin: *fish*
42 Sean Calder-Potts: 'Iago'
43 Paul Mulvany: 'Market Gallery'
44 P.J. Harrington: 'Paddy Joes': *cobbler and tailoring*
51 Frank Hederman: 'West Cork Smoke-House'
52 'K. O'Connell Ltd': *fish*

Oppostie page: The Grand Parade and Princes Street Markets as shown on the Goad Insurance map of 1953 (Cork City Library). The Princes Street Market is incorrectly titled the English Market.

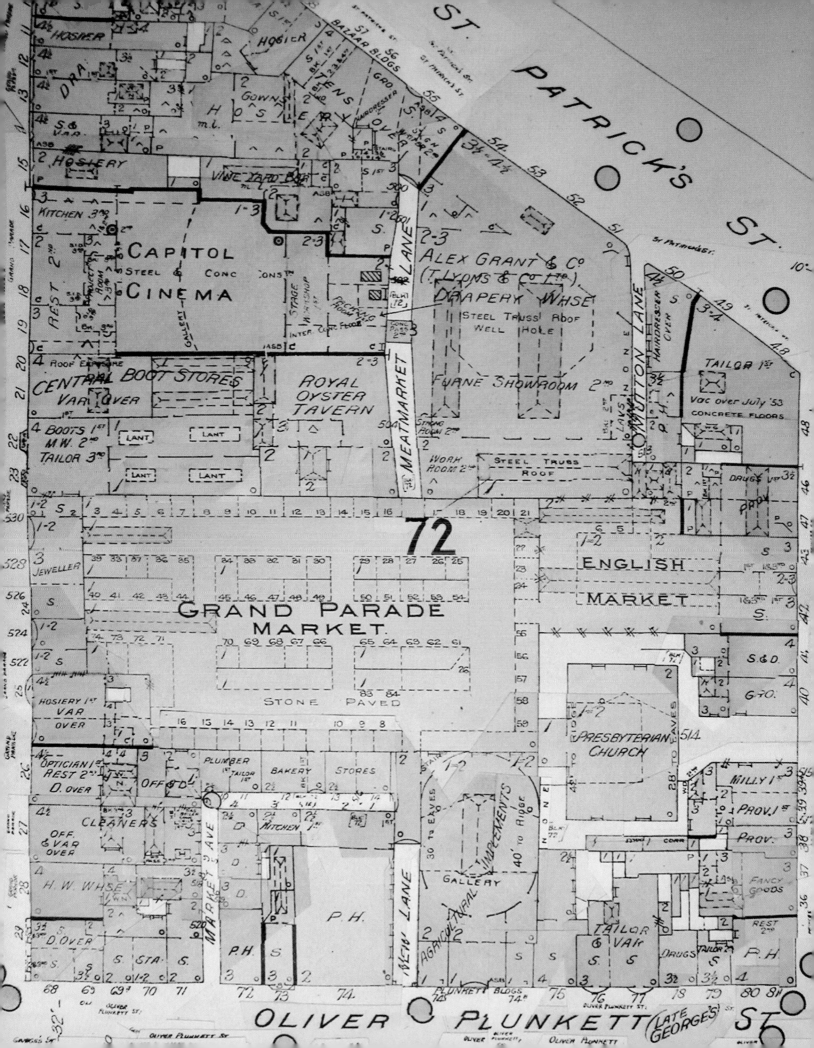

Late eighteenth-century Cork
from a map by John Rocque (Cork City Library)

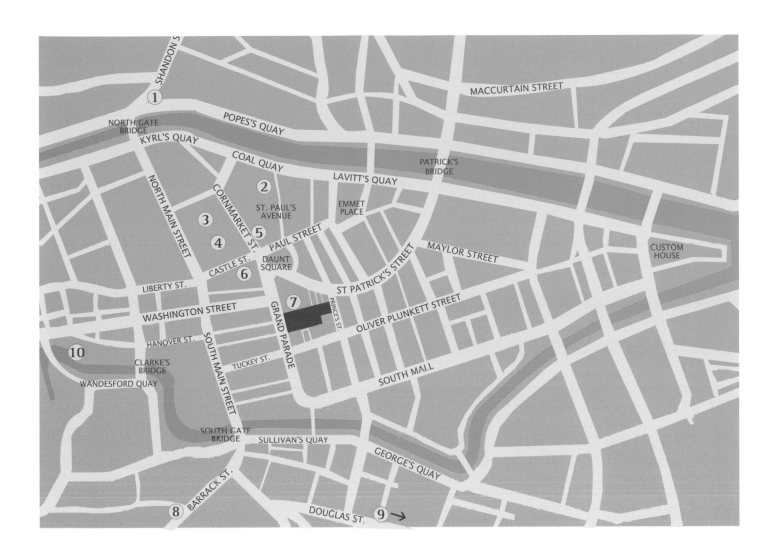

Locations of principal markets, eighteenth to twentieth century

1 North Shambles
2 Harpur's Lane Market
3 St Peter's Market
4 Bazaar Market
5 Street market, Cornmarket Street
6 Castle Street Shambles
7 English Market
8 South Shambles and St Finnbarr's Market
9 St John's Market, Douglas Street
10 Fish Market

NOTES AND REFERENCES

PREFACE
1. *Irish Examiner*, 11 December 2004.

CHAPTER 1 Cork: the making of a city
1. This section is based on a reading of a range of sources on the historical development of Cork, including: Francis H. Tuckey, *The County and City of Cork Remembrancer* (Cork, 1837); Henry Alan Jeffries, *Cork: Historical Perspectives* (Dublin, 2004); Maurice F. Hurley, 'Below Sea-Level in the City of Cork', pp 41-54, and Maura Cronin, 'From the "Flat o' the City" to the Top of the Hill: Cork since 1700', pp 55-68, in Howard B Clarke (ed.), *Irish Cities* (Cork, 1995); Gina Johnson, *The Laneways of Medieval* Cork (Cork, 2002); David Dickson, *Old World Colony: Cork and South Munster, 1630-1830* (Cork, 2005); Colin Rynne, *The Industrial Archaeology of Cork City and its Environs* (Dublin, 1999); Colman O'Mahony, *In the Shadows: Life in Cork, 1750-1930* (Cork, 1997); John Bradley and Andrew Halpin, 'The Topographical Development of Scandinavian and Anglo-Norman Cork', pp 15-44, A. F. O'Brien, 'Politics, Economy and Society: The Development of Cork and the Irish South-Coast Region c.1170 to c.1583', pp 83-154, John B. O'Brien, 'Population, Politics and Society in Cork, 1780-1900', pp 699-720, A.M. Fahy, 'Place and Class in Cork', pp 793-812, Kevin Hourihan, 'The Evolution and Influence of Town Planning in Cork', pp 941-962, in Patrick O'Flanagan and Cornelius G. Buttimer (eds), *Cork: History and Society* (Dublin, 1993); Andy Bielenberg, *Cork's Industrial Revolution 1780-1880: Development or Decline* (Cork, 1991); William O'Sullivan, *The Economic History of Cork from Earliest Times to the Act of Union* (Cork, 1937); Richard Caulfield (ed.), *The Council Book of the Corporation of the City of Cork, from 1609 to 1643 and from 1690 to 1800* (Guildford, 1876); Charles Smith, *The Ancient and Present State of the City and County of Cork,* vol. I (Dublin, 1750); Cn., 'Cork City in 1748', *Journal of the Cork Historical and Archaeological Society* (*JCHAS*), vol. 9 (1903), pp 69-72; Eugene Carberry, 'The Development of Cork City', *JCHAS*, vol. 48 (1943), pp 67-81; Helen Ryan, 'Two Inscribed Stones', *JCHAS*, vol. 49 (1944), pp 60-1;
2. William O'Sullivan, *The Economic History of Cork from Earliest Times to the Act of Union* (Cork, 1937), p. 148; Thomas Campbell, *A Philosophical Survey of the South of Ireland* (Dublin, 1778), p. 174.
3. Richard Twiss, *A Tour in Ireland in 1775* (London, 1776), quoted in Cornelius Kelly, *The Grand Tour of Cork* (Cork, 2003), p. 43.

4. Joseph Rogers, *An Essay on Epidemic Diseases* (Dublin, 1734), p. 37.
5. Quoted in Colman O'Mahony, *In the Shadows: Life in Cork, 1750-1930* (Cork, 1997), p. 52 (no source cited).

CHAPTER 2 A City of Markets
1. A.F. O'Brien, 'Politics, economy and society: the development of Cork and the Irish south coast region, c.1170 to c.1583' in Patrick O'Flanagan and Cornelius G. Buttimer (eds), *Cork: history and society* (Dublin, 1993), pp 93-4.
2. This map is reproduced in F.H. Tuckey's *The County and City of Cork Remembrancer*, first published in 1837. The caption beneath states that it was engraved 'from a Copy of an ancient Sketch in the Tower of London'.
3. Richard Caulfield (ed.), *The Council Book of the Corporation of the City of Cork, from 1609 to 1643 and from 1690 to 1800* (Guildford, 1876), entry for 27 January 1695.
4. Sean Daly, *Cork: a City in Crisis – a history of labour conflict and social misery 1870-1872* (Cork, 1978), p. 256; Henry Alan Jefferies, *Cork: Historical Perspectives* (Dublin, 2004), pp 132-3.
5. L.A. Clarkson and E.M. Crawford, *Feast and Famine: Food and Nutrition in Ireland 1500-1920* (Oxford, 2001), pp 256-7.
6. 'Regnum Corcagiense, or a Description of the Kingdom of Cork. With Remarks on the Ancient and Present State thereof by Sir Richard Cox', *JCHAS*, vol. 8, 1902, pp 65-83 and 156-179.
7. Quoted in Clarkson and Crawford, *Feast and Famine*, p. 258.
8. *Council Book* (hereafter, *CB*), 11 April 1693.
9. It is called a 'Fishambles' in the *Council Book* entry for 20 August, 1695. This was probably an error, a misreading or misspelling of 'fleshambles', though there was also a fish shambles on the site
10. *CB*, 13 June 1710 and 8 April 1712.
11. *CB*, 7 January 1711, 10 December 1713 and 12 September 1715.
12. Charles Smith, *Ancient and Present State of the City and County of Cork* (1750), p. 404.
13. *CB*, 17 August 1772.
14. *CB*, 22 November 1733, 28 May 1737 and 22 February 1738.
15. Cn., 'Cork City in 1748', *JCHAS*, vol. 9, 1903, pp 71-2.
16. Smith, *Ancient and Present State*, p. 404.
17. *CB*, 4 March 1735.
18. *CB*, 19 March 1789, 15 July 1791, 26 August 1791 and 3 February 1792.
19. *CB*, 22 November 1733 and 28 May 1737.

20. *CB*, 29 September 1747.

21. *CB*, 31 July 1754.

22. Colman O'Mahony, *In the Shadows: Life in Cork 1750-1930* (Cork, 1997), pp 268-9.

23. *CB*, 2 September 1756.

24. Johnson, *Laneways*, p. 50.

25. *CB*, 1 August 1695, 1 March 1713, 14 October 1713 and 13 May 1717.

26. Johnson, Laneways, pp 118-9.

27. *CB*, 4 November 1706, 3 November 1718, 23 August 1758 and 29 August 1760.

28. *CB*, 28 September 1787 and 23 January 1790.

29. Smith, *Ancient and Present State*, p. 413; *CB*, 2 June 1786 and 23 February 1787; House of Commons Parliamentary Papers (1835): *Appendix to the first report of the commissioners appointed to inquire into the municipal corporations of Ireland – Report on the City of Cork*, p. 44.

30. See, for example, entries for 16 November 1699, 13 June 1712, 8 April 1712 and 22 November 1733.

31. *Report*, p. 47.

32. *CB*, 22 February 1738.

33. *CB*, 28 August 1780.

34. 'Proclamation by Samuel Rowland, Mayor', *Cork Hibernian Chronicle*, 5 October 1786.

CHAPTER 3 The English Market 1788-1899

1. *Census of Ireland*, 1851, 1861, 1871.

2. *Cork Constitution*, 30 October 1855.

3. Cork Corporation Tolls and Markets Committee minute books, Cork Archives Institute (hereafter, TMC minutes): entry for 2 February 1887. On 29 August 1894 there is reference to 'the condition of the English Market', and on 27 November 1895 the removal of refuse from 'the English Market' is mentioned.

4. 'The Cork Directory for the Year 1787' by Richard Lucas, *JCHAS*, vol. 72, pp 135-157; *Holden's Triennial Directory for 1805, 1806, 1807* (London, 1805), pp 62-75; William West, *Cork Directory 1809-1810* (Cork, 1810); *Pigot's Commercial Directory of Scotland, Ireland, and the four most northern Counties of England for 1820, 1821 & 1822* (Manchester, 1820); Angela Fahy, 'A Social Geography of Nineteenth-Century Cork' (MA, UCC, 1987), pp 164-279 and 'Residence, workplace and patterns of change' in P. Butel and L.M. Cullen (eds), *Cities and Merchants: French and Irish Perspectives on Urban Development* (Dublin, 1986), pp 41-7.

5. Richard Lovett, *Irish Pictures* (London, 1888), p. 96.

6. Richard Caulfield (ed.), *The Council Book of the Corporation of the City of Cork, from 1609 to 1643 and from 1690 to 1800* (Guildford, 1876), entry for 19 January 1786 (hereafter, *CB*). On 16 August 1786, the corporation took an 800-year lease on the grounds, houses and premises of the late Richard Marrett from his heirs at the yearly rent agreed to earlier.

7. *CB*, 8 August 1786.

8. *CB*, 16 August 1786.

9. Francis H. Tuckey, *The County and City of Cork Remembrancer* (1837; Cork, 1980 edn.), p. 194.

10. *CB*, 14 March 1787.

11. *CB*, 27 September 1787 and 9 June 1788.

12. *CB*, 17-18 July 1788, 1 September 1789; Tuckey's *Remembrancer*, p. 194.

13. *Cork Hibernian Chronicle*, 25 December 1788.

14. *CB*, 17 July 1789 and 18 March 1791.

15. Dan Murphy's 1789 map of Cork shows no entrance from Princes Street. The *Council Book* records a decision of 10 March 1789 to open a passage from Princes Street into the market. This passage is marked in William Beauford's map of 1801.

16. *Cork Hibernian Chronicle*, 20 October 1791.

17. *The Hibernian Chronicle*, 18 May 1797.

18. Tuckey's *Remembrancer*, pp 200-1.

19. *Flynn's Hibernian Chronicle*, 26 May 1800.

20. Horatio Townsend, *Statistical Survey of the County of Cork* (Dublin, 1810).

21. Thomas Sheahan, *Irish destitution in 1834; or the working classes of Cork* (Cork, 1824), pp 17-24, cited in Fintan Lane, *In search of Thomas Sheahan: radical politics in Cork, 1824-1836* (Dublin, 2001), pp 28-9.

22. Maura Murphy, 'Cork Commercial Society 1850-1899', in Butel and Cullen (eds), *Cities and Merchants*, pp. 233-4, and 'The Economic and Social Structure of Nineteenth-Century Cork', in David Harkness and Mary O'Dowd (eds), *The Town in Ireland* (Belfast, 1981), p. 128.

23. Cormac Ó Grada, *Ireland: A New Economic History* (Oxford, 1994), p. 265.

24. Regina Sexton, 'I'd ate it like chocolate!': the disappearing offal food traditions of Cork City', in Harlan Walker (ed.), *Disappearing Foods* (Devon, 1995), p. 174.

25. J. Windele, *Historical and Descriptive Notices of the City of Cork and its Vicinity* (Cork, 1840, 1844, 1848), pp 121-2.

26. *Henry and Coughlan*, p. 232.

27. Townsend, *Survey*, p. 167; *Pigot & Co.'s City of Dublin and Hibernian Provincial Directory* (London and Manchester, 1824), p. 241; Samuel Lewis, *A Topographical Dictionary of Ireland* (London, 1837), p. 170.

28. *Southern Reporter*, 15 December 1827; House of Commons Parliamentary Papers (1835): *Appendix to the first report of the commissioners appointed to inquire into the municipal corporations of Ireland – Report on the City of Cork*, p. 46.

29. Valuation Lists, 1855-84, Valuation Office, Dublin.

30. *Cork Mercantile Chronicle*, 7 October 1814.

31. *Cork Constitution* (hereafter, *Constitution*), 26 October 1826 and 15 September 1827.

32. *Commissioners' Report*, pp 33-57.

33. *Commissioners' Report*, pp 45-6.

34. Ian D'Alton, *Protestant Society and Politics in Cork, 1812-1844* (Cork, 1980), p. 179

35. *Cork Examiner* (hereafter, *Examiner*) , 20 November 1843.

36. *Examiner*, 20 November 1843; Alexander Aldwell, *The County and City of Cork Almanac* (Cork, 1844), p. 122.

37. *Examiner*, 6 March and 20 November 1843; Peter Foynes, 'City, Street, Market', unpublished paper, pp 20-22; Aldwell, *Almanac*, p. 122.

38. *Examiner*, 8 May 1844.

39. *Examiner*, 18 February 1842.

40. Colman O'Mahony, *In the Shadows: Life in Cork, 1750-1930* (Cork, 1997), p. 144.

41. *Constitution*, 30 May 1846.

42. *Constitution*, 6 June 1846.

43. Sean Daly, *Cork: a City in Crisis – a history of labour conflict and social misery, 1870-1972* (Cork, 1978), pp 262-270; Emmet O'Connor, *A Labour History of Ireland, 1824-1960* (Dublin, 1994), pp 1-6.

44. Lane, *Thomas Sheahan*, pp 35-6.

45. Daly, *City in Crisis*, p. 312.

46. *Cork Daily Herald*, 18 October 1864.

47. Emmet O'Connor, *A Labour History of Waterford* (Waterford, 1989), pp 91-2.

48. Maura Murphy, 'Cork Commercial' p. 236.

49. Maura Murphy, 'The Economic and Social Structure of Nineteenth-Century Cork', pp 131-2.

50. TMC minutes, 8 February 1872, 6 March 1878, 17 May 1893 and *passim*.

51. See Appendix, 'Stallholders, 1845-2005'.

52. James S. Donnelly, *The Land and People of Nineteenth-Century Cork* (London, 1975), p. 73.

53. Donnelly, *Land and People*, p. 83.

54. *Constitution*, 15 and 17 April 1847.

55. Marita Foster and Larry Geary, 'The Great Famine in Cork' (pre-publication MS), in John Crowley *et al* (eds), *The Atlas of Cork City* (Cork, 2005); O'Mahony, *Shadows*, p. 166; Donnelly, *Land and People*, pp 86-7.

56. *Examiner*, 14 June 1847; O'Mahony, *Shadows*, pp 166.

57. *Examiner*, 11 August 1847.

58. *Constitution*, 15 April 1847.

59. *Examiner*, 21 May 1847; O'Mahony, *Shadows*, p. 166.

60. O'Mahony, *Shadows*, pp 168-9.

61. *Constitution*, 15 July 1847.

62. *Constitution*, 22 December 1855.

63. *Report of the Commissioners appointed to inquire into the State of the Fairs and Markets in Ireland, Part II*, (Dublin, 1855) (hereafter, *1855 Markets Report*).

64. *Royal Commission on Market Rights and Tolls: Final Report of the Commissioners* (London, 1891), p. 14.

65. *1855 Markets Report*, p.192.

66. *1855 Markets Report*, p.193.

67. *1855 Markets Report*, pp. 210-211.

68. *Constitution*, 6 May 1862.

69. *Examiner*, 26 November 1861.

70. *Examiner*, 29 November 1861.

71. *Constitution*, 1 September 1862.

72. *Constitution*, 10 May and 17 June 1862.

73. *Examiner*, 5 March 1862.

74. *Constitution*, 5 August 1862.

75. *Constitution*, 8 November and 20 December 1862; *Examiner*, 28 November 1862.

76. *Examiner*, 20 December 1862.

77. *Constitution*, 22 September 1862.

78. *Constitution*, 22 December 1862; *Examiner*, 17, 31 January and 28 March 1863.

79. *Examiner*, 16 July 1881.

80. TMC minutes, 5 August 1869 and 14 March 1871; *Examiner*, 11 February and 14 March 1871.

81. *Examiner*, 26 June 1876; www.crawfordartgallery.com.

82. TMC minutes, 17 October 1877, 20 March 1978, 3 April 1878, 3 July 1878, 15 January 1879, 21 May 1879.

83. *Examiner*, 23 October 1880, 9 July 1881 and 16 July 1881.

84. Bryan A. Cody, *The River Lee, Cork, and the Corkonians* (Cork, 1974 – orig. publ. 1859), p. 99.

85. TMC minutes, 2 August 1881 and 25 April 1883.

86. TMC minutes, 19 April 1882-12 October 1887.

87. Corporation of Cork, *Report of the Inspector of Grand Parade and Princes Street Markets for the year 1889* (Cork, 1890) – Cork City Library.

88. TMC minutes, 11 April 1894.

89. TMC minutes, 2 August 1893.

90. *Report of the Inspector, 1889*.

91. TMC minutes, 2 August 1893.

92. TMC minutes, 23 March 1892, 1 February 1893, 7 February 1894 and 23 January 1895.

93. TMC minutes, 2 February 1887-14 March 1888.

94. TMC minutes, 10 April 1895-17 June 1896.

95. *Royal Commission on Markets and Tolls: Final Report of the Commissioners* (London, 1891).

96. TMC minutes, 31 August 1892-21 December 1898.

CHAPTER 4 **Market People 1830 - 1925**

1. *Cork Constitution*, 23, 26 October and 6 November 1830.

2. Tolls and Markets Committee Minute Books, Cork Archives Institute, 30 January 1872 (hereafter, dates refer to entries in these minute books, unless otherwise indicated).

3. 20 August 1872.

4. 23 January 1872.

5. 20 June 1872.

6. 2 August 1872.

7. 17 June 1874.

8. 6 February and 6 March 1878.

9. 17 July 1878.

10. 17 October, 1883.

11. 11 June 1884.

12. *Corporation of Cork: Report of the Inspector of Grand Parade and Princes Street Markets for the year 1889* (Cork, 1890), Cork City Library.

13. 28 November 1894.

14. 10 July 1895.

15. 31 July 1895.

16. 4 September 1895.

17. 11 September 1895.

18. 27 December 1899.

19. 9 January 1901.

20. 27 May 1903.

21. 30 July 1872.

22. (Clothing Committee), 30 July 1874.

23. 16 August 1867.

24. 16 December 1867.

25. 2 July, 20 August and 11 December 1872.

26. 20 August 1872.

27. 16 February 1881.

28. 12 September 1883 and 30 January 1884.

29. 31 December 1884.

30. 30 July and 31 December 1884, 5 August 1885, 11 August 1886.

31. 19 September 1994.

32. 11 January 1899.

33. 28 March 1900.

34. 15 May 1918.

35. 11 December 1872 and 3 December 1873.

36. 7 January 1874.

37. 8 July, 1874.

38. 26 August and 8 September 1874.

39. 6 October and 23 December 1874.

40. 25 March 1874.

41. 3 December 1873.

42. 7 January 1874.

43. 25 March 1874.

44. 11 January 1899.

45. 3 February 1875.

46. 8 April and 15 July 1885.

47. 5 August 1885.

48. 28 October 1885.

49. 13 July 1887.

50. 16 January and 6 February, 1918 and 29 April, 1920.

51. 15 January 1924.

52. 4 March 1885.

53. 7 and 28 September 1887.

54. 18 and 25 March 1896.

55. 15 August 1883.

56. 7 June 1921 and 27 May 1927.

57. 18 March 1824.

58. 19 November 1873.

59. 17 August 1904.

60. 17 July, 1907 15 July, 1908, 16 July 1919.

61. 17 August 1904.

62. 30 July 1873.

63. 3 September 1873.

64. 7 January 1874.

65. 3 June 1874.

66. 30 March and 18 May 1881.

67. 18 February 1885.

68. 16 June 1886.

69. 5 September, 1894.

70. *Cork Constitution*, 22 December 1855

71. *Cork Constitution*, 3 August 1858.

72. 6 and 27 May, 23 June 1869.

73. 31 January 1871 and 11 December 1872.

74. 2 April 1874.

75. 11 August, 15 September, 6 and 27 October, 1875.

76. 3 October 1883.

77. 6 October 1897.

78. 17 November 1897.

79. 10 August 1898.

80. 31 August 1898.

81. 7 September 1898.

82. 5 and 12 October 1898.

83. 8 August 1898.

84. 15 June 1898.

85. 22 and 29 June 1898.

86. 10 August 1904.

87. 14 March 1906.

88. 28 March 1906.

89. 19 May 1905.

90. 2 October 1909.

91. 16 March 1910.

92. 5 April 1911.

93. 26 May 1911.

94. 15 May 1912, 5 and 19 March 1913.

95. 18 June and 2 July 1913.

96. 2 May 1917.
97. 6 June 1922.
98. 7 January and 25 February 1874.
99. 28 May 1884.
100. 11 and 18 June, 30 September 1884.
101. 5 August 1885.
102. 9 February 1887.
103. 4 and 25 July, 8 and 22 August 1900.
104. 13 March 1901.
105. 13 August 1902.
106. 29 August 1902.
107. 12 November 1902.
108. 26 November 1902.
109. 10 December 1902.
110. 2 April 1879.
111. 16 April 1879.
112. 14 June 1882.
113. 6 November 1895.
114. 6 July 1881.
115. 12 September 1894 and 13 March 1895.
116. 4 July and 7 November, 1917 and 6 February, 1918.
117. 6 June 1883.
118. 25 January 1893.
119. 24 March 1897.
120. *Cork Examiner*, 5 October 1880.
121. 25 May 1892.
122. 24 August 1892.
123. 8 March 1893.
124. 2 June 187.
125. 30 August 1876.
126. 6 September 1876.
127. 26 July 1893.
128. 2 August 1893 and 20 March 1894.
129. 10 April and 13 June 1900.

CHAPTER 5 **Market Trends 1900 - 2005**

1. Tolls and Markets Committee Minute Books, 27 May 1903 (hereafter, unless otherwise indicated, dates refer to entries in these minute books).
2. 10 June 1903.
3. 22 May 1901 and 1 April 1908
4. February 1904.
5. 25 September 1901, 14 March 1906 and 20 January 1909.
6. May 1912.
7. 22 February 1905, 30 November 1905, 16 December 1908 and 5 October 1910.
8. 6 January and 7 April 1915, and 15 May 1918; The Commonwealth War Graves Commission, 'Casualty Details', www.cwgc.org.
9. 3 June 1916 and 4 July 1917.
10. 5 and 18 April and 6 September 1916.
11. Information from Cork Journeyman Butchers' Society Minute Books (CJBSMB), courtesy of the Independent Workers' Union.
12. 6 November 1918, 16 July and 1 October 1919 and 16 March 1920.
13. CJBSMB, 1919-20.
14. 20 March 1918.
15. 16 July 1919; Dermot Lucey, 'Cork Public Opinion and the First World War' (MA, UCC, 1972), p. 140.
16. Cork Corporation, Council Minute Books (hereafter, CMB), 9 January 1920 (Cork Archives Institute).
17. 20 July 1920 and 1 March 1921.
18. 7 and 21 September 1920.
19. CJBSMB, 3 November 1920.
20. 18 January and 19 April 1921; CBM, 16 February 1921.
21. Michael Bannon, Joseph Boland and Eunan O'Halpin, *City and County Management 1929-1990: a Retrospective* (Dublin, 1991), pp 119-121; Henry Alan Jefferies, *Cork: Historical Perspectives* (Dublin, 2004), pp 206-7.
22. 3 July 1923 and 24 April, 6 May and 28 November 1924.
23. CMB, 23 September 1941.
24. *Food Hygiene Regulations, 1950 (S.I. No. 205)* (Dublin, 1950).
25. CBM, 11 December 1951-18 January 1961, *passim*.
26. CBM, 19 May 1953-16 November 1954; Simon O'Flynn interview, June 2004.
27. CBM, 24 March 1959-26 May 1964, *passim*.
28. *Cork Post*, 23 January 1973; Cork *Examiner*, January 1973; May 2005 interview with Simon O'Flynn, MTA chairman, 1972-3.
29. *Cork Examiner*, January 1973.
30. *Cork Post*, 23 January 1973.
31. *Cork Examiner*, January 1973; O'Flynn interview.
32. Information from Cork Operative Butchers' Society (COBS) minute books, 1975-77 and 1986, and an unpublished paper on the strike by Noel Murphy, former secretary of COBS.
33. *Cork Examiner*, 23 August 1977.
34. Much of the detail regarding the restoration work comes from Gerry Cahill, 'A Princely Market', *Architect's Journal*, 18 April 1984, pp 45-50.
35. Ibid, p. 50.

TRADITIONAL FOODS OF CORK

1. The information for this section comes mainly from: Regina Sexton, '"I'd ate it like chocolate!": The Disappearing Offal Food Traditions of Cork City' in Harlan Walker (ed.), *Disappearing Foods: Studies in Foods and Dishes at Risk* (Devon, 1995), pp 172-188; Cathal Cowan & Regina Sexton, *Ireland's Traditional Foods: An exploration of Irish local and typical foods and drinks* (Dublin 1997); Regina Sexton, *A Little History of Irish Food* (London, 1998); Alan Davidson, *The Oxford Companion to Food* (Oxford 1999).

2. '"I'd ate it like chocolate!", p. 174.

Photography

Numbers indicate the page on which the photograph appears, the letter indicates the position of the photograph beginning, 'a', from the top left hand corner and proceeding clockwise .

Copyright of photographs is held by those credited below.

Courtesy of *Irish Examiner* – Cover a, Backcover, 6, 58, 81, 98/99, 118/119, 135(detail) 168, 169, 178 a–b, 179b, 183, 235.

Diarmuid Ó Drisceoil – 34, 36, 65b, 66a, 67, 72, 95a, 104b, 127a, 127b, 129, 145, 146, 151, 187, 228.

Stuart Coughlan – Cover c–e, Back flap, 49, 61b, 92 a–d, 95b, 95c, 104a, 104 c, 148, 184c, 194, 199b, 200, 201, 203 a–b, 206 b–c, 207b, 208, 209, 210 a–g, 211, 219b, 221b, 223 a–c, 226, 227, 245 d–e.

© **Chris Ramsden**, from *Forgotten Cork*, The Collins Press, 2004 – 57, 66b, 70/71, 82, 90b, 138, 147.

Janice O'Connell – 60a, 188.

Wendie Young – Cover b, Cover f, 60b, 74, 110, 124, 128, 132, 141, 155, 159, 166, 172, 175b, 184 a–b, 193, 196, 199a, 202 a–b, 204 a–b, 206a, 206d, 207a, 212, 214 a–c, 215, 216, 220, 221a, 225, 230, 244, 245 a–b.

Daphne Pochin-Mould – 77, 78, 87, 112, 113, 123, 136, 170, 175a, 177, 179a, 180, 182, 190 a–b, 219a, 238.

Tony O'Connell – 107, 184d, 198b, 218.

Dori O'Connell – 142

Claire Keogh – 176, 205, 207 c–d, 229 a–d, 245c.

Gloria Monteleone – 222.

K. Aherne – 84, 86.

The mural shown on the back flap and page 223 is at Mutton Lane. Titled *'The Pana Shuffle'* it was painted by **Anthony Ruby** in 2004, www.anthonyruby.com

INDEX

Italicised page numbers refer to picture captions